NICHOLAS

By the same author

A Fez of the Heart: Travels Around Turkey in Search of a Hat
The Snakebite Survivors' Club: Travels Among Serpents
Treachery at Sharpnose Point: Unraveling the
Mystery of the Caledonia's Final Voyage

NICHOLAS

THE EPIC JOURNEY FROM

SAINT TO SANTA CLAUS

JEREMY SEAL

BLOOMSBURY

To Anna and Lizzie

Published by Bloomsbury Publishing, New York and London
Distributed to the trade by Holtzbrinck Publishers

All papers used by Bloomsbury Publishing are natural, recyclable products made
from wood grown in well-managed forests. The manufacturing processes
conform to the environmental regulations of the country of origin.

Library of Congress Cataloging-in-Publication Data

Seal, Jeremy.
Nicholas : the epic journey from saint to Santa Claus / Jeremy Seal.—1st U.S. ed.
p.   cm.
ISBN-13:   978-1-58234-419-5 (hardcover)
ISBN-10:   1-58234-419-1 (hardcover)
1. Nicholas, Saint, Bp. of Myra.   2. Santa Claus.   I. Title.

BR1720.N46S43   2005
270.2'092—dc22
2005011875

First U.S. Edition 2005

1 3 5 7 9 10 8 6 4 2

Typeset by Westchester Book Group
Printed in the United States of America by Quebecor World Fairfield

1

A MAN REACHES FOR a high window.
He wears a cowl, and holds something in his outstretched hand. The object is indistinct, more or less spherical, more likely a cannonball, to judge by the man's stooped posture, than a soap bubble. In the yellow-lit interior beyond the window, three young women embrace. They are dressed in nightgowns and caps, though these bedtime preparations are plainly mechanical; they are distressed and there is no prospect of sleep. The distracted father sits apart, head in his hands. There is no sign of the mother. Crisis looms.

This antique scene is insistently ecclesiastical. It is the subject of frescoes, icons, the illuminated pages of breviaries, psalters, and saints' lives. It has been worked in stained glass and carved in stone and wood. It's a still from a seventeen-hundred-year-old story, one that has been recounted many times, with minor variations, across the Christian world, a staple of devotional iconography. Even so, it can hardly claim the universal familiarity of a Crucifixion or a Nativity scene, leaving those who do not recognize it to seek clues in the image as a means of making sense of the wider narrative the moment is wrapped in. There's a cypress tree in some renderings, and often a cross-topped cupola. The scene, typically Byzantine, is bathed in significant moonlight; the cowl is not merely customary, then, but clandestine. Even so, it's inconceivable that this nighttime visitor intends malice. He is not in the business of breaking and entering. He is not about to shatter the window with the object in his hand, whatever it is, to incite a pogrom or inflame a vendetta. Nor, though the girls are beautiful, can it be a billet-doux that he is delivering. For one thing, as the cannonball stoop indicates, the object is heavy. For another, there's a purpose beyond the merely lovelorn about this visitor.

The story can wait, except in one detail. Draw back the cowl, as the narrative will duly culminate, and a man is revealed by the name of Nicholas;

St. Nicholas Endows Three Impoverished Maidens with His Inheritance (panel), by Fra Filippo Lippi (c. 1406-69), in the Martelli Chapel. (Church of San Lorenzo, Florence, Italy/The Bridgeman Art Library)

or, to begin his identification, Nikolaos in the Greek transliteration. A Byzantine Greek at a window, then, delivering something significant. So significant that Nicholas' biography depends upon this episode. It has proved the defining moment of his life, the one action, above all others, that made him. Only, posthumously.

Nicholas' great journey had barely begun when they laid him in his sarcophagus at Myra, in what is now southwestern Turkey, in or around A.D. 352. The year is contested; the day of his death, December 6, is far better established. As vampires shun daylight, so saints are distinguished from ordinary mortals by the anniversaries they keep. The date of their death rather than their birth is commemorated. With death, they fledge. Whatever saints achieve during their lives, they graduate to their true

calling—as influential intermediary between God and men—only on their deaths. When the Byzantine saints went to work among the celestial kingdom's porphyry halls, banqueting tables, and golden balconies, they had one overriding ambition: to convince the living that the ear of God was theirs. Saintly survival was achieved by acquiring the necessary devotees from among the living; and what attracted people to a saint beyond his character or piety was demonstrable access to the Almighty and an impressive intercessional record with Him, whether in delivering God's relief from aching teeth or from potato blight, in ensuring successful conception or the obliteration of enemies on the battlefield. Beatification was no guarantee against oblivion in this fiercely competitive and pointedly modern environment. The world is littered with the lost and broken shrines of forgotten saints. Sometimes, their constituencies stalled or were dispersed by upheaval; others could not adapt their specializations to change. Many had their moments, shining in remote corners of the saintly firmament before they were extinguished by new operators across their territories.

So it was that Nicholas entered such a world one distant December day, and set about surviving. Seventeen hundred years later, a million invocations to Nikolai rise from onion-shaped domes across the Russian steppe. He is revered across the Hellenic world, across Catholic Europe and the Balkans. In the former Yugoslavia, it has long been the convention that marriages may not take place between families who have adopted the same patron saint, but an exception is necessarily made in the case of Nicholas, whose popularity might otherwise endanger the institution of marriage itself. He has protected generations of sailors on their voyages; not only Greeks, but Bretons, Croatians, and Liverpudlians, Bari fishermen and Volga boatmen. He has been the patron of a wide range of trades, and also assisted with marriages and conceptions. His name was given to one thirteenth-century saint, Nicholas of Tolentino, whose mother finally bore him after a visit to Nicholas' shrine at Myra. Nicholas has spawned generations in his name: popes in Rome and doges in Venice, princes and kings in the Balkans, tsars in Russia and despots in Romania, but also millions of ordinary boys; not only Nikolaus and Nikolai but Nicolas in France and Nicola in Italy, Nigul in Estonia and Mikulas in the Czech Republic, Nick or Colin in England, Klaus in Germany and Klaas in Holland. And in all these countries and beyond, these boys and their sisters await his secret visits as the year draws to a close. He would seem, on current evidence, to have surpassed all expectation.

And so to Nicholas' life, the seed of his posthumous success. Saints must achieve one thing in their earthly span, which is to commend themselves for sainthood; there's a self-evident Darwinian truth at work here. Most of Nicholas' Christian contemporaries achieved this in the last, and most brutal, of the persecutions by suffering torture and execution at the hands of the pagan Romans; only the unluckiest of martyrs were passed over for sainthood. Others performed astounding miracles or condemned themselves to a life of desert asceticism which led them to heaven via filth, chronic fleas, and an unremitting diet of fallen fruit and nuts. Nicholas took himself to a Byzantine window.

Which brings us to ask what he is doing there. Making a secret gift, quite without commitment. Nicholas expects nothing from it, except the knowledge that it will change lives. What he cannot know, even if he doubts that he will succeed in keeping the gift entirely secret, is that it will never be forgotten. On a moonlit Byzantine night late in the third century, a young man does the right thing, and so starts something big. He reaches for nothing less than immortality.

2

IN EARLY DECEMBER, I took my daughter to see the man whom Nicholas had become.

We made for Santa's Kingdom. The Kingdom lay to the north, though not the deep north; near Birmingham, in fact. It was also at London and Glasgow, where some of Anna's friends would see Santa at much the same time. Not that this troubled my six-year-old, who had long since accepted Santa's essential omnipresence as the natural consequence, though the phrase was not hers, of his compressed calendar commitments. What was more likely to wreck her belief was the fact that the Kingdom was reached by the M5 where Santa had installed himself, for one month only, at the National Exhibition Centre; and I doubted that wide-eyed wonder would flourish in the NEC's prosaic tilth. Beyond the wipers, frantic against the rain, the headlit traffic was heavy in the submarine gloom.

I was getting to know Santa Claus all over again. The man was cyclical, but doubly so; an annual returnee, of course, but also a generational one, describing a wider orbit to leave the awareness on a long fade at the end of childhood, then return with a vengeance in the first years of parenthood. What had brought him back to me were my two daughters. The shift of perspective occasioned by one's own inexorable slide down the generations transformed the experience of Santa. I had lived Santa last time round; this time, my role was to supervise Anna and Lizzie's relationship with him. Like walking and talking, like the respectivity of trouser legs (a particular problem for my girls), Santa was another early-life experience that was learned as a child and taught as a parent. To all of us, it seemed, he presented challenges.

The Kingdom's marketers had thrown a vast advertising trawl net, which had snagged Anna among a million-strong shoal of kids in the weeks preceding Christmas; there was no denying my older daughter. She was approaching her devotional peak, breathlessly receptive to the promises, but not yet tainted by the least doubts about the man she insisted on calling Father Christmas. The name her parents knew Santa Claus by, a peculiarly English usage, sounded quaint from Anna—a sure sign that its time was short. Even so, the old name had a distinct resonance, evoking a time when they had barely begun to mine Santa's merchandising potential.

All that had changed, of course; we were driving through a singularly venal world. The forces of commerce, adept as kidnappers in the exploitation of parental love, had ticketed objects of childhood adoration accordingly. I had not troubled Anna with the fact that it cost a lot of money to enter Santa's Kingdom. I was more concerned by the Kingdom situation that was developing: the Kingdom that I anticipated and the one that Anna in her innocence imagined were set to collide, and in about two hours' time; my daughter was not prepared. It was not long after we had left home (in fact, the petrol gauge was still inching toward a reading) that she looked from the window and remarked that it looked the same as ever: the roundabouts and the retail warehouses, the housing estates still settling into their freshly excavated plots, the roadside thickets of plastic tubes containing freshly planted saplings, as if a few trees might redeem England's benighted suburbs, and the pubs lit with premature Christmas decorations and the reflected flickery glow of fruit machines.

What Anna had expected was some give in the landscape, a slide toward a truer north along empty roads that ran through birch and spruce, just us and a dance of flakes in the headlights as we moved toward magic. When she next checked, a motorway service station reared at the window.

"We're not there yet." But even as I reassured her, I knew that we never would be. The darkness came as a mercy, shielding her from an obstinately ordinary world. I wondered if this might be the night; six-year-old Anna was approaching the age. I feared that the experience that we were fast closing on might shatter her belief in Father Christmas. Then, only the tooth fairy and the mermaids, about which she nursed a particular conviction, would stand between her and the loss of her own magic kingdom.

It was hard, getting reaquainted with Santa. To the child, he might be the man who brought secret presents. But once that child became a parent, there was a significant payback to be endured. Santa would continue to protect the innocence of the next generation so long as the previous one agreed to be privy to a ruthless acknowledgment of the loss of its own; this meant assuming logistical and financial responsibility for the entire rite leading to its culmination on Christmas morning. And it seemed to this parent, as it must surely seem to all, that Santa had inveigled him, by appealing to the feelings that he once felt for him, into an intention which now seemed monstrous: to inflate the material appetites of his offspring. Was a man who won children's devotion with the promise of excessive gifts—a promise he then left the parents to honor—really to be trusted?

"We're here," I whispered as the car drew to a halt, my voice humble with apology. Anna hauled herself to the window and was silent. She had conjured her own visions of how Santa's Kingdom might look; a vast car park, with the rain flailing about the lamp lights, had not figured among them. As we made our way to the Kingdom, we ran into a countercurrent of show dogs hauling their owners back to their vehicles: Labradors and Spaniels, Dachshunds and Alsatians that had recently been immaculately groomed but were now merely soaked.

"Does Father Christmas like dogs?" asked Anna. Her belief had survived the car park, and even found an explanation for the dog show in the adjacent exhibition hall; I feared that greater tests lay ahead.

A plastic Christmas tree announced the entrance to Santa's Kingdom. Its fairy lights were only intermittently operational. They resembled the flashing activity outside an accident and emergency department. A posse of elves slapped yellow tags around our wrists. We were being hospitalized, interned to a backing track of Christmas medleys. Inside, crowds waited to be transported to the Kingdom. They had gathered about a stage where Frosty the Snowman, a penguin, and some majorettes danced and sang, which was not what Anna had expected. Her lower lip began to tremble. We retreated to a nearby booth, where I fortified my daughter with a cup of hot chocolate.

"We have to go by rocket to reach the Kingdom," I told her brightly. Anna liked rockets, which made me grateful for this one, even though it demonstrated that the Santa's Kingdom story line was increasingly scrambled.

Anna had, however, become wiser. "A real rocket?" she asked, her eyes narrowing. "Well, it should feel like a real rocket," I offered.

It didn't. When it was our turn, which we knew by the color of our wrist tags, we gathered in an abbatoir file before taking our seats on the "shuttle" to Santa's Kingdom. We took off to a rising rattle from concealed speakers. A short video shot us past the Eiffel Tower and the Sydney Opera

House, which was hardly the obvious route north. As we touched down, the lights came up with a lurch; a choreographic equivalent of a rough landing which was followed by music, solemn, enchanted, and a right provocation since it suggested that we were embarked on some marvelous odyssey. We were filing down a passageway walled with chipboard to which fairy lights had been stapled when Anna asked when we were going on the rocket. The passageway led to the cavern of the Snow Queen, who appeared from a cloud of dry ice. "Are you being good?" she asked in a Yorkshire accent. "Looking forward to seeing Santa?"

"What are you doing here?" asked Anna, who was used to her favorite characters keeping to their own books.

We continued among our tightly packed fellow passengers, topped and tailed as we were by elves. The elves smiled a lot, but they also maintained their station, which lent their smiles a sinister cast. It was clear that they were there to prevent us running up against passengers from other rocket arrivals, as if to preserve some kind of illusion. At Santa's toy factory, more elves were making rocking horses and drums. At his post office, Anna queued to write a postcard, which she dutifully dropped into the red pillar box. The Sugar Plum Fairy smiled; the Sugar Plum Fairy asked whether Anna was looking forward to seeing Santa. Then we arrived at the reindeer. These were at least relevant, and real, though they were suffering from what I took to be flu. I stroked one of them. It sneezed on my sleeve. I wiped off the sneeze on a drift of plastic snow.

We emerged among booths variously stacked with chocolates, pink rabbits, Santa hats, and plastic reindeer. The area beyond was carpeted in machine-made snow. Desultory snowballs flew and toddlers examined their mottled hands, which they extended to their parents that they might be relieved of the unfamiliar discomfort. It was their first experience of the white stuff, which was fast becoming a northern exotic in England. These days, a series of muddy footprints usually led to Father Christmas.

So it was at Santa's Kingdom, where he lived beyond a curtain. The curtain was flanked by nine identical curtains. When Anna's turn came, she found herself propelled into a booth with walls of green baize slung with fairy lights. It looked like a poorly decorated workstation. Father Christmas sat on an office chair which did not fit him; his thighs extended over the sides in red felt rolls. Father Christmas did not look like the sort of man who usually went out of his way to be nice to children. I wondered what had happened to the man at the window. In a few days' time, with a journey to Nicholas' beginnings in Turkey, I might start to find out.

Father Christmas asked Anna if she had been a good girl, and she barely had time to answer before we were being ushered out. Anna was silent on the way to the car, clutching the plastic doll that Father Christmas had given her. She made no further attempts to incorporate the latest surroundings into her Santa world, which was sensible since a concert crowd dressed in fezzes, winklepicker shoes, and string ties was gathering.

Anna had enough dolls; she neither needed nor wanted another one. She unwrapped it from the plastic packaging to discover a leg had come loose from its socket. This one might at least provide her with a challenging repair even as she nursed hopes of something better.

"Will you bring us presents when you come back?" It was a reminder that the girls customarily got gifts after my trips away.

And then, irritated: "I can't get this leg back in."

And then: "Dad?"

"Yes."

"That wasn't the real Father Christmas, was it?"

I intended to find out in Turkey.

3

I SAW SANTA CLAUS again a few days later. This time, however, he was in a half-buried basilica in Demre, southern Turkey—not his usual habitat. In his grotto, history could not touch him; so, it seemed, he had broken out to reacquaint himself with his own story at its very source. He might even have called the basilica his own, except that he had been away so long and changed so much in the process that few among the Orthodox gathering acknowledged his claim to the place or even recognized in him anything of the man he once was, a Byzantine by the name of Nicholas. So it is with lengthy absences. Odysseus, another fabled Greek, had disguised himself as a nondescript to go unnoticed among his rivals on his return to Ithaca after the Trojan Wars. When Marco Polo and his father, Nicolo, returned to Venice in 1295, they seemed so foreign in accent and bearing that they were initially turned away from their own home. But whereas Odysseus and the Polos had been away for ten and twenty-six years respectively, Santa had been traveling for many lifetimes.

The time away had all but transformed the man; not only his outfit and manner but even his name, which bore only a garbled, foreign-language echo of its original. A Dutchman might have recognized Santa Claus as the Americanized form of Sinterklaas, the common Dutch agglutination of Sint Nicolaas; but it was no surprise that the Greeks and Russians venerating their fixed and unchanging Orthodox saint in the basilica should neither have known this godless hybrid from the West, nor wished to. Even so, Santa would not be denied. Dressed in his red, white-bobbled hat and a jacket bordered with fluffy white trimmings and cuffs, snowy beard, broad shiny black belt and patent-leather knee-length boots, he had taken up a prominent position in the apse between propped icons of his former self. And all while an Orthodox liturgy was in progress.

It was rare these days that Christian services were held in Demre, a scruffy market town in what was now Muslim Anatolia. Demre had a Turkish present, with its skyline spiked by minarets, but an overwhelmingly Christian past, when it was commonly known as Myra. The service, grudgingly licensed by the Turkish authorities in the name of religious freedom, bore contentious political traces, which Santa Claus' presence only inflamed. This left the man who played him, a Turkish actor in the employ of the Ministry of Tourism and Culture, to endure the cold stare of Orthodox disapproval.

The visiting Greeks and Russians who had gathered here to celebrate the feast day of St. Nicholas, fourth-century bishop of Myra, were living reminders of the fallen empires of Orthodoxy: the Byzantine Greeks had once ruled Anatolia, and the Russians had long coveted it. The upheavals of the early twentieth century had finally caused the deportation of Anatolia's Greek Christian population during the 1920s. Their sorry removal to Greece and elsewhere marked the end of Anatolia's ancient Christian tradition, not to mention the loss of St. Nicholas' original constituency from the land of his birth.

December 6 meant little, of course, to Santa. Santa had long since moved on, securing himself another date almost three weeks later in the year. How well that new date, among the most prominent in the Christian calendar, had served him. This emigrant had prospered; he had now returned to remind himself of the distance he had traveled from his origins. Hard to believe that this was how Santa Claus had begun; hard, too, for the bishop Nicholas, if he had ever imagined a divided future all those centuries ago, to imagine that Santa Claus was what half of himself was set to become. Saint and Santa shared a beginning; but while the saint had remained unchanged, Orthodox to the last, his errant half had long since acquired a life of its own and would one day emerge as Santa. The one who stayed and the one who left: each was the other's alternative story.

Few facts attest to St. Nicholas of Myra. His foundations are slight to the point of subsidence. Even his dates, A.D. 280 to A.D. 352, are shrouded in speculation. He cannot be reached by his own words; anything he may have put to parchment has long since been reduced to dust. Nor is his name mentioned by contemporary chroniclers—third- and fourth-century Eusebius or fourth- and fifth-century Jerome.

A single reference secures him. It dates from the late sixth century, some

250 years after Nicholas' probable death, and occurs in the written life of another saint from the Myra region—another Nicholas, as it happens, who seems to have taken the name as a tribute. St. Nicholas of Sion, sixth-century abbot of the eponymous mountain monastery above Myra, will repeatedly tangle with our Nicholas. This other Nicholas, an undoubted narrative distraction, is at once a crucial blessing in that a detail included in his written life serves almost single-handedly to substantiate the life of Nicholas of Myra. St. Nicholas of Sion's life was not only written by a close associate, but was completed shortly after his death. The reference the life contains to our Nicholas in a description of a visit Nicholas of Sion made to Myra—"And going down to the metropolis of Myra, he went off to the martyrium of the glorious Saint Nicholas"—is therefore reliable. Here is his anchor; confirmation that the man who would become Santa once existed.

I had arrived in Demre the previous afternoon. In what passed for the town's hotel, an aging maid with emphysema showed me to a room. It contained an iron-frame bed topped by a folded blanket and a naked bulb hanging above a basin. I dropped my bag on the bed, which doubled-up at the modest load, before following the maid into the corridor. Coughing seismically into an oddly fresh pink handkerchief, she handed me a dangled room key.

Inland, a risen moon illuminated the peaks of the Bey Mountains, a final southwesterly spasm of the Taurus range, suspending their snowcaps above Demre's main street. The chill evening was scented with grilled lamb and onions. The basilica was in the center of the town but closed, hunkered down against the call of the muezzin. In the gardens beyond the railings stood a modern statue. It was of a bearded man, head cowled and a sack slung over his shoulder. A ringlet of children, their carved hands clasped, buttressed him at the knees.

Nearby, some shivering stallholders had persisted beyond their usual hour, hopeful that the special significance of the following day might throw up a last wandering pilgrim or tourist to provide them with some evening tidbits. Their ill-lit trestles were festooned with infidel knick-knacks. To the fore were key rings, medallions and beaded pennants, miniature plastic frames and hinged triptychs; they all bore images of St. Nicholas. Something of the original aura of these iconic Orthodox representations, as direct gazes from another time, had somehow survived their mass manufacture. Nicholas was no longer the young man, the one at the window, but had been represented in the full flowering of his venerability. Ordained as a bishop famously young, he wore the vestments of the Orthodox church: a turquoise, gold-edged mantle or omophorion over floral-patterned robes, a bejeweled bracelet, and a medallion of office around his neck. In the hand that once had delivered the mysterious sphere he now cradled a Bible, while he offered a blessing with the other. His hair was gray and receding but patriarchal; thick, burnished, and brushed back against the ears to reveal an expansive forehead. Beneath his strong nose a thick mustache fell vertically like the tucked wings of a plummeting falcon (the sort of mustache that allows its owner a shorthand claim, merely by stroking it, to Confucian wisdom), melding into an expansive but tidy beard in which the first specks of white were showing.

Beyond his obvious authority, however, a fixity pervaded St. Nicholas' expression. Strict conventions have always prowled the perimeter fence of Orthodox iconography, guarding the original image against the intrusions of artistic experimentation, stylistic development, and individual expression. Thanks to the faithful replications of generations of steadfast icon painters, with their pots of egg tempera and walnut wood panels, I was looking at Nicholas just as he was first represented when his image began appearing some three centuries after his death, around fourteen hundred years ago. The man who stared out at me was immunized against revision, captured in the aspic of an unchanging faith.

Which could not be said of Santa. His merchandise had colonized another expanse of nearby trestle to which the stallholder, finding me unproductive, soon directed my attention. Santa Claus stood in ranks of painted clay and meerschaum figures. His image had been lacquered onto dried pumpkin gourds whose own shape conveyed his generous girth. It was also on fridge magnets and key rings, stickers and trinkets; on slippers and doormats, and on hearth rugs fringed with a white parabola of wool strands which had been left long to serve as his beard.

The sheer variety of forms and the unchecked proliferation of Santa styles suggested an evolution of almost profane impurity that was quite at odds with the adjacent saint. Even so, their proximity prompted me to

Ο ΑΓΙΟΣ   ΝΙΚΟΛΑΟΣ

DEMRE   ANTALYA

St. Nicholas of Myra icon. (Author's photo)

check them for likeness, as if they were ancestrally linked portraits where persistent genetic traits might be revealed. There was the beard—the one my daughter Lizzie regularly conjured from bubble bath on her two-year-old chin whenever the Santa impression was demanded of her—though Santa's had grown more unkempt than Nicholas' with the years. It had also turned completely white and, particularly on a fridge magnet that caught my eye, was slung from one ear to the other in a hammock shape that masked much of Santa's face. What remained of the face once the low brim of his hat had annexed the forehead—the pink cheeks and the wide-apart eyes—suggested mirth, even high living, which was not the case with St. Nicholas. And where the saint's arms were arranged in clerical quietude, Santa's stubby limbs were regularly flung wide in a gesture of joy. The differences were considerable. Still, who was to say what each was destined to become? Who could know the potential for personal transformation? I marked the moment, with Solomonic wisdom, by buying one of each, a Santa fridge magnet and a small plastic icon of St. Nicholas. The stallholder appeared confused, as if each figure had its own incompatible constituency, but banknotes at the end of the day soon unknotted his brow.

Back at my hotel, I set about furnishing the room by slapping my magnetic Santa Claus against the iron bedstead. Then I hung St. Nicholas off a nail that protruded from a shadowed rectangle of wall which an unknown image—a sylvan glade, startlingly colored perhaps, or a Koranic inscription—had once occupied. Thrilled by this minor act of subversion, hanging an icon of its former saint on a wall of this once-Greek city, I fell onto the bed, which promptly enfolded me in a sandwich of mattress. I only knew I had slept when I awoke, to a dawn chorus of coughing from the ground floor that was punctuated by a rhythmic rasping. I straightened myself and rubbed the frost rime from the window; the noise was the work of the maid, who was sweeping the step with a stiff broom. When I went downstairs, she brought me a glass of tea and bemoaned the absence of her only son, whom the bright lights of Antalya three hours' drive to the east had seduced. Was there comfort to be had, I wondered, in the fact that her son was not alone? That people had always left Demre? That even the local saint had moved on?

Demre squatted on an alluvial plain, its flat-topped roofs spiky with sprouts of rusted iron rods. The shops sold tractor parts, plastic piping, and rolls of transparent plastic sheeting. The town, renowned in the 1960s for its wheat fields and for its oranges and lemons—a few dusty groves survived—had recently been overrun by hothouses. Tomatoes, peppers, and eggplants now shot from the summer earth. These vast hangars covered the winter plain. Beyond their polythene cladding, which wind and sun had shredded, stood the sagging blackened stems of dead tomato plants. Smoke rose from the chimneys in vertical plumes that still day, intent on height so that they might pick up breezes to transport them, in the way of mercy missions, to more uplifting landscapes.

Myra had been listed among the six leading cities of Lycia in the first century B.C. and was awarded the title of metropolis in the second century A.D. Under the emperor Constantine—at the time of Nicholas—it was even made the capital of all Lycia. In subsequent centuries, however, it fell victim to earthquakes, plagues, Arab attacks, pirate raids, famines, and malaria. Its port at nearby Andriake silted up. By the eighth century, a protracted period of decline had set in. Complete abandonment threatened.

It was then that all trace of the ancient city began to disappear, but gradually. It was not water (Atlantis) nor lava (Pompeii) that caused its erasure but silt, borne to the plain by spring meltwater and rainstorms. In its prosperous years, the city had resisted with ease the silt's stealthy advance. It was only when the population fled that the brooms went unwielded in their season, and the silt began to gather. It started as brown wainscots which collected against the walls of abandoned buildings. They rose with every passing summer to wedge gates and doors. During the summers, dust clouds found their way through high windows and settled in layers on damp marble floors, forming an earthen crust where weeds sprang. House martins and hornets nested in the eaves. Beetles and termites addled the roof joists, causing dust plumes to fall with every earth tremor or with the hooves of passing cattle.

The silt lapped at sills, spilled through windows, and inched up sagging domes. It advanced up the trunks of flood-weakened cypress trees, so that it seemed as if the earth was reclaiming them. In the afternoon silence, the clatter of sliding tiles caused the storks to abandon their roosts in ungainly flurries. Another year might see a portico tip earthward with a massive thud. And so the city slid beneath the rising earth until it fed hothouse tomatoes and eggplants whose roots twisted down, as if to entwine the fallen statues and fountains and capitals far below.

The city that St. Nicholas knew had all but disappeared; the one building to have survived the rise of the plain was the basilica that bore his name. It stood in a deep pit, like a coffin awaiting interment. A slope led into the pit, whose sheer sides indexed Demre's history of flood. Earth and gravel from upland streams and riverbanks had reached here on a whitewater charge to be laid down as the alluvium rose and the scoured mountains fell, plain and peak inching toward each other.

History first records a church here in the early fifth century, some fifty years after Nicholas' death. The church was subsequently damaged in a succession of Arab raids, then restored and enlarged by various imperial patrons, notably in the 1040s. It subsequently fell into disrepair and, with piracy and malaria depopulating swaths of coastal Lycia, was all but forgotten until the nineteenth century.

European explorers, surveyors, and cartographers began to explore the southern Anatolian coast and its hinterland during the nineteenth century. Except for customs posts and military billets, and the nomadic Yoruk tribes who wintered at sea level, the place was deserted beyond the few towns. A resident Christian presence had persisted, however, at Myra. A French architect, Charles Texier, found three monks stationed at the basilica in 1836. It was plainly a beleaguered settlement. The monks, burying a malaria victim on the morning of his visit, told Texier that they had not seen a European for over a year.

The basilica was restored by the Russians in the mid nineteenth century—the tsars had been taking an interest in the heritage of their patron saint for centuries—but had once more sunk into decrepitude by 1906, when the German Hans Rott visited. The silt had buried the basilica almost to the tops of the ground-floor arches so that only the rounded apexes protruded from the earth, like the wheels of a covered wagon buried beyond the axle. The doorways had long disappeared beneath the earth. The basilica was entered through an upper window, which gave onto a gallery where stairs descended. The groundwater reached the German's waist and covered the sarcophagi to their lids; Rott explored the interior in thigh-high fishing boots.

Even so, as Rott observed, the priest performed regular mass here. Worship continued as it had done since the time of the saint himself, albeit in a crudely constructed chapel that had retreated skyward with the rising earth and that now abutted a half-buried arcade wall. The basilica's hull had settled deep, but it had remained afloat. Earthquakes and raids, malaria, famine, and silt had not quite sunk it. Now, as the Turkish officials drew back the gates and the saint's Greek and Russian devotees passed through for the liturgy, I was struck by the basilica's will to survive. It spoke of the saint's own singular tenacity.

I followed the crowds into the basilica. This agglomeration of half-buried arcades and aisles, chapels, narthexes, and courtyards arranged around the nave suggested a pilgrimage center of once considerable importance. Greek women, their gray hair tightly sprung beneath black shawls, removed icons of St. Nicholas from the plastic bags they had brought them in, and propped them on alcoves. A priest positioned two more icons against the wall, on the top step of the marble synthronon, the stepped semicircle that filled the apse like a miniature amphitheater. In a gloomy adjacent arcade, a hushed crowd had gathered before a sarcophagus where it was supposed that the saint had once rested. The sarcophagus lay in an arched alcove and was of finely worked marble, its lid sepia stained where a reverent multitude of hands and lips had brushed against it. The pilgrims had adorned it with sprigs of green foliage and planted its cavernous interior with candles so that it glowed like a Christmas crib ringed with lambent faces.

"But it's an antique!" an outraged local official exclaimed, mindful of the building's designation as a museum. The Greeks ignored him in their haste to repossess, for what little time they had, the church that had been taken from them eighty years before.

The service began. The closely packed congregation crossed themselves repeatedly as a procession of black-swathed, bearded priests holding Bibles and icons aloft passed among them. A thurible swung with a yo-yo rhythm. At the stone altar a bishop in gold-braided robes, palms raised, stood to receive them. It was as the responses rose from the congregation that there was a brief flurry of color; a figure in red had peeled away from a group of Turkish officials to position himself at the top of the apse, between the two propped icons of St. Nicholas. The wintry light that entered the church through the three arched windows high in the apse hardly illuminated the liturgy. Instead, it fell upon the newly arrived Santa and all but gave him the floor. But this was not the Christmas grotto of a distant department store on Fifth Avenue or Oxford Street, and these were not children. To the congregation, Santa seemed impiously off-station. Placing himself at the head of the basilica like that, where a wall painting or icon (or stained-glass window in the West) of Christ or the Virgin, a major saint at the very least, usually presided; it was to hijack an event that was no business of his.

Santa Claus had enjoyed an association of sorts with Demre since the 1950s, when archaeological excavations had first brought the basilica to international notice; its labeling as the real home of Santa Claus was inevitable. Santa had been a fixture on December 6 at Demre since the 1990s, when the authorities had first allowed the feast of St. Nicholas to be celebrated. He came with civic banners bearing the exultation "Santa Claus, a Love Born in Anatolia and Exported to the World." It was not the Greek visitors, however, who had invited him but the Turkish authorities; they had deployed him, under a touristic pretext, as sanitized soundproofing against the territorial vibrations that the mass caused. Santa served to muffle St. Nicholas in a warm, apolitical wadding of the sort his grotto was padded by. The authorities had long been wary of the saint's special significance. St. Nicholas was a reminder of Anatolia's Christian heritage, one that predated the Turks' own emergence from the steppes of western China by at least five hundred years. He also happened to be the patron saint of Turkey's two traditional enemies, the bastions of Orthodoxy which had long believed this land to be theirs. St. Nicholas was a symbol of Greek loss and Russian frustration.

It was no surprise, then, that the Greeks should have resented Santa's presence at Demre. What they would not see was what they had in common with him. Like their own forebears, Santa had suffered displacement and been compelled to adapt. He himself was a Greek who had been forced to leave Anatolia, fleeing before an earlier Turkish advance; the difference was that he had left posthumously. Even so, his was as much a migrant's story as theirs. He had had no choice but to leave. What they shared were journeys which had begun here, without knowing where those journeys would take them or what they themselves might become.

4

THE GREEKS AND RUSSIANS did not linger. They had made their pilgrimages and would now be tourists, visiting what remained of the ancient city, which had survived the silt by virtue of its position on the rocky hills a mile north of the modern town: a fine amphitheater littered with fallen columns and a cliff face dotted with Lycian rock tombs. They then filed onto their coaches and were gone, leaving the town to the Turks. I returned to the basilica, empty except for a museum worker in a blue boiler suit kneeling before the sarcophagus. He levered wax from its floor, each piece as irregularly shaped as the pitted surface where it had puddled except for the smooth crescent curve formed by the candle base. With the removal of these last vestiges of Christian reverence, which soon joined the sprigs of holy foliage and the candle stubs in a nearby bucket, the basilica reverted to a museum.

I squatted before the sarcophagus and ran a tentative hand along the horizontal rim of the lid where it was buffed by devotional touch, seeking an initial contact. The sarcophagus was early Byzantine. Its façade took the form of a mansion, with scrolled columns supporting a series of porticoes, though little of it remained beyond a gaping hole where the sarcophagus had been stove in—or ram-raided, in the sarcophagus' own metaphor. The local claim was that the hole dated from 1087, when sailors from Bari in southern Italy removed St Nicholas' relic bones in a daring raid. The truth was that the damage hardly substantiated the identification: all Lycian sarcophagi tended to take a hammering. The claim, furthermore, is all but disproved by the lid, which takes the form of a reclining couch where a Byzantine couple, somewhat battered, lie in effigy. Nicholas, an insistently single saint, is not given to sharing couches.

So much for the initial contact. It might have surprised me that the whereabouts of the saint's original resting place could even be in doubt, not least since his shrine had been the specific draw for countless pilgrims over the centuries. In fact, the uncertainty was ancient, and deliberately nurtured. Obfuscation, for which the Byzantines supposedly had a special talent, had served to keep the saint intact despite those who might covet his remains or wish them harm whenever the rule of law slackened in these parts. With the growth of St. Nicholas' fame, the basilica's sentinels learned to be guarded or expertly vague when dealing with certain foreign visitors—those, for instance, who came equipped with objects that could not be considered devotional, like heavy hammers. Arab raiders who desecrated the wrong tomb during the ninth century were not the last to be misled by the wily Myra priesthood. The strategy was destined for eventual failure, as the relics' absence demonstrated; but long after the bones' disappearance many would claim, Venetians and Russians among them, that the Bari sailors had themselves been duped into removing the wrong ones back in 1087.

Nicholas' bones and sarcophagus were clearly elusive, but this was at least consistent with the man himself, who did not seem to emerge, except as an hagiographical cipher, from the lives and legendaries he inspired in increasing volume from the ninth century (he was hardly chronicled until five hundred years after his death). Every saint of any consequence generated these manuscript lives or synaxaries, which circulated in Greek, Armenian, and Syriac, in Latin and Slavic. The earliest were based on oral tradition, or were recalled from earlier texts destroyed in the iconoclastic purges of the eighth century; in the manner of icons, their representational equivalents, later versions barely deviated from their predecessors. Their authors were exclusively clergymen in cities like Constantinople, Naples, and Rome; archimandrites, deacons, hymnographers and panegyrists based in scriptoria and schools of rhetoric who strove to fashion formulaic encomia, riveted together with stock flourishes and familiar narrative devices that conveyed unchanging Christian verities through the saint's example. A life described the saint's origins, birth, childhood, education, and death, and offered the miracles the saint had performed as proof of intercessional ability with God. These lives were designed to be read aloud to congregations on the feast day of the saint they honored. They bore repetition, year after year, like narrative rosaries. These chronicles, it need not be said, did not aspire to biography in the modern sense. They did not seek to express individuality nor to illuminate the human experience. Indeed, any such element that may have clung to the account was routinely eroded as succeeding lives honed the saint to uniformity within the essential saintly types: the hermit ascetic; the reformed prodigal; the apostle; the visionary; the martyr. The fixed expressions I had noticed on the icons of St. Nicholas now made sense. They conveyed an abstracted ideal, offering no clue to the man: Orthodoxy's "No comment."

In the case of St. Nicholas, however, the hagiographers had left the door ajar; only ever so slightly but enough to cause them to fail in their best efforts to close it upon the last traces of his humanity. They had discovered in their subject a complexity of character which prevented them from reducing him to a fit in any of the established saintly categories. He would duly be seen as a pointedly early example of a new type, the confessor, which might even have been invented for him. The Latin-derived term referred to those who bore witness to God's work by the example of their lives. Confessors lived lives of social value; the notion was surprisingly uncommon at the time of Nicholas, largely because sainthood was mostly achieved through the manner of death. If he was to have imitated the example of the great majority of his canonized Anatolian contemporaries in the early fourth century, the defining feature of Nicholas' life should have been its brutal termination. He should have been a martyr saint.

Martyrdom was the ultimate avowal of faith in the early church, and the very imitation of Christ's own example three centuries previously. Eusebius evoked willing Christians lining up to denounce the pagan gods. They refused to burn incense at the statues and derided the sacrificial rites before offering their sunburnt napes to the sword; this may have appeared brave but was more likely an attempt to provoke a mercifully straightforward end. Instead, they must expect to be stripped naked and scourged before salt and vinegar were rubbed into their wounds where bones protruded. They might be confined with leopards and bears, bulls and boars enraged by the application of red-hot irons; suffer sharpened reeds to be driven beneath the fingernails, molten lead to be poured across the torso; or be strung by the ankles between two trees that had been roped together: young poplars perhaps, still vibrant with the sap that would catapult them apart upon their release.

St. Nicholas is not entirely absent from these gory scenes. The lives state that he suffered imprisonment under Diocletian, whose commanders were responsible for the most extreme persecutions from A.D. 303. They also state, however, that Nicholas died in his bed at the end of a long life. All of which suggests that he was not where he should have been, especially since the bishops, as the church's very sinew, were a particular target of the persecutors. This made him the Byzantine equivalent of the able young man enjoying himself in the clubs of Piccadilly in the summer of 1916. What could have caused him to dodge the martyr's draft, save a lack of moral courage?

It was no surprise that martyrdom should have guaranteed canonization; it not only represented the ultimate personal sacrifice but also served the Christian institution in its struggle to become established. Martyrdom functioned as the religion's recruiting officer, refreshing it with the force of admiring new converts. Tertullian called the blood of the martyrs the seed of the church; it was their unwavering belief that sowed doubts among the pagan prosecutors and caused the baying crowds to fall silent in the arena. But martyrdom's effect was cumulative; to ensure the fall of the pagan gods, this spectacular coup de théâtre was required to play repeatedly. Martyrs were their religion's cannon fodder. Their sheer weight of numbers condemned the mass of them, like the fallen at Ypres, to collective memorials—and individual oblivion. There were admittedly plenty of surviving martyr saints, like St. George, the Christian officer in the Roman army who was beheaded at Nikomedia for protesting at the persecutions in A.D. 303. But more typical were the long forgotten Juliane, also beheaded at Nikomedia, in A.D. 309, for refusing to recant, and Methodius, bishop of Olympos, whose own martyrdom had not prevented obscurity claiming him while his episcopal counterpart at nearby Myra set about a glorious future.

I venture that a private thought may have occurred to Nicholas; that there were less painful ways of serving the faith—or aspiring to sainthood—than martyrdom. The work of the martyrs, like that of the horseback regiments, was in the past now; and the Faith, by their extraordinary sacrifices, had acquired a momentum that would lead the empire under Constantine to embrace Christianity in A.D. 313. Was this the basis of Nicholas' moral courage? That, as Christianity stood on the brink of endorsement, he should now live and devote himself to the world, even though dying for one's belief remained the glamour choice as the preeminent expression of Christian virtue?

I stepped across tarnished brown and gray mosaics into the empty nave, and looked up. I uttered Nicholas' name, hearing its echo loop around the vaulted roof above me, then tried it in a Greek accent as I had heard it during the morning's mass: Nikolaos. I listened for something beyond the echo, but there were only the noises of a distant tractor and a radio playing in a ticket booth. And a rhythmic scratching, like a noisy cicada, that I could not account for. I followed the sound from the basilica, tracing it to the far side of a plywood board that sectioned off part of the complex. I peered through a gap, straight into the eyes of a man holding a dusty scalpel. He was an archaeologist whose name was Ridvan Bey, and he opened a makeshift door to let me in. I found myself in a narrow room on the south side of the complex; it was a secret arcade with a series of deep arched alcoves, flanked by marble pillars, set into both walls. Vaulting arced upward from the pillars to end in space; the roof was long gone, the whole now protected by yellow plastic sheeting. On all sides were scaffold platforms where young students scraped at the plaster walls with their scalpels; here was the source of the strange scratching noise.

"This entire room, probably a mausoleum, was buried in the earth for many centuries," explained Ridvan Bey. "And all that time, the plaster attracted a crust of whitish calcite which the floods carried from the limestone mountains. We are slowly removing this crust." The crust hid frescoes from the twelfth century.

"They are secco," Ridvan Bey continued; the images had been painted onto dry plaster rather than by the usual method which was to apply them when the plaster was still wet, sealing the image more durably in place. "They are very fragile." But they were there; it was as if the calcite crust had fortuitously come to the protection of these delicate frescoes. I was reminded of the English Puritans whose intended destruction of church paintings, by daubing them with whitewash, had inadvertently preserved them for more tolerant times. I stood back and looked around at the faint images as the restorers coaxed them from the walls, like shy things blinking in the light. The effect was fragmented. The plaster had long since fallen in many places, reducing the paintwork it bore to dust. The restorers had concentrated their energies on small sections where the plaster remained intact. These recovered squares and rectangles appeared as windows where the paintings' original colors—vermilions, lemon yellows, cerulean blues—showed through; they also had the effect of illuminating the fainter surrounding frescoes by imaginative extension. I began to make out haloed heads, robed and kneeling figures, crosses and crowds, bearded faces, a ship's bow.

I was standing before a visual representation of St. Nicholas' life, a legendary in pictorial form. It was a rare thing; the only such life, or narrative cycle, known to have survived in the saint's Anatolian homeland, and only now emerging after centuries in hiding. I had seen such cycles in the West. They commonly featured as many as fourteen episodes and took various forms and arrangements. They often appeared as wood-framed painted panels along nave walls, or as a predella, a paneled altar base, depicting multiple episodes. Sometimes, the episodes appeared on stone tablets where they were carved around a central iconic image of the saint. The Russians enameled them in miniature, the English worked them in stained-glass church windows, and on the Lido at Venice they were carved as wooden reliefs on a set of choir stalls. They functioned as billboards, and this one put Nicholas' life up in lights at the hub of his cult. As I stared, identifiable episodes began to emerge from the walls. Here Nicholas appeared in a vision to reassure three commanders as they languished in prison, falsely accused and awaiting death. Here, he stayed the executioner's arm above the bowed head of an innocent. In one, he stood beside a young boy he had rescued from Arab captivity; in another, he calmed a heaving sea. Of one episode, however, there was no sign: the moment at the window was missing.

It was the most popular of all the stories, a staple of the cycles. Symeon, Nicholas' preeminent chronicler, called it "the most charitable and the best known" of all the saint's deeds. The episode must once have appeared on these walls; either it was on a section of plaster which had long since fallen, or it was still concealed beneath the crust. Only the restorers could answer that question, and in their own time. But in its absence, it was left to Symeon to reveal the narrative either side of the moment at the window:

A prosperous nobleman of Patara, a city of Lycia, fell into poverty. He eventually determined, since no suitors could be found for his three beautiful daughters in their impecunious state, to sell them into prostitution. The nobleman was already making preparations to this end when God sent Nicholas to his aid. Nicholas, not wishing to be identified in his philanthropy, went to the nobleman's house in the dead of night and—the moment of the image—threw a bag of gold through the window. In the morning, when the man found the mysterious gift, he was elated and married off his eldest daughter forthwith, using the gold as her dowry.

In time, it came to Nicholas' attention that the nobleman was now proposing to sell his second daughter into prostitution. He once more returned at night to throw a bag of gold through the window. The second daughter was married off accordingly. On the third occasion, when the gold thudded against the floor, the nobleman stepped outside and pursued the donor to discover who was responsible for these great kindnesses. The cowl was removed to reveal Nicholas, who bound the nobleman never to divulge his generosity.

"Three Daughters," as the story was commonly known, was not entirely without precedent. Cyprian of Carthage, a Christian lawyer and teacher and subsequently a bishop martyr, had liquidated all his worldly goods and given the proceeds to the poor around A.D. 240. The act was remarkable, largely because a hollowness was perceived to have prevailed in the application of philanthropy under the pagans. Ignatius, the bishop of Antioch, wrote how the pagans "do not care for acts of love, they don't care about the widow, the orphan, the distressed, the afflicted, the prisoner, or for him released from prison, neither do they worry about the hungry and thirsty." Carthage once again exemplified Christian charity when an epidemic broke out in A.D. 251. The Christians tended the sick and the dying, even those who had persecuted them. It was as if Christianity had reoriented the pagan notions of charity, directing them beyond family and friends to focus on the needs of strangers.

Nicholas, caught red-handed, insisted, in the modern phrase, on anonymity; an instance of personal discretion which some have used to explain his absence from documented history. He didn't get his anonymity, of course. He didn't get anything like it. It may even have been that the nobleman was quick to break his vow, telling his three daughters, as well as prospective sons-in-law and friends that he woke with urgent whispers at their own high windows; and that the story of Nicholas' charity began its long journey into the world the very night he was discovered.

Things to note: an arrival at night, bearing secret gifts to the young.

I thanked Ridvan Bey, left the hidden arcade, and made my way to the hotel. I retrieved my bag from the lobby and was stepping into the street when I heard the maid call from an upstairs window. I looked up to see her at the window of my room. "You forgot your Noel Baba," she said,

laughing, and tossed me the Santa magnet which I had left on the bedstead. I was about to ask for the icon as well, which the maid had not noticed, but thought better of it at the last moment. I would leave the saint
in possession of the town; after all, he who had stayed in Orthodox Anatolia all those centuries ago could stay a while longer. By the same token,
it seemed fitting that Santa should come with me; it was, after all, his own
journey. So I thanked her, pocketed the magnet, and slipped away through
the darkening streets.

5

I HAD NOTICED AN antique marble slab propped among the stacks of numbered masonry in the weed-strewn courtyard of the basilica. The slab had lost its upper corners, perhaps as the result of an earthquake or inundation (or even the attentions of a Muslim zealot; it bore the motif, in raised relief, of a cross). What interested me was the intact lower section. From either side of the vertical at its base, pointed flukes bent upward to recast the cross, with the connivance of the horizontal, as a ship's anchor.

The road to the sea, two miles from Demre, passed beyond the hothouses and crossed bleached winter grasslands strewn with heaps of rubble and ancient ashlar footings. It then dropped into a shallow river valley under a sky leached of all color. Herons speared mussels on chill mudflats which were strewn with tiny islets, their dark green salt bushes neat as topiary. Concrete benches molded in the shape of bark-covered timbers announced the port of Andriake. Along the quayside, a mean wind fretted at the shrouds of the blue fishing caïques. Nearby wooden gulets were moored; these Anatolian freighters had lugged oranges and lemons to Fethiye and Antalya before being adapted as tourist cruisers.

The port had been stripped bare, leaving only its history. In A.D. 62, a ship carrying St. Paul had put in here to embark him on an Alexandrian vessel bound for Rome. A little way inland, among the pine trees and olive groves, were the ruins of riverbank warehouses, walls, and cisterns, and what remained of numerous basilicas including an apse that had survived the collapse of its nave, its brick innards rudely exposed. The whole settlement was dominated by a massive edifice enclosed by high ashlar walls: the great second-century granary of the Emperor Hadrian. Interior walls divided it into bins, ruinously open to the sky and choked with myrtle and olives, where the produce of inland Lycia was once stored.

Andriake had flourished by virtue of its position on the sea route east.

Ships hopped between the islands of the Aegean, but when these stepping-stones dwindled at Rhodes they sought in Anatolia for their landmarks and ports of call: Makri, Patara, the close-to-shore island of Kastellorizo, and Andriake. At Andriake, shipping heading for the great ports of Beirut, Sidon, Tyre, Jaffa, and Ashkelon (for Jerusalem), Suez, or even Alexandria found the open sea finally beginning to insist. A southeasterly bearing, passing to the west of Cyprus, would bring ships straight to the Holy Land. Which made it the natural point of final departure for the East; and a noted seat of the sailors' gods who would preserve them on their passage.

Sailors leaving Andriake were subjected to a fading coastline. It was an unfamiliar sight after the abundantly littered islands and islets of the Cyclades and the Dodecanese; perhaps even one that some of them, particularly the archipelago Greeks, had never experienced. Greek sailors have long had a reputation for hugging the shore, which Alexander Kinglake, voyaging east from Smyrna in 1834 on a Greek brigantine, was well aware of. "I knew enough of Greek navigation," he wrote in the classic *Eothen*, "to be sure that our vessel would cling to earth like a child to its mother's knee, and that I should touch at many an isle before I set foot upon the Syrian coast." In the land-encompassed world of the fourth century, the departure from Andriake was alarmingly vertiginous, just as weighing anchor at Lisbon, Cádiz, or Brest for the Atlantic was liable to be in latter centuries.

No surprise, then, that sailors should have sought particular protection before leaving Andriake. In ancient times, seafarers made regular visits to the shoreline temples of Poseidon and Ephesian Artemis there, framing their appeals in accordance with the particular marine fears that preyed upon them: navigational misfortune; unfavorable winds, such as sudden onshore southerlies blowing from the Sahara; or the sea demons that dragged ships beneath the waves, the nymphs who lured unwary sailors into their submarine embrace.

With the imperial adoption of Christianity in A.D. 313, the old gods were gradually driven out. Veneration was to be focused upon Jesus Christ, but polytheism had deep roots, which no doubt reflected the workaday tendency to specialization. It was the way of the world that solutions to a wide range of problems were not to be found in one place. Experience taught that the shipwright's assistance was not to be sought when it came to earache, nor did the soapmaker know much about the prevention of fruit blight. So it was with divinities; it was asking too much of Jesus Christ, may his name be praised, that he should be a universal panacea, with power over everything from warts to sea demons. The old gods did not die, then, but were simply repackaged, as saints. They were reinstalled in chapels, which were built on the sites of former temples. So it was with Nicholas, saint of the shoreline.

Nicholas' marine influence spread throughout the Mediterranean, the Aegean, and the Adriatic, into the Black Sea and latterly across the oceans. Trading ships and caïques took his name or hung his icon in the cabin, honoring it with a burning lamp. On the brig that bore Alexander Kinglake to the Holy Land, an image of St. Nicholas, enclosed in a glass case, was "hung up like a barometer at one end of the cabin." Until the Reformation, nearly every coast throughout Europe and Russia had its churches and chapels of St. Nicholas where sailors would light candles and leave crabs' shells painted with his image. Just as ships' cabins tended to resemble shrines, so there was much of the ship or the chandlery about the mariners' chapels, with coiled cables, anchors, buoys, navigation lamps, and strips of sail strewn about as votive offerings. There were ships' models, in bottles or under glass domes, or arranged as lamps that were suspended from the ceiling by the vessel's shrouds.

These offerings were not designed to insure sailors and shipowners against future mishap, but were given in settlement, as testimony that divine protection had actually been provided. They did not anticipate the saint's intercession but demonstrated his power to deliver. The chapels of St. Nicholas were commonly hung with votive ships shaped out of silver or wax, and with painted sea scenes. These paintings depicted dire events: foundering ships, stormy seas, flailing sails, and lee shores. They were pledged by crews at the moment of their greatest need, on the understanding that the saint would deliver them. Each picture was commissioned on the crew's safe return, not only providing a visual record of its plight but also including written details of the date and place of the celestial intervention. It also contained an invariable break in the storm clouds, often in the top corner, where St. Nicholas hovered in the reassuring manner of a coast guard helicopter.

Nicholas, no doubt, was in the right place at the right time to make a play for the influential territories of Poseidon and Ephesian Artemis: a topranking Christian at a hub of sea-god veneration just when personalities from the new faith were being sought to fill the old tutelary roles. Even so, Nicholas did seem woefully short of what can only be called relevant experience. In the narrative cycles, he was increasingly represented as a maritime rescuer, but only under the self-perpetuating influence of his burgeoning sea cult. The earliest surviving legendaries do not suggest that Nicholas was much of a sailor; they rarely place him at Andriake. On one instance the bishop did walk down to the port, but only to quell a disturbance that had arisen when accusations of pilfering were leveled at some visiting sailors. He hardly ever put to sea during his life and then only in visionary form (hardly what could be called hands-on experience); once, to persuade a grain merchant to bring his cargo to famine-starved Myra, and on another occasion to quell a storm that was threatening a ship off Andriake. Nor did he delay after that storm in returning to Myra, where the sailors found him back in physical guise when they put ashore to thank him for his assistance. The top sea job went to a man who never knowingly set foot aboard a ship.

Nicholas seems to have been assisted on this occasion—not the only time—by the same man who had confirmed his very historical substance, Nicholas of Sion. Sion was a proper sailor. He made two sixth-century sea pilgrimages to the Holy Land, taking ship once at Andriake and once at nearby Tristromo (modern Üçagiz). He learned through experience to quell storms and to reorient problem winds. Not that Sion's nautical know-how was to benefit him. In the course of the saints' entanglement, his hard-won ability passed straight into the bloodstream of his more illustrious namesake. Sion, deprived of his master's certificate, headed for comparative oblivion while Nicholas established himself as the saint of choice among seafarers, a breed of devotees unmatched in their ability to get themselves—and those they carried—to far-off places. In the matter of saintly advance, no patronage was more significant.

Did Nicholas ever imagine, on those rare visits to Andriake, that sailors might one day carry his name out into the world from this very quayside? It is the case that every instance of his name, which litters the charts even today, originated here. Harbors, sheltered bays and islets are called Agios Nikolaos (St. Nicholas) all along the coast of Greece and its islands: in the Mani and on the Gulf of Corinth, in the Cyclades—on Tinos and Naxos—and on Hydra and Samos, Symi and Karpathos, Zakynthos, Rhodes, Crete, and many others besides. His name snagged on rocks off

Sicily and reefs off Valencia. It caught on coastal monasteries and forts, capes and peaks among the splintery archipelagoes off Croatia. Ports and moles, shoreline towers, shoals and river mouths, channels and headlands from Nigeria to Florida, from Haiti to the Philippines, from California to the Cape Verde Islands bear his name. It reached Morbihan, Brittany, and Quebec, Canada, and Venezuela and Mexico. It attached to islands off Cornwall and Berwick-upon-Tweed on the Scottish borders. The saint gave his name to fishing boats, ferries, and freighters, and even to an English light vessel. Churches and chapels dedicated to St. Nicholas crowd the water's edge. In Britain, they are to be found at Deptford and Chiswick on the River Thames in London; and at Southampton, Romney, Ilfracombe, Bristol, Gloucester, Liverpool, Aberdeen, Newcastle, Great Yarmouth, Ipswich, and numerous smaller ports. Elsewhere, they dominate great ports such as Bari and Venice, Amsterdam and Hamburg, Tallinn and St. Petersburg, Helsinki and New York.

I watched a fishing boat returning to port, and thought how Myra and its hinterland had depended upon Andriake for two thousand years. The patronage of sailors had not only spread Nicholas' name across the world; its first job had been to spring him from the confines of Myra's alluvial plain. Hemmed in by mountains, Myra depended upon Andriake just as Rome relied on Ostia, and had continued to do so until recent times. The only natural link with the interior was by the deep gorge of the Demre river, an arduous fifteen-mile route which the traveler D. E. Colnaghi had negotiated in 1854, taking seven hours and fording the river on twenty separate occasions in the process. Even at that time, though the Lycian coast was largely depopulated, the people of the uplands continued to ship their produce from these ports. Colnaghi witnessed pine logs and plank loading at Olympos to the east of Andriake, and a grain cargo at Dalyan to the west. The region's produce left by its ports as surely as the silt found its way there by the rivers.

I walked down the quay to meet the fishing boat, its red and white pennant of crescent moon and stars fluttering from the shroud, and considered the traders and sailors, crusaders and pilgrims who had called at Andriake over the centuries. Some left with cargoes: cedar, sacks of grain, amphorae of wine. Others, buoyed by spiritual sustenance, merely provisioned themselves with a replenished water jar, with bread and figs. But few would have neglected to take with them the blessing of the local saint, protector of seafarers, whose shrine lay a short journey inland. Andriake's greatest export had always been Nicholas of Myra, and the sea was the saint's formidable delivery system.

I hailed the fisherman and asked him whether he would take me along the coast. It would be good to follow in the wakes of the old cargoes— acorns, sponges, and oranges and, long ago, a casket containing a saint's revered bones. By this simple act, I would commemorate all those former departures that had carried Nicholas' name out of this port to put him ashore in distant lands. The fisherman just looked at me and said through a mouth of slewed teeth, "Fakat yol var": But there's a road.

6

THE FISHERMAN MIGHT HAVE indulged me, especially since banknotes had been proffered. But he was right about the road. A broad, surfaced highway secured Demre to the outside world fore and aft. On the west edge of town, beyond the tattered lemon groves, it headed for Fethiye; and on the east side, beyond the petrol stations, it wound around the headland toward Finike and Antalya.

But the time it had taken arriving: the terrain was viciously contoured. In the 1830s, a French officer in Charles Texier's party had attempted to walk east to Myra from Simena, one of the shore villages at nearby Kekova, a distance of just fifteen miles. But he soon lost his way among bouldered gorges, dry stream beds, and pine forests, and walked for two days and nights without water or food before being returned to his colleagues in a state of distress by some considerate Yörüks. Demre continued to depend upon Andriake for its links with the outside world until the 1960s; it was then that a ten-meter-wide ribbon of tarmac began to be laid along the dynamited hillside cuttings on either side of the town. Demre's produce began leaving by lorry, piled unfeasibly high so that the wooden cartons often spilled on the hairpins, to leave a roadside mush of tomatoes, tinder, and whirring wasps. And so Andriake died.

The road to the west had been recently widened. A twenty-meter strip of highway climbed effortlessly through rocky hillsides of pine and myrtle, turning back on itself with a flourish to present a final view of the town far below. The alluvial plain momentarily resembled a patchwork of paddy fields before the silvery rectangles revealed themselves as hothouse roofs, all except one, which bore a distinct tinge of yellow (as if the paddy had been pissed in): the plastic awning over the basilica. The fanciful Cathay illusion quickly faded, but a residual sense of something Levantine,

even Arabian, clung to Demre and its port. I had spotted it in the accounts. Texier had disembarked at Andriake to the Oriental vision of an
African and camels that bore him, pasha-like, to Myra. There were further traces in the 1950s when the British writer Freya Stark noted how the
Arabic expressions which Turkish has absorbed—"Yaalah!" "Salaam
aleikum!"—were used here with an almost indigenous familiarity. It was
also notable in the absence of the Hellenic character that prevailed at
neighboring Kas and Kekova, in their bougainvillea-clad cottages, with
terra-cotta-tiled roofs and whitewashed walls. At Myra, Nicholas was
touched by the East; which was what would duly draw him, in the way of
opposites, to the West.

The road began to climb. On the seaward side, gorges fell away to
thickly forested floors, where I imagined the long-ago wanderings of an
increasingly confused French officer. The road crossed a narrow plain
where pebble-dashed fields huddled, giving way to inland limestone jags
where the scrub thinned toward the white peaks. Suddenly, thin flakes
drifted out of a pearly sky. I glanced at the rearview mirror where I had attached my Santa fridge magnet; the snow, even this thin fall, prefigured
the landscapes that would unfurl around Nicholas by the end of his journey. It seemed that the scenes of Nicholas' life, olive trees throbbing with
cicadas and the sound of goat bells on sun-bleached scrub slopes, were
fading even now as he began his voyage west and north, toward whiteout.
Cold is the price, as lowland Pakistanis in Connecticut and muffled Kurds
in Oslo have discovered, of forced migration.

The snow had barely dusted the pine branches, however, before the
road peaked and plunged toward the sea beneath a clearing sky. I passed
Kaş, where the Greek island of Kastellorizo lay two miles offshore in a
puddle of winter sunlight. Beyond Kalkan, more high ground sent the
road switchbacking through the pines before it coiled down into the Xanthos valley. At the end of a narrow track, sunless waves drove up the beach
where loggerhead turtles nested during the summer. They laid their egg
clutches in sandy holes that they dug with their flippers during the night.
Above the beach, where the turtles had hatched in the autumn, a line of
dunes was gradually backing through protective eucalypts into what remained of Patara. The turtles shared the place of their birth with St.
Nicholas.

Patara had been an important city—at the time of Nicholas' birth, it was the capital of all Lycia, famed for its elegant baths, monumental gateway, and theater. Its temple was home to a revered oracle, and an imperial granary to rank with Myra's stood by the harbor's edge.

That was then. The dunes were now repossessing the ancient theater. The sand skittered inland on the bitter wind. It dusted the exposed black and rubbery roots of the eucalypts, crested the acropolis hill, and plumed over the banks of marble seats, which earthquakes had shunted into unusual angles. I perched on a fallen column. Nobody was about. Not that I was looking for company, only a spark that might evoke something of a late-third-century child innocent of the earliest intimations of sainthood. This was not biographical whimsy. The key to Nicholas' very meaning lay in his childhood. Without it, he would once more bring a serious shortage of relevant experience to a position of extraordinary influence. The sailors' saint who had never been to sea, and now the children's patron whose own childhood could not even be sensed?

The lives, predictably enough, did not help. Symeon introduced Nicholas' childhood by describing his father, as if the parental example alone would suffice; wealthy, but admirably incapable of owning anything for his own selfish purposes. As for Nicholas himself, he proved prenatally miraculous, leaving his mother sterile from the moment of his conception as if Nature, in Symeon's words, having lavished such bounty, could offer no more. In his thirteenth-century life, Jacob of Varazze had it that Nicholas' parents resorted to celibacy thereafter. The lives were generally agreed that the infant Nicholas wasted no time before demonstrating the virtues of abstinence, confining himself twice a week to single daily feedings from his mother's breast.

It was up to me, then, to draw out the boy from another time. I tried to conjure him on the quayside, counting the ships out of harbor, catching a fig that a sailor lobbed at him as his barque drew clear, bound for Ostia. Or receiving a cup of wheat from the man at the granary to feed his caged finches. Or awakening to a traditional gift from his parents—a pottery figure, perhaps—on the morning of Saturnalia, the great winter festival of the Romans: the boy who at least knew what it felt like to receive. But the gulf was too wide and the images did not stick. Reeds and silt had long since claimed the harbor, Patara's free-flying finches were in Africa, and the boy would not emerge. When my mind did finally settle, it was not on Nicholas' childhood but on one in which he had played a dominant part: my own, in 1960s England.

Every Christmas Eve, we sent letters up the chimney. Occasionally, when bouts of creativity and greed combined, the letters would be adorned with objects cut from the color supplements: cars, campers, puppies, bikes, even jet fighters, and once a stairlift were all pasted into place. These dispatches might have seemed at one with the decorative festivity—the holly and ivy from the garden, the wreath and tree, the Christmas cards hung over a string that was slung in shallow loops from the banisters like a washing line. They were in fact calculated in their intent, which was to close off Father Christmas' usual loophole—supplying toy miniatures in place of their full-size equivalents—by providing him with photographic evidence of our requests. That way, there could be no room for misunderstanding.

The chimney in the sitting room was big. It generated an impressive draft, which easily dealt with the standard folded notes, whipping them in a stream of sparks straight to Father Christmas. These pasted documents were a different matter. Getting them airborne was a challenge to his scouting skills that my father could not resist. My father was not the type to rely on the popular fallback, that Father Christmas could divine messages in the rising smoke of burned letters, especially if the challenge of delivering them entailed the exciting possibility of setting fire to himself. He threw on more logs and stoked the blaze before balancing a letter upon the pronged poker, which he extended high up the chimney. He then gave his arm a practiced flick which launched the letter, for better or worse, like a fledgling toppled from its nest.

Persistence paid off; the letters eventually disappeared up the chimney. Months later, however, when nesting birds or equinoctial winds disturbed the letters from the chimney ledges where they had lodged, they were liable to return, damning those in the know. All through the spring, my parents kept a watching brief on the hearth, dreading the reappearance of soot-stained, rain-streaked pages illustrated with Labrador puppies and Mercedes cars: a notice to their children that the ways of the world could be downright suspicious, as well as a reminder that the puppies and the cars, despite those unambiguous letters, had not been delivered.

At bedtime, we laid out the biggest socks we could find. These were our father's knee-length ribbed hiking stockings. Rumor had it that they used pillowcases at Bruce's house. There was something so flagrant about this ploy to increase capacity that I never quite got over the disappointment of discovering that Father Christmas had not taken my friend to task over this. The depressing discovery that Bruce's haul was as large as ever would not, however, be made until Boxing Day. In the meantime, there was the delightful sensation of waking to a weight upon my toes; a disembodied leg, one contorted as if by carbuncular contusions. Not that the stockings' contents varied much from year to year. A few years in, I was able to predict that the unpacking would begin with a rolled-up spring-bound notebook. This not only lent the upper calf an agreeable smoothness absent in the lower leg but worked as a welcome sock extension where a few final items, often a sugar mouse and a pencil eraser—I had a lot of stationery from Father Christmas—could be securely lodged. Farther down, where the leg went lumpy, I would find the bouncy ball, the flat-ended pencils and pencil sharpener, the chocolate soldiers, and the spring-loaded plastic insect, often a ladybird. A six-inch transparent plastic ruler usually functioned as a prosthetic Achilles tendon, supporting the ankle where a tangerine nestled in the heel. There was a pack of playing cards and a string bag of chocolate coins wrapped in golden foil. Finally, there was a walnut and a square of sugary fudge; I knew these to be seasonal staples because my mum made the same fudge, from condensed milk, sugar, and vanilla essence, and also bought walnuts at the supermarket in the days before Christmas.

Thirty years later, I watched my own children make sense of Father Christmas. Unlike the 1960s, when Father Christmas rarely made it in person beyond the city department stores and was all but unheard of as a visible presence in our village, he ranged far more widely now. Anna and Lizzie encountered him throughout December. He made appearances in the shops, at school, and on the streets as every organization and association pressed him into service. It was the fact that Father Christmas was so obviously a multiply incarnated figure which had allowed Anna, at six, to work out that they must all be phonies, except for one. By this logic, she was able to discard those Father Christmas experiences that did not live up to expectation—notably, her recent visit to Santa's Kingdom—without undermining her belief in the man.

Last Christmas, Anna thought she was on to the real Father Christmas when he appeared one afternoon at the allotments where the local gardeners grew their vegetables. Here, they had prepared a grotto for Father Christmas in one of the sheds, which they had emptied of tools and seed trays, and hung with greenery. The children did not much like the allotments; parents who grew their own vegetables tended to insist that their children should eat them. Even so, they formed an orderly queue that snaked between lines of wilted spinach. When Anna emerged from the grotto, clutching a box of crayons, the light in her eyes spoke of mysteries solved.

"I think that's the real one," she said. "He knew that I like drawing." The magic did not reside, then, in flying reindeer, miraculous chimney descents, or the dizzying rate at which the man worked; the real Father Christmas was the one who knew her mind.

Nicholas' largely invisible childhood was followed by a typically hagiographical adolescence, where his chroniclers blithely fended off the usual awkward human preoccupations that might have distracted their subject from his studies. He attended school, at nearby Xanthos in some sources, where he excelled. Symeon again: "In a short time Nicholas mastered the many disciplines . . . [He] avoided immoderate companions and consorting and conversing with women. Refusing even so much as to turn his eyes in their direction, he bade them goodbye . . . and spent all his time in holy churches." Symeon and his like, casting Nicholas in the values of their own worlds, did him no favors. Certainly, insufferable piety was something Nicholas couldn't be stuck with in the long term, not if he was to endear himself to children at the far arc of his future.

It was not long after he completed his schooling that Nicholas moved from Patara to Myra, which would be his base for the rest of his life. It was a first demonstration of the attribute which would serve him much better than sanctimony: an uncanny positional sense. This opportunism, already implied in Nicholas' adroit acquisition of seafaring's patronage, persisted beyond his death and would duly become a defining characteristic of his progress through the centuries.

The sense behind the move was not immediately obvious. Indeed, the striking similarities between the two ports—the granaries; the harbors where St. Paul had called (and which would subsequently silt); the theaters and the basilicas—suggested an incomprehensible sideways maneuver. What appeal could Myra hold that would cause him to abandon the place of his birth?

The answer was, Opportunity. It was at exactly this time that the emperor Constantine removed the Lycian capital from Patara and instead conferred it on Myra. Exit Nicholas, smartly abandoning a waning city for its rising replacement. This strategic relocation would duly serve as the model for a whole series of posthumous ones, except in one regard: it would prove to be his only move east. After Myra, his future bearing was set—westward, with some north in it, all the way.

Nicholas had not quite finished with Patara. The city of his birth was the setting for his defining act of charity. Self-interest might have caused Nicholas to leave Patara, but not before he had dispensed with a fortune to save a family there. At Patara, Nicholas' adolescent piety was erased by the generosity for which he would henceforth be known. No documentation confirms "Three Daughters" as historical fact, but what distinguishes the story from many of the other Nicholas episodes—visionary appearances, adolescent zealousness, abstinence at the breast, storm calming—is that it steers strikingly clear of stock characteristics of hagiography. "Three Daughters" is a misfit, depending neither on the saintly planks of celibacy and asceticism nor on the miraculous, which may explain how it makes the tricky cultural traverse to the modern age with such ease. It immediately finds expression in modern phraseology: the anonymous donation. The act is not only credible and humanly feasible but persistently admirable. All of which lifts it from mere hagiography to insist on its basic truth. The story seems to have its origins not in religious rhetoric but in life itself. Something of the actual man otherwise lost seems to have survived in "Three Daughters"; the Nicholas kernel is carried forward in the one story whose events may have actually occurred.

This was the story that began among these ashlar walls back when they gave shade and shelter to the living. It began with a father whose tongue was loosened with gratitude. It initially circulated, no doubt, with a certain whispered discretion, in a partial attempt—already doomed!—at respecting Nicholas' own wishes: a bolt withdrawn in the early hours and a

Fra Angelico, *The Charity to the Three Girls*, detail from the Perugia Triptych. (© Photo Scala, Florence)

tale breathlessly told, one that was under no circumstances to be repeated, of family salvation. Those who heard it pledged their silence but perhaps presumed exceptions in cases of wives or brothers. Or even discreet friends. Or well-connected acquaintances who regarded the latest gossip as currency and were sure to repay. Which was to say that no time had passed before it began to seep out beyond those whom it had saved. Now, the discretion that attached so firmly in earlier tellings grew weak, not least because the man's generosity was to be celebrated. Everybody was to know what Nicholas had done. Once the story reached the streets, it began to gather pace. It no longer passed from one whispering adult to another, but gripped whole audiences at market stalls and at the bathhouses. These groups splintered to seek out those who had not heard. The story had soon saturated the city. Where the houses thinned at the city's edge it waited for soldiers, shepherds, and envoys to carry it inland to Tlos and Pinara. It soon found its way to the port, which it left with sailors and traders bound for Phaselis and Telmessus. It may even have beaten its subject, who was shortly to arrive there, to Myra. And so it circulated on the back of ten thousand Lycian conversations and even embarked for other shores in the care of traders and pilgrims.

This, of course, was only the beginning. If the story was to really flourish, it needed Nicholas to die.

7

I CONTINUED WEST TO Fethiye, which was known to the ancients as
Telmessus and to more recent residents as Makri, where a sarcophagus
stood in the middle of the road. With its rounded gray back, which rose to
a pronounced spine ten feet clear of the ground, the sarcophagus might
have been an itinerant elephant. Its effect was startling but also practical,
disentangling this port town's traffic streams, temporarily at least, even as
it reminded me of the local genius for carved funerary monument. As the
landscape's numerous sarcophagi and rock tombs testified, the ancient
Lycians did not dispose of their departed so much as set them up in
posthumous residences of unstinting splendor.

With their pitched lids and protruding beam ends, the sarcophagi clearly
represented roofed houses. The lids' keeled spines also lent them a strong
resemblance to capsized ships, which seemed like a spry enough metaphor
for demise among these coastal people; better, anyway, than elephants.
They occupied the plains just as the rock tombs, with their ornate doors,
pillars, and lintels, had colonized the available cliff faces, notably at Myra
but also all over the crags directly above the traffic-island sarcophagus at
Fethiye. The tombs' very forms were evidence that the Lycian afterlife was
insistently material. It was experienced, like life itself, not in some abstracted space but in a meticulously worked representation of home (or
ship, albeit inverted), though treasure hunters had long since smashed
their way in through house's façade or ship's hull, leaving the occupants'
bones for the leopards. Such desecrations awaited Nicholas. At Myra a
long life was drawing to a close, one so garlanded with admirable achievements, interventions, and acts of kindness that sainthood was guaranteed.
Death was merely the moment of transition, delivering him full-time to
the saintly condition that, the lives would subsequently claim, he had regularly visited as a provident vision during his earthly existence: to the
sailors in their foundering barque; to a group of falsely accused, bringing

them comfort in their cell; and even to Constantine himself, to alert the emperor to a grievous injustice. Symeon again: "When he came to the very advanced age, full of days both heavenly and earthly, he must needs comply with the common law of nature, as is man's lot. He was ill but a short time. In the grip of that illness, while rendering those lauds and thanksgivings up to God which are said in death, he happily yielded up his spirit."

Nicholas' tomb is hazily described. Symeon furnishes no details, except to mention that Nicholas was borne to his temenos—his holy precinct—by the local clergy in a torch-lit procession. Jacob of Varazze merely mentions a "marble tomb." We can be sure it was impressive, though, not only because the bishop was revered, but because he had passed his life among a people who excelled at funerary monument. In this respect Nicholas had served himself well yet again, for an eye-catching tomb was essential for a man with extensive posthumous plans. Nicholas had a long time ahead of him being busily dead, and his shrine was less a mere casket for his remains than a springboard for the great journey that lay ahead of him. Which is where we leave him, the lid closing over his remains, as he begins the lengthy process of converting his earthly reputation into the fuel of immortality.

I stopped at a garage to fill up on petrol and bought an air-freshening Christmas tree; the car smelled fine but the tree would provide Santa with familiar surroundings. Beyond the sarcophagus, the road led inland through pine-clad hills before emerging on a bowled plain that the Turks knew as Kaya. It passed between olive groves and plowed fields, and ran beneath the hillside ruins of the town of Levisi, then continued as a pot-holed slalom, throwing wide coils to slow its descent to the sea. I drew up above a short beach at the head of a deeply indented bay where the water had the sheen of chrome. Fishing boats nudged against a rickety wooden jetty. A few hundred meters from the shore, a high-sided island rose to a peak at its western end. Indistinct ruins protruded from its rocky outline. Between island and mainland a strait ran where a breeze barely penetrated; through the summer, gulets competed for this superb anchorage, which the tourist age, unusually enough, had not yet resettled.

The strait lay empty now, its surface so smooth in the lee that the deserted island was reflected in it, the ruins' surviving regularities of arch and ashlar sharp against the random lines of rock and olive trees. It was the sort of place that sailors had always known; like other places where his name had tended to lodge—from Ionia to Brittany and Sicily to the Caribbean—the island was called St. Nicholas.

The name first appeared in the portolanos, or nautical almanacs, of medieval Greek and Genoese sailors, as Agios Nikolaos or San Nicola. It was not the island's only name, of course, which was often the case in Lycia. The Turks knew it as Gemiler, or Boats, and the Greeks as Levisi, which was to say that it shared its Greek name with the abandoned inland town I had passed on the way. As for the compilers of the portolanos, they were referring to a ruined settlement that had flourished and failed the best part of a millennium before their own time. The island ruins, and those along the shore opposite, are reckoned to date from around the 400s, or a century after Nicholas' death. Here, just a hundred miles to the west of Myra, was a first glimpse of posthumous activity as the saint stepped beyond his shrine to secure a secondary foothold on the era's preeminent sea route.

The place is not mentioned in antiquity. The excellent anchorage must, however, have been known to trading sailors for at least fifteen hundred years before Nicholas. A Phoenician wreck found off Kaş in 1984 dated from 1400 B.C. It was not, however, until around the fifth century that the place was developed to cater to a new breed of visitor, the Christian venturing to the holy places to do his devotions there. These pilgrims were pioneering types, courageous, independent of means, and instinctively evangelical. Most important, they were mobile, taking the accounts of their pilgrimages—the holy sites, the places of devotion along the way—home to rapt audiences starved for new stories. Nicholas, newly established on the saints' circuit, needed these people to progress; he must win their devotion.

Christians first began visiting the Holy Land in the late second century, notably when Bishop Melito of Sardis, near Ephesus, set out to establish whether the available facts on the ground tallied with the claims of the Scriptures. Melito, though he traveled in a spirit of inquiry rather than of blind veneration, effectively pioneered the path of the preeminent Christian pilgrimage route. Nothing is known of the bishop's chosen route, though his point of departure, hard by the western coast of Anatolia, almost amounts to confirmation that he traveled by sea. Melito's barque would have passed along this coast, and perhaps even called at the island, the bishop offering up the first Christian prayers in a place that would return them a thousandfold in subsequent centuries.

The pilgrimage concept was given the royal imprimatur by Constantine's mother, Helena, who visited the Holy Land in A.D. 326. She identified the sites of Jesus' crucifixion and burial and had them cleared of buildings and temples, and also recovered from a ditch the Holy Cross and the nails that secured it. Constantine confirmed the work of his mother—the two often share church dedications, particularly in the Orthodox world—by commissioning holy shrines at the major sites in A.D. 335. The Church of the Holy Sepulchre at Jerusalem, built on the site of Christ's burial, was followed by the Church of the Nativity at Bethlehem, and the Church of the Ascension on the Mount of Olives. The Holy Land, previously a geographically remote source of religious inspiration, was now a vigorously promoted destination for the intrepid, complete with an array of visitor sites; and pilgrims arrived from far-flung corners of a rapidly expanding Christendom. At the end of the fourth century, Paulinus of Nola explained how visitors were inspired by seeing the manger of Christ's birth, "the river of his baptism, the garden of his betrayal, the palace of his condemnation, the column of his scourging, the thorns of his crowning, the wood of his execution . . ." More and more holy relics were revered; the sanctity of objects associated with the Scriptures, however doubtful their provenance, preoccupies traditional Christianity even today. They were then coveted; at the Church of the Holy Sepulchre, where a casket containing timbers from the Holy Cross was displayed to receive the kisses of the faithful, one pilgrim began a disreputable tradition by carrying away a mouthful of relic into which he had secretly sunk his teeth.

It was no surprise that the new religion should by then have been established in Palestine and the Nile Valley, Syria, Asia Minor and Mesopotamia, but it could be said that Christianity truly announced the extent of its intentions on the day in A.D. 333 when a pilgrim from Bordeaux turned up. The Roman empire, as we have already seen, had given Christianity the best of starts by persecuting it. The empire indulged every would-be martyr's wish to play the Messiah, and allowed their sublime displays of faith to play to packed houses of potential converts at the local arena. It had also put its efficient network of roads and shipping routes at the new religion's disposal, enabling missionaries to follow in the footsteps of St. Paul, who had preached at Ephesus and Iconium (modern Konya),

Athens, Thessalonika, and Rome. The Christian Word accordingly reached Bordeaux; and a pilgrim of that city, like a returning echo, retraced the journey to the East.

The Bordeaux pilgrim had journeyed overland to Jerusalem, by Milan, Constantinople, and Tarsus. But the sea passage, with its venerable service record as an ancient trade route, held its own—so much so that Nicholas, showing every sign that his natural opportunism had actually been honed by the small matter of his death, now began to appreciate the true potential of his position. His Myra shrine was excellently placed from the trade perspective; he now understood that it happened to lie on a prominent strand in the emerging weave of pilgrimage routes to the Holy Land. Admittedly, it was the inhabitant of another shrine entirely, and one far more exalted than he, who was causing all the pilgrim traffic. Venerating Christ should not, however, prevent them from making secondary devotional acquaintances in the course of their voyage, especially when these were as prominently positioned as Nicholas. Those who chose the sea route might know nothing of Nicholas when they left home, but the saint would do all in his power to ensure that they returned with word of him. And one way of doing so was to expand beyond Myra. The brand—though he did not yet see himself in such terms—was ready for rolling out.

On that wintry day, among the out-of-season detritus around the beach cafes—a glass-fronted refrigerated cabinet with a tangle of exposed wiring, a pile of roof matting, a huddle of olive oil catering cans that now contained withered geraniums—Gemiler seemed remote and without consequence. It was abandoned except for a fisherman in the bowels of his boat who hammered at a recalcitrant engine. This one quickly agreed to ferry me across—there was no road this time—and insured against engine trouble by packing a pair of oars that a goat had nibbled down to the paddles' cuticles.

The arrhythmic engine slumped and surged. The fisherman spoke over it only once, to pronounce the island the former home of a fair-skinned queen. Such local lore was all that was known of the place until the 1980s, when the first archaeological investigations made tentative inroads into its obscure past. Along the island's sheltered inland shore, stone Byzantine quays and jetties had sunk beneath the strait. The waterline was dotted with cubed stone cisterns where the rainwater from the island's upper slopes drained by a complex network of pipes. These were supplemented by a water cistern on another scale entirely—it was the size of a basilica—which stood nearby. With the provision of fresh water, scarce along much of this coast, the island of St. Nicholas was able to serve more than just the spiritual needs of passing ships.

I stepped ashore and watched the boat make its jerky return to the beach. A rocky path led uphill through olives and laurels hung with ancient cobwebs. Ruins were all about; rubble walls, graves, gateways, mosaic puddles of red and gray tesserae showing through the dirt, and a broken marble column with a cross carved upon it. I soon arrived at a ruined church, with a surviving half-domed apse and its three arched windows above a synthronon, or semicircular stepping, that unusual architectural feature of the sixth century that I'd seen only at Myra. From one of the church exits, where a vaulted walkway ran for a few meters before subsiding into rubble, I stopped and looked up. I soon found what I was looking for in the plasterwork above my head: the faint fresco remains of a figure, the familiar face and halo partly visible, above the legible title—"Osios Nikolaos," Bishop Nicholas.

I continued to the island summit. From the top I looked east, to the massif of Baba Dağ, Father Mountain, and south to the open sea. I was standing among the ruins of another church, where the island's most extraordinary feature began—or, more probably, ended, for the purpose of the remarkable walled, once covered walkway was to bring visitors to this summit church rather than lead them away from it. I was experiencing this cloistered corridor in reverse as I left the church by a domed vestibule and began descending toward the island's eastern end. The corridor was several hundred meters long, in many places piled high with the rubble of its fallen roof vaulting, and with view-filled arches to either side.

I took the local myth, the fisherman's single contribution, as an imaginative popular attempt to comprehend the function of this unique structure: the covered corridor must have been a kind of parasol for the island's albino queen. It seemed to me, as I walked down its entire length, rather more like an extended Byzantine drum roll set in stone, a warm-up act prior to arrival at the significant summit.

What seemed certain, from the ubiquity of ruined churches—not only the four on the island but more on the nearby islet of Karacaören and the mainland opposite—was that the settlement had proved a major draw to pilgrims. But what had encouraged them to make the ascent to the summit? I initially wondered whether the island, with its comparatively accessible altitude, might have touted itself as a pilgrim's crows' nest offering encouragement to the faltering: a panorama of the sea unfurling in the direction of the Holy Land. I soon rejected the idea, which seemed too reflective for an age that confirmed its beliefs through material objects like relics; besides, Baba Dag obstructed much of the view. There must have been a shrine at the summit.

The island's archaeology was extremely uncertain; probably it was developed as a Christian settlement in the course of the fifth and sixth centuries and dedicated to the protection of Nicholas. A far-sighted choice, in that Nicholas had not been around long, but an insistently obvious one, too, given that he was local and had already established his name on the water. A reassuring presence, he particularly appealed to the less seaworthy of the pilgrims who came this way. Those who viewed the sea with the least misgiving were liable to be tempted by the island, with the protection its Nicholas association promised, much as they might now be drawn to establish as their first onboard priority the whereabouts of the lifejacket lockers.

But what was the precise nature of the Nicholas association? In what sense was Nicholas on the island? Pilgrims, through the example of Helena and others, had come to expect a material relic presence at the sites they visited. And Nicholas, although he had demonstrated a visionary omnipresence, was restricted to a single set of physical remains. These lay at Myra. Even so the island shrine, with the momentous promise of its covered approach, must have contained something of religious significance (or, at least, claimed to: the first signs of the relic trade's descent into charlatanry would not be long in showing). It may be that Nicholas and those who served him had worked out, as others duly would, the benefits that accrued from the division of saints' bones. It is known that improvements were made to the basilica at Myra about a century after Nicholas' death; a disturbance, an earthquake perhaps, may have occasioned the repairs. Did this represent an opportunity for the removal from the remains at Myra of a pliant bone, manageably desiccated now, and its transfer to the island settlement? Was it sold, or even made available, gratis, by a far-sighted bishopric at Myra looking to erect a signpost a few headlands before the main event?

There was another possibility. The island, initially at least, may not even have been in Nicholas' domain. Cue Nicholas of Sion. Let us return to the surviving island fresco—not to the faded and unrevealingly hieratic saint's image there but to the inscription, "Osios Nikolaos," "Bishop Nicholas." This may suggest that Nicholas had yet to achieve full recognition as "agios" or saint; the date of his canonization is unknown. It may alternatively suggest that the island was actually dedicated to Sion, perhaps shortly after his death in A.D. 564. Sion's Life chronicles visits to Symbola (now the tourist haven of Ölüdeniz), just around the corner from the island. The Life also reminds us that Sion was bishop of nearby Pinara during his later years. We might not take this any further, except that Nicholas had used his lesser namesake to his advantage before; which only invites the proposition that the man who had borrowed Sion's nautical credentials had now lifted his island. Nicholas was learning early what it took to survive as a saint. He absorbed, by sheer weight of influence, Sion's possessions along with his cult. Certainly, by the time of the portolano writers, no trace of the island's original occupant remained.

Nicholas' new appointment as deliverer of pilgrims to the Holy Land by sea was soon to be interrupted. The seventh century saw Byzantine supremacy in the eastern Mediterranean come under threat from Persians, Avars, and Slavs, and subsequently from Arab fleets under the banner of nascent Islam. Byzantine Cyprus was attacked in A.D. 625. Slavic raiders sacked Myra the following year. Rhodes and Kos fell. When the Byzantine fleet was defeated off Finike, just east of Myra, in A.D. 655, with the loss of five hundred ships, there was a danger that Nicholas' name, with its shallow coastal roots, would not even survive the seventh century.

All over the island, even in the churches, I noted high walls and bricked-in windows: doomed attempts at defense. A watery dark age rapidly descended on this contested coast, where life became fraught with the threat of raids. The seas passed into the hands of pirates and brigands. Myra and Patara, Aperlae and Telmessos declined. Trade routes withered. The pilgrims that the island of St. Nicholas had come to serve stayed away. Nicholas' fortunes suffered a sudden slump. The island community might have gone the same way as Myra, the dispersal of the populace but for a few dogged guardians at the shrine. What made the difference here was geography. Inland, beyond the gaze of raiding Muslims, lay a fertile hidden valley, which had supplied the island settlement with produce from its earliest days. Now that the sea was dangerous and no longer provided a harvest of pilgrims, the people of Levisi sought refuge in their inland kitchen garden. They took their settlement's name with them.

8

THE FISHERMAN RETURNED ME to the mainland, where I drove back to the valley of paddocks, smallholdings, tobacco plots, and olive groves; I was following the line of Levisi's retreat, perhaps begun by the pirate raids all those centuries ago. The refugees had sited the new settlement across a rocky hillside. It was as if they had chosen the setting, overlooking the flat plain to the north, to recall the view of the strait's still waters they had surrendered to the pirates. More likely, they had simply been necessarily quick to appreciate that, having been recast as farmers, they must leave the fertile plain for the cultivation of vegetables and grain. What was all too clear was that the second place to bear the name of Levisi had duly gone the way of the first.

The Greeks of Anatolia, who had once numbered millions, were known as Rums. The term was Turkish for Roman; it acknowledged them as descendants of the Byzantines, whose own beginnings went back to the Roman empire. The Rums, whose communities were scattered across Anatolia, had lived as subject peoples of the Ottomans since the 1400s. By the late 1800s, as the Ottoman empire declined, the Turks had begun to regard the Rums with increased suspicion. The rise of Greece, which had wrested its independence from the Ottomans in the 1820s, served to divide Rum loyalties, especially as Greece began dreaming of a pan-Hellenic state that would include western Anatolia. In the aftermath of the Great War, when the Ottoman empire was on its knees, the Greeks occupied the port of Smyrna (modern Izmir). Their forces then marched inland in a bid to secure western Anatolia: a new nation around the rim of the Aegean.

The Greeks, who had the support of the western allies, might have succeeded. They were scuppered when the Turks in eastern Anatolia reached an understanding with the Russian Bolsheviks facing them across the Caucausus. Stark notice was served to the western allies that the Greek push into Anatolia might have wholly unintended consequences: a closer alliance between Turks and the Bolsheviks, leading to Russian control of Turkey which the West had always feared. By late 1921, the western allies' enthusiasm for the Greek adventure had waned. By August 1922, when the Turks were finally able to counterattack, Greece found herself alone. Her wilting armies were driven back to Smyrna to join the fleeing Christian population along the crowded quaysides.

There had been a significant Rum community at Levisi, but one that had not, finally, been spared by its inland retrenchment. I walked the cobbled paths of the place the locals knew as a ghost town; Levisi had been home to some 6,500 people in the early 1920s. Two thousand houses, some fronted by subterranean water cisterns topped by mosaics of black and white pebbles, stood derelict. Window frames and doors had been removed and the roofs had all disappeared, their tiles and timber reused by Turkish neighbors and by refugees from Macedonia who had latterly settled their smallholdings across the plain. The chimneys had survived. They were of stone and rose to roofed apexes, with tiny square vents, like windows, on all four sides. They were a suspicious sort of chimney: the smoke might escape, but nothing was going to get in. The design might have suggested that Nicholas had been left with no choice but to deliver his dowries through the window; a better explanation was that anything approaching a recognizable chimney was a thousand years from being invented in the late third century.

Eighty years of abandonment had removed every scrap of whitewash from these houses, stripping exterior walls to stone and render. They appeared to have reached a state of ruin without ever being completed, which was often the case with Turkish constructions that ran out of money or hit unexpected planning hitches. The truth was that these houses had been rich with lives. Inside the doorways, where fig and pine trees now grew, there were expanses of old paint, a rusty red or the characteristic faded blue of the islands. There were hearths with rounded cowls and bellied chimney breasts. There were alcoves where icons had once been propped.

Levisi was rich in chapels. Its two basilicas were dedicated to the Virgin Mary and to St. Nicholas. Its religion would prove its downfall. Turkey followed its defeat of the Greeks in 1922 by arranging for the exchange of its religious minorities with those of its former enemy. The 200,000 Rums who remained in Anatolia were to be exchanged for the Muslim minority in mainland Greece and the islands. Centuries earlier,

Muslim raiders had driven the people of Levisi inland; now Turkish nationalist politicians would finish the job by driving the town's every last Christian from Anatolia.

Ayşenina lived in a shadowed copse on the other side of the plain. Her ramshackle cottage was hemmed in by fig trees. Its roof had sagged to a deep bow where displaced tiles had puddled. An exterior wooden stairway bearing patchy repairs led to a first-floor covered balcony hung with dried chilis that ran the length of the cottage. Loose planks lifted with the weight of my boots to clobber me about the knees as I climbed the steps. Ayşenina, who knew to avoid the offending planks from her daily descents to the well at the side of the cottage, tried to warn me with a series of little squeaks, tutting in apology. The Turkish widow sat shawled in the weak winter sunshine, a dog by her side. Her limbs had turned thin, and her weathered tan had retreated to leave her skin translucent in the valley floors of deep wrinkles which the sun could no longer reach. Her eyes were flecked and milky, complex with the impurities of age. She was ninety-five years old and had lived in the valley all her life. She had been fourteen when the Rums left.

Ayşenina fossicked for a few remaining memories. She remembered how the order had come from Atatürk one day, and "how the Rums had all left for Fethiye a few days later, women and children mostly"; all Christian men of fighting age had been dispatched during the Great War to join the labor battalions deep in Anatolia, and few had made it back. She remembered the noise the cats had made the night the town was first abandoned. She remembered how the few refugees who found their way to the valley, mostly Macedonian Muslims expelled in the exchanges, had refused to settle the abandoned town. Mostly peasants, they preferred to surround themselves with land they could farm, so they built on the fertile plain. Some claimed the town had been cursed by the departing Greeks; darker rumors circulated. The owls and goats moved in.

Ayşenina remembered nothing of the final days. It may be that she was shielded from them by her parents, and had never known anything of the priests and old men gathering to make sense of the expulsion orders; the deals hastily done with those Muslims honorable enough to offer prices that were not downright derisory for the businesses, land and cattle, carts, tools, and harvests of the expelled. It may be that she was spared the farewells that her parents made with those Greeks they counted as friends, and knew nothing of the procession that gathered below the town one morning: the carts and donkeys piled high with pots, blankets, and trussed chickens, the old men clutching their deeds, the women their children and the icons of their protector saints. The deportees had gathered; now the soldiers gave orders and the procession moved out, disappearing through the pine trees on the road to Makri. It carried Ayşenina's friend into exile.

Ayşenina beckoned me into the front room. It was here that she lived and slept; her florally patterned mattress roll was pushed back against one wall. The room was otherwise empty except for floor rugs and a wooden trunk, which was pushed against another wall. The lidded chest was as square and simple as the room itself, except for the floral motif carved on the front. It was a Greek wedding chest. It had once belonged to her friend Maria. The chest, which the carts had not had space for, had been left in Ayşenina's care.

Eighty years had passed. Ayşenina did not know what had happened to her childhood friend. Maria's family might have ended up in Greece; the settlements of Nea Levisi and Nea Makri, oriented in a striking echo of their Anatolian originals, sprang up near Marathon. Or they might have gone, like many other Rums, to the nearby island of Kastellorizo en route to Perth, Melbourne, or New York. What was probable was that Maria's life, wherever she had lived it, was over. She would never return for the chest. It had long since ceased to be an object kept in trust and was no longer even a relic of a life that had passed, on the orders of others, elsewhere. Its original contents, silks and cottons intended for a Christian wedding, had long since been discarded as Ayşenina claimed the chest for herself, for her one remaining purpose. She lifted its lid to reveal two objects: a gray funeral shroud and the clay pot with which her corpse would be washed.

I left Ayşenina by the steps, taking plank blows to the calves, and made my way to the Church of St. Nicholas. It stood at the foot of the town where the plain pushed up against the ruins, a handsome basilica of reddish ashlar with tufts of grass growing across the roof. I stepped inside the empty shell and watched plumes of powdered plaster fall as if in an hourglass from the stucco ceiling where the empty nests of house martins were wedged. The ornate marble iconostasis had taken a battering, but remnants of painted scenes of angels, Christs, and miracles

survived in gilt-framed relief. On many, however, the heads had been
obliterated. At Levisi, it was impossible to identify Nicholas in his own
church.

But there were other churches. Nicholas had made sure of that.

9

THE POPULATION EXCHANGES OF 1924 marked the end of Anatolia's Christian presence after almost two thousand years. The loss of this territory, which was second only to the Holy Land in its historical Christian significance—it had seen St. Paul's great missionary journeys, and was home to St. John in his later years—was grievous to the Faith; and a blow to St. Nicholas, shunted from the land of his birth.

Orthodox Christianity ran deep among the Rums. It was no surprise that they should have taken their saints with them when they were banished from Anatolia. In the case of St. John the Russian, whose bones were revered by the people of Prokopi (now Ürgüp) in Cappadocia, the accompaniment was literal: the Rums took the saint's relics to their new home at Nea Prokopi on the Greek island of Evvia, where a new church in his name was built to house his relics. The people of Karvali (now Güzelyurt, or Beautiful Place), also in Cappadocia, had long since lost the bones of their revered St. Gregory the Theologian to Constantinople, but they never gave up on him; their new settlement of Nea Karvali, outside the port of Kavala in northern Greece, soon became popularly known as Agios Gregorios. Refugees from Nicaea (Iznik) and elsewhere even transported masonry from their churches and incorporated it in the new churches they raised to their saints. The difference with Nicholas was that he had ceased to a be local saint. His bones had long since made the same journey westward, where he had been operating across a wide front for centuries. This left the Christians of Lycia, of Levisi and Myra among them, with only icons of St. Nicholas to clutch when they went into exile.

Nicholas first broke out of Lycia some fifteen hundred years ago; the first reference to a Constantinople church bearing his name occurs in a sixth-century text. The obvious route was by sea, rounding Anatolia's southwest corner at Knidos, then north through the Aegean islands to the Dardanelles on an unknown vessel, but one whose crew could have had no inkling of the historical significance of their journey. A merchantman, perhaps, that had put into Myra or Levisi and picked up a party of pilgrims there along with their invisible stowaway: a local saint, but one with ambitions. Was Nicholas' name initially heard along the quaysides of the Golden Horn as those pilgrims stepped ashore, giving thanks for their safe return from the East? Or did Nicholas first set foot in the Imperial City only by implication, with a sailor remarking how old Poseidon had changed of late in Lycia—covering his nakedness at last—and in the vestments of the new faith—and clutching the holy book instead of the trident, so only the beard remained?

There was no such boat in my case. The modern journey to the city meant overland arrangements: leaving the car at the city of Denizli and joining the night train there. At the carriage window, framed in varnished wood, the Turkish steppe flickered in fragments that the darkness soon bore away—a strip of snow at the foot of a high wall that had cloistered it from the sun, a line of bare poplars that ran alongside the train before departing on a steepening diagonal, and the lights of a village, low against the night, that set glints in the windows and along the etched outlines of roofs and chimneys.

By dawn, the train had descended from the frozen plateau to close on a damp Istanbul Sunday. Now the windows revealed a collage of stained ashlar and concrete façades, all pasted over with balconies and rusting air-conditioning units. The train eased into Haydarpaşa Station where the Bosphorus signaled the end of the line, and the end of Asia. Outside the station a ferry was straining at its warps, smokestacks streaming. I boarded with the last few passengers and palmed away the damp grime at the window. Winter had leached the city's European shore of all color; in the gray wash of hoarding boards, high-rise hotels, and office blocks, only the yellow taxis stood out.

Nicholas had hardly begun—he had not even died—in A.D. 326, when the emperor Constantine began rebuilding the city that would take his name. Byzantium had been contested by Sparta and Athens, Persia and Rome for nine hundred years; Constantinople would continue to draw armies of Goths, Huns, and Bulgarians, Arabs and Slavs, Pechenegs,

Latins, and Turks to its walls. The modern city in turn attracted its own straitened invaders: Anatolian peasants, Romanian hawkers, and Russian prostitutes who arrived on the bald tyres of overnight buses. It was a metropolis that people had always coveted, whether they raised armies to force the walls or arrived at dawn with only a cousin's promise of a floor, for a few nights at most, while they sought a living from the place.

Constantine began to transform his namesake city by plundering the ancient world of its stone and statuary. He then set about establishing Constantinople's Christian credentials by adorning it with holy relics, which, in the Byzantine estimation, were no less than points of contact with the divine. He had his mother to thank for the prize pieces from the faith's defining drama, Christ's Passion, which Helena had brought back from Jerusalem: a portion of the True Cross and pieces of the two crosses that flanked it as well as the lance that pierced Christ's side, the sponge that bore vinegar and myrrh to his dying lips, and the Crown of Thorns. Constantinople soon secured the table on which the Last Supper was taken; the "column of flagellation" where Christ was whipped; and the stone of unction on which his corpse was embalmed.

The city soon widened its interest in these revered collectibles by turning its attention to the Nativity. It acquired the infant Christ's swaddling clothes along with the mortal relics of the three Magi and the vessels that had contained the gifts of gold, frankincense, and myrrh. It then went general in its interest, securing the Virgin's veil and girdle, the head of John the Baptist, and the bones of three Apostles: Andrew, obtained from Achaea in Greece, and Luke and Timothy from Ephesus. Other notable relics included the twelve baskets in which the leftovers from the feeding of the five thousand were collected, the ax with which Noah built the Ark, and the bones of the church fathers St. John Chrysostom and the Cappadocian St. Gregory the Theologian. Constantinople was the world's great reliquary; by A.D. 500, with Goths and Vandals running amok in Rome, it was also the world's finest city. It had hundreds of monasteries, over a dozen palaces, and magnificent moated walls, and would soon be crowned by an incomparable dome: the basilica of St. Sophia, whose name means holy wisdom, begun by the emperor Justinian in A.D. 537.

Nicholas, meanwhile, was making a reasonable name for himself at Myra and Levisi. He might have been content to secure his Lycian beachhead, safe in the knowledge that the sea routes to the east would continue to nourish him. Lycian consolidation appeared a perfectly rational, if somewhat provincial, course of action, but one that Nicholas was saved from taking by a strong intuition: that Lycia was about to experience a dramatic decline which was liable to stall him before he had barely begun.

Nicholas knew all about the frailty of fortune; he also knew that all were subject to it. He had witnessed instances both epic and private, the fall of the old gods and the plunge into poverty of a Patara nobleman. Nor, it seemed, had the lessons of Nicholas' life been lost with his death. He understood that he would have risked being marginalized, even—as Islam advanced—stranded behind enemy lines, if he stayed. Lycia, though he might just survive there, meant stagnation and withering. In the long term, as the twentieth century was to demonstrate, Lycia would fail him wholesale. He must establish himself elsewhere.

Besides, Nicholas meant to do more than merely survive, and for a saint intent on contending, there was only one place to be in the late fourth century. That great port commanded a promontory that was bounded by water on three sides, providing it with an unrivaled defensive position. It also stood at the axis not only of two continents but also of two seas, the Mediterranean and the Black. So narrow was the Bosphorus, the waterway that divided Europe and Asia, that the city could control all traffic across it as well as along it. For much of the first millennium, no spot anywhere on the planet was of greater consequence. It was where Europe and Asia came to parley and trade. It was also the key to the vast north, with its river-veined plains of black earth and birch land—though Nicholas' extensive plans as Russian Nikolai would not be hatched for centuries. Suffice it to say that the city was a strategic base that dwarfed Myra and Patara. And so to that first boat.

Nicholas is not actually recorded in the city until A.D. 555, but the reference, by Justinian's historian Procopius, relates to repairs to a Nicholas church; say, with some retrospective latitude as to when Nicholas' arrival in the city prompted the building of his first church there, a round figure of A.D. 500. This church stood beyond the Palace of Blachernae on the banks of the Golden Horn. Procopius noted that the restorers' scaffold platform protruded over the sea, which invites the fanciful notion that the church was built on the spot where those first pilgrims trumpeted his arrival, as well as the more substantial idea that his sea cult had continued to flourish. Procopius also observed that Nicholas shared the church's dedication with another saint, Priskos, a contemporary of Nicholas and one of the forty martyred at Sebaste (modern Sivas) in central Anatolia in A.D. 320. Poor Priskos, doomed to fail, would at least provide the useful caution that no saint was free from the ever present threat of obscurity; the precise spur, no doubt, that had brought Nicholas to Europe only 150 years after his death, providing him with a foothold vital to his westward ambitions, especially from the seventh century when the trouble he foresaw—pirates, earthquakes, Muslims, and silt—would undo his home ports forever.

Nicholas duly spread beyond the waterfronts to secure other church dedications, as many as twenty-five over the centuries. These churches have mostly disappeared. One was built by the patriarch Anastasius in the eighth century, and another stood close to St. Sophia. Many, as might have been expected, were sited next to the water. One was built in gardens on the Golden Horn near the original Nicholas church during the twelfth century, and another stood at nearby Balat. There were others on the Bosphorus—at Yenikapı and close to the waterfront at Galata.

Even so, these achievements actually suggest that Nicholas' impact upon Constantinople was oddly muffled. At no time was his name attached to the city's preeminent church, not least because of the supreme shadow St. Sophia had cast since A.D. 537. Nor were any of his churches even in the second rank, which included the likes of St. John Studius (where the Baptist's head resided), or St. Mary of the Copper Market (home of the Virgin's girdle), or the Holy Apostles, where Byzantine emperors were crowned, or St. Polyeuctos, so richly endowed that even its masonry was carted off to Venice during the Fourth Crusade of 1204.

Nor did the city's reliquaries, even at their apogee, have much of Nicholas to show. Venice, Rome, and Santiago de Compostela, which housed Saints Mark, Peter, and James respectively, demonstrated that nothing cemented city to saint quite like quality relics. There was at St. Sophia a carpet that, according to a Russian archbishop visiting in 1200, had belonged to Nicholas. But Nicholas was no Aladdin, his life being conspicuously short of significant rugs; the devotional point of this particular relic must have been hard to divine. As for Nicholas himself, the city had only extremities. There were a few teeth, but the provenances of relic teeth were dubious, notoriously. There was a single finger, which was also housed at St. Sophia until its removal in 1204; it ended up at Halberstadt in eastern Germany. The earlier service history of this lonely digit is unclear, but it seems probable that it was a late arrival, reaching Constantinople after Nicholas' removal to Bari in 1087, when the saint's formerly intact remains first underwent something of a diaspora. Bari's Catholics most likely presented the finger to Constantinople as a peace offering, perhaps as one of numerous attempts to heal the schism between the Greek and Latin churches that had gaped so spectacularly open in 1054. No doubt, however, that the offering came with the crowing subtext that a future for Nicholas had already been decided elsewhere.

It must have been clear, long before Bari gave Constantinople the finger, that saint and city were not the perfect match that had been widely predicted. What had gone wrong? Had the city rebuffed Nicholas? Constantinople was replete with saints, certainly, but selectivity had not lain behind its emergence as the world's greatest reliquary. Constantinople's could not be described as a discerning collection, abounding as it did with the relics of passing fancies and two-bit eccentric cults like that of St. Euphemia, martyred when a soldier drove a ram's horn through her neck. Besides, as a port city Constantinople was not about to turn away an attested sea specialist like Nicholas.

Had Nicholas been the lukewarm one? The provincial bishop playing it cool, perhaps to mask the fact that he did not fancy his chances against the resident saints? Certainly, there were among the eccentrics some formidably impressive names. There was not only St. Sophia but Michael the Archangel, who had cult sites all over the city, and the Magi, among the first to have witnessed the infant Jesus. Then there were the Virgin Mary and John the Baptist, often to be found in their privileged positions either side of Christ on the city's icons. In the case of the Baptist, Nicholas was also up against the physical fact of the saint's severed head, which was a reminder to him (and to those whom he might consider potential constituents) that he was a mere confessor among any number of heavyweight martyrs, including three of the Apostles, one of whom, Andrew, was established as the city's patron saint. He might have felt, for he could hardly know everything the future held, even Priskos breathing down his neck.

It might have been plausible—Nicholas missing the moment on account of a failing sense of worth—except that this saint was beginning to demonstrate a genius for survival that was almost viral. He seemed acutely sensitive to the first signs of falling off. Whenever obscurity threatened his existing territories, it seemed he could summon agents of transmission to establish his name in new ones. This was the man who had stayed one step ahead, moving to Myra just as Constantine made it the new capital; the man who died among a people with a genius for funerary monument—a significant saintly leg up—and who got time and place just right to assume the role of Poseidon even as that dying deity vacated it. Then there was Levisi, and the foothold he'd been quick to acquire at Constantinople as Lycia went into decline. Was this sure-footed saint one to allow a lack of self-esteem to come between him and his destiny? The truth was that Nicholas had discerned, though he was not about to say so, Constantinople's glaring deficiency.

Constantinople, the greatest city site on earth, would always be coveted. It is the nature of walls, however high they tower, that they will one day be breached; and so it was with Constantinople. Nicholas was privy to the city's future, not by magical divination, but as a simple reflection of its past, which had been a series of sieges. This could only mean more sieges and then more of them, from the Slavs during the sixth century to the Turks in the fifteenth, and any number of others in between. The city would fall, and the saints that then reigned supreme would fall with it: the Baptist's head, captured by the Turks and displayed to this day at the sultans' palace of Topkapı, and Andrew, poor Andrew, legendarily carted off to the Scottish golf town that bears his name.

What Constantinople's second-rate Nicholas churches and token relics indicated was a presence that was merely consular; he was the one man, it might be said, who had bigger plans than the coveted city on the Golden Horn's southern shores. History has proved Nicholas right. I looked across the water to the domes of the old basilica, which had kept its name—Aya Sofya in the phonetic Turkish—but was stuck with the minarets that proclaimed its forced conversion. When Mehmet II's great siege finally sprang the city's defenses in 1453, the sultan was quick to turn the great basilica into a mosque and to cleanse it of all relics and images. Many other churches duly followed, including the Church of St. Savior in Chora and the Church of the Pammacaristos, seat of the patriarch himself. Mosaics and frescoes were plastered over. Icons were removed and a mihrab, a prayer niche, was created hard by the existing high altar. Christianity did not die in the city, but after ruling for twelve hundred years, it was shunted out of the sun, a subject religion. Those saints who had invested their all here, trusting in high walls to keep them safe, had only centuries of contraction before them.

The ferry approached the jetty at Karaköy, where the north shore of the Golden Horn meets the Bosphorus. Above the stern waters, boiled by the reverse thrust of the engines, a mob of gulls swooped for thrown crumbs of the sesame bagels called simits. Karaköy was the shore district of Galata, the promontory on the north shore of the Golden Horn which lay beyond the Ottoman imperial city. Galata had been the city's commercial powerhouse under the Byzantines. It was here that many of the dispossessed Rums removed under the Ottomans. Mehmet II largely left the infidels of Galata to their own devices, except to ban the peal of their church bells, which were deemed to pollute the call of the sacred muezzin.

To this Christian enclave, with its warehouses and merchants' houses, dockside bars, gambling dens, and brothels, Nicholas also retreated. His eighteenth-century church still stands in the middle of Karaköy, though it fared badly in the twentieth century. A high wall, built to seal off the docks, had deprived it of its sustaining waterfront. More recently, a fire had gutted it; no key would have turned the rusted padlock that hung from its door. It was opposite this dead church, however, that I had been advised to stop and look skyward; so I stepped ashore among fishermen's trestles where anchovies and sprats were arranged in circular petalled blooms, and made my way toward it.

I passed along the arcades that ran between fin-de-siècle tenements, the haunts of chandlers, ironmongers, and shipping offices hung with signs in Cyrillic. Above the high wall rose the rust-flecked superstructures of ships from Sevastopol and Kherson. The cabin windows were obscured by merchandise: rolled mattresses, bundles of folded track suits, and boxed electrical goods. These bargain acquisitions from the city's flea markets seemed like the sorriest guttering of a mighty imperial ambition. Long before Russia adopted Byzantine Christianity in the tenth century, its traders had shipped furs, honey, and slaves down the Dniepr, Don, and Dniester Rivers to the Black Sea and thence to the city. The waters of those rivers gathered at the entrance to the Bosphorus, as if to insist, by the sheer weight of the current they generated, on the right of the shipping they had carried from the steppes to continue unhindered to the Mediterranean. To this end, Russia regularly sent armies to the walls of the city. From the time of Peter the Great, the occupation of Constantinople and control of the Dardanelles was imperial Russia's foremost territorial objective.

Arriving at the burned-out church of St. Nicholas, with its mandorla of the saint peering down from the portico, I did as I had been told. My rising eyes took in the crumbling neoclassical cornices of the block opposite. From the windows, poles angled out like bowsprits rigged with complex washing lines. When my gaze reached the pitched roof, I should have expected no more; certainly not round ashlar walls, with tall arched windows, topped by a scalloped cornice below a verdigris onion dome on which a Russian Orthodox cross was planted.

The place had once been a *podvoriye,* or Russian pilgrims' hostel, a way station for the faithful headed for Mount Athos, the Holy Land, or Bari. It was built in 1870, just as Russian roubles were restoring the basilica of St. Nicholas at Myra, when an expansionist Orthodoxy still coursed through the veins of tsarist Russia. The podvoriye was known as St. Andrew's, taking its name from the monastery on Mount Athos that had founded it. Nor was it alone. Russia's three other Athonian monasteries soon commissioned their own hostels nearby. Between the docks and the old Russian embassy on the hill at Beyoğlu a quartet of closely packed green domes had sprouted, marking out an enclave of old Orthodox Russia. The domes had all survived, to varying degrees, though the rooms beneath them had long since settled into low-rent troughs.

I entered the podvoriye and climbed the gloomy marble staircase.

Through the doors of the former pilgrims' rooms, I glimpsed washing lines and smelled the reek of vegetables. From one such room, a hunched lady emerged and began climbing the stairs. With her faded blond hair and cardigan she was clearly not Turkish. Madame Shura, as she called herself, was Russian. And she was on her way to church.

Madame Shura's father had been in Constantinople at the time of the Russian Revolution. He remained in the city, where Shura was born in 1924 and where she had lived all her life. Her home for the last twenty years had been a room in the podvoriye which was hung with icons, family photographs and a portrait of the last tsar. The block's last surviving Russian resident, she still sold candles during the services at St. Andrew's rooftop church.

We reached the top landing, where a canvas represented the Hermitage of St. Andrew. Grime had robbed that settlement of its celestial shine, lending it rather the cast of a Siberian mining town. I followed Madame Shura through an open door. I found myself beneath the dome I had seen from the street, its arched windows inset with crosses of purple stained glass and its richly painted biblical scenes mottled by mildew. A quartet of turquoise and gilt iron columns supported the dome, which was hung with a glass chandelier. Some of the peeling walls depicted processions of painted saints, often bisected by wavering seams of plaster-filled cracks. Other walls, painted turquoise with a mosaic band, were hung with icons and decorated with silk and plastic roses. There were round arched windows with turquoise and scarlet stained glass. There were red velvet braided banners. The icon stands were hung with white damasks edged with gold braid, their embroidered crosses complete with the Orthodox angled bar. The thickets of Madame Shura's candles that had been planted in the raised brass receptacles of sand illuminated the gilded iconostasis; it was hung with saints' images and lamps, and topped with a portico where the Cyrillic letters X and B—representing the words "Christ is *risen!*"—were arranged in red lightbulbs. It was as if all the building's life and color had forsaken the lower floors, leaving them monochrome, and gravitated upward to make a last stand in the one place that mattered.

Even so, my eye was drawn to a single secular detail: the stove in the middle of the floor, whence a long pipe, lagged by a shimmer of heat, dallied vertically and horizontally before exiting the church by the wall. It was a necessity in December Istanbul, but it seemed to have a more telling function, serving the deep well of wintry Russian nostalgia. It evoked cart-crossed frozen rivers and thin birchwood light, and the steppe churches with their steeply pitched roofs and spires, and the cupolas cinched below bulbous overhangs, all designed to deny purchase to the falls of snow. For the émigrés who gathered at St. Andrew's, it was the stove that bore them home.

I began to observe the imagery around me, recognizing in the size of the icons, in their number and arrangement, a Russian disposition toward particular saints. There was Russia's own St. Vladimir, who had introduced the nation to Christianity, and his murdered sons, Boris and Gleb; and the Oumilenie, an icon type much loved among the Russians, which features the mother and child in an affectionate clasp. Then there were the favored Byzantines, notably the Archangels Gabriel and Michael, and Basil of Cappadocia, and St. Andrew who was supposed to have made missionary journeys in Russia. And Nikolai, not only in the church but also in the rooms of the building's last Russians, just as he occupied millions of rooms across Russia: a talisman of the household and Russia's most reliably approachable saint.

Nicholas enjoys a vast popularity in Russia. "If anything happens to God, we've always got St. Nicholas," goes one proverb. "Net ikon—kak Nikol"—There's no icon like Nicholas'—claims another. The saint is known as Chudotvorets, the Wonderworker, and Morskoi (of the Sea). So close is the attention paid him that icons distinguish him seasonally, with a winter version in which he wears a miter. Thursday prayers in the Russian liturgy have always been dedicated to Nicholas, as the representative of all the saints. He is also the only saint to be represented as statuary in the Russian faith.

When Russian merchants and traders first bore Nicholas home from Constantinople (along with an enthusiasm for bathhouses and cupolas), they unsurprisingly situated the churches they built in his name on the banks of navigable rivers, the trade routes of the Russian hinterland. The earliest was on the Dnieper at Kiev in A.D. 882, and was intended as the mother church of the Russian state. Others followed, at Novgorod on the River Volkhov in 1113; on the Pskova, at Pskov; on the Kamenka at Suzdal, and on ten thousand other willowy river bends where towns and villages had gained a purchase. At Yaroslavl, where the Volga is half a mile wide, ten churches still bear Nicholas' name. One was (in a typical devotional act) built by a rich merchant as a token of his gratitude to the saint; Nicholas, as a natural extension of his nautical patronage, had begun moving into cargo haulage. The merchant sited his church on the banks of the river that carried his goods from Pskov to Yakutsk and Astrakhan, making him a fortune from consignments of grain and fish, tobacco and flax.

Certain adaptations were to be expected. The people were not Byzantine; nor were the landscapes. In the vast Russian hinterland the comparative calm of the inland waterways meant that Nicholas was rarely called upon to pull off the usual maritime rescues. The Russian staples were one-off river incidents involving tipsy ferrymen and lovelorn swains. Freed from onerous maritime service, he expanded his patronage to all travelers. Russians carried his medallion with them on journeys, and his icon adorned railway stations—as well as barracks and shops—all over the empire, until the Revolution.

It was, however, his homegrown reputation for practical charity which was his greatest attribute. It gave rise to his most common Russian epithet: Nikolai Ugodnik, Nicholas the Helper. Nicholas moved beyond his Byzantine brief to assume new steppe functions, protecting houses from fire, guarding the crop and keeping the shepherd company in his vigil against wolves. He was a common source of general assistance, once wading in to free a bogged cart while St. Cassien held back lest soiled garments delay his entry into Paradise. It was on account of his willing assistance, Russian lore had it, that Nicholas was granted two saint's days there: on May 9, the date of his relics' arrival in Bari, as well as December 6. St. Cassien, by the same token, was assigned the punitive February 29, which confined him to leap-year appearances.

A flock of sorts, a fluctuating half dozen, had gathered at St. Andrew's. They were served by Father Symeon, the bearded image of St. Nicholas himself, who occasionally appeared from behind the iconostasis in a gold robe embroidered with vermilion grapes. It was the elderly church officers, however, who held my attention as they tottered about the church: eighty-year-old Madame Shura and the white-haired church-warden, Igor "Harry" Norregaard, who had been four when his Danish father and White Russian émigrée mother moved to the city in 1936. They were exotic reminders that the *podvoriye,* built to serve Russian pilgrims, had soon come to house refugees from the Bolsheviks.

In November 1920, the last of the White Russian armies under General Wrangel and the civilians under its protection evacuated Sevastopol in the Crimea before the Bolshevik advance. One hundred twenty-six ships bearing almost 150,000 Russians arrived at Constantinople. The new arrivals were billeted in stables, in cheap hotel rooms, and in cellars. The Karaköy *podvoriye* were soon requisitioned as dormitories where privates and generals, counts and liverymen sheltered side by side. And in the rooftop churches, the exiled faith continued as the Bolsheviks set about abolishing it in the mother country. All across Russia the Reds destroyed icons and opened coffins to expose as old bones the supposedly incorruptible relics of saints. In 1921, the Russian church was ordered to hand in all consecrated valuables such as golden chalices. The following year, the local soviets were instructed to strip the churches of all valuables. In the ensuing clashes, some seven thousand priests, nuns, and monks were killed. Churches were closed by the thousands. By 1924, Nicholas had not only lost Anatolia to the Turks but Russia to the atheists; his two great bastions of Orthodoxy were all but wiped out in a few short years.

The congregation gathered about Father Symeon to take bread and to chorus "Christ is risen!" Then the priest disappeared behind the iconostasis, which was promptly covered by a falling curtain like a shuttered shop front. A lamp was lowered on a chain. The service had come to its abrupt end.

As I left, I noticed a printed icon of St. Nicholas that hung above the door outside the church. Around the central image of the saint were arranged episodes from his life, forceful reminders of what the Russians had seen in Nicholas. Staying the hand of the executioner, breaking the chains of the falsely imprisoned, saving a sailor from drowning, and stretching an arm to a window; this Byzantine had devoted his life to the needs of others. Here was a saint who could break their chains and dispense justice, law, and money: a man who could help them.

It was less clear what had drawn Nicholas to Russia in the first place. For the first time, I sensed something had distracted Nicholas from his single-minded purpose. Russia's bearing was off; Russia did not serve the grand trend that compelled Nicholas toward Europe. It must, I thought, have been the depth of Russian veneration, which Nicholas had found hard to resist. Either that or, mindful of what the future held, he was acclimating to the cold.

10

A TWO-MINUTE WALK from the *podvoriye* brought me to a steep alley-
way flanked by plane trees where Karaköy's notorious *genelev,* or
brothel, stood. High concrete walls enclosed a maze of alleyways where
prostitutes lolled behind windows, striking provocative poses that could
not disguise their shabby dishabille, at least according to the lupine youth
in the leather jacket.

"Instead I get you pretty girl," the pimp assured me, waving a dismissive
hand at the brothel entrance. Policemen milled around an X-ray machine
that screened a steady stream of young men; a bomb planted by Islamic
fundamentalists in a *genelev* rubbish bin had injured twelve people in
1998. I did not join the queue. Istanbul's main sex bazaar was quite without the least trace of raffish glamour. What had brought me here was
Nicholas, who had saved three girls from prostitution and, it now appeared, had established an enclave of sorts right alongside the city brothel;
the inklings of a pattern, then, but one that would not become insistent
until Amsterdam.

I was reminded of the brothel later that day, when I arrived at the Ecumenical Patriarchate in the formerly Greek suburb of Fener. The resemblance was superficial but striking: the Patriarchate, headquarters of the
Greek Orthodox church, had exactly the same entrance security, including
the X-ray machine, and stood behind its own high walls. The compound,
a target for Islamic and nationalist zealots, had also known occasional
bombings, not to mention regular broken windows, Molotov cocktails,
and threatening graffiti. Prostitution and the Rum church, though the Patriarchate might not care for the comparison, were at once the oldest and
the least welcome of the modern city's institutions.

The walls surrounding the Patriarchate, shrunken descendants of the
great bastions that had once preserved an entire Greek metropolis, offered
a pitiful reminder of Christianity's reduced circumstances in the city. The

city's 400,000 Rums, exempted from the population exchanges as non-Anatolians, had suffered withering taxes in the 1940s and pogroms in the 1950s. By the 1960s, the Rum population had dropped to under 100,000. Now, fewer than three thousand Greeks remained in the city. History had proved Nicholas right; his future lay elsewhere.

I had come to see Nicholas' successor. The Myra bishopric had outlasted the Ottomans and so far survived Atatürk's republic; it seemed to me that something of the saintly archetype—the venerable age, the direct eyes, and the gray beard—had also endured in the present bishop of Myra, Metropolitan Chrysostom, whom I recognized from the December 6 service at Demre. The nature of the job, however, had certainly changed. Chrysostom, Myra's bishop since 1996, ministered to a diocese quite without Christians. He did so largely from the shores of another continent. It might have depressed him except that Myra, by comparison with other Anatolian dioceses, was positively vibrant with Christian activity. Many of the Patriarchate's bishops served remote eastern dioceses, Sivas for example, where even token celebrations of Christian faith were not tolerated. Metropolitan Chrysostom not only had offices in Demre, but had held some ten masses there during the last year. "It is not so far"—he smiled—"and I am always happy to go there if St. Nicholas should wish it."

It was not until the 1990s that the authorities had allowed services to be held at Myra. I took this to indicate a recent religious latitude on the part of Ankara. The bishop shrugged. "It is clearly the wish of St. Nicholas that it should happen," he said, putting Nicholas at the helm again. The metropolitan told me that he had undergone an operation two weeks earlier, and when the surgeon reassured him that he was in good hands, the bishop had corrected him: only St. Nicholas would see to it that the operation worked out all right. He had a similar relationship with the skipper of his boat, which he kept on the northern Aegean island of Imvros (Turkish Gökçeada), putting his real trust not in the captain but in the saint whose icon hung in the small cabin. The metropolitan saw his early predecessor not merely as the outstanding example of how the job should be done, but as nothing less than an active miraculous organizer of the way things turned out.

I asked the bishop what made the saint so special.

"He lived his life among the people," said Chrysostom. "He was not remote or detached. He helped them in their distress, whether they were poor or endangered, persecuted or hungry. The Russians believe that St. Nicholas took over from Jesus Christ the job of saving mankind. And I carry a small piece of him with me." The wood-carved engolpion, or locket, that the bishop wore around his neck contained a tiny certificate-wrapped shard of relic. The relic had once belonged to the Russian metropolitan Nicholas of Krutitska and Kolomna, murdered by the Bolsheviks at the monastery of Kolomna in Moscow. Quite how the relic had reached Moscow, or how it subsequently passed into the hands of the previous metropolitan of Myra, who had passed it on to his successor, Chrysostom did not know.

What seemed likely, however, was that Nicholas had wished it so.

I took the ferry to Yalova the following morning. A mean winter wind stirred the Sea of Marmara, twisting the tops from the breaking crests. Fragmented waves struck the cabin windows with such power that the water forced past the seals surrounding the glass. The fattening drops that slid to dampen my sleeve tasted of salt. The sleeve soon left its moist mark on the seat arm of a rattling bus, which climbed through rounded hills dotted with chestnut trees, into ancient Bithynia. The road closed on a wind-scratched lake lined with straight ranks of brush-bare poplars before arriving at Iznik. Legend has it that some 1,675 years ago, when the city was known as Nicaea, Nicholas visited here.

The bus entered a ceremonial gate through the formidable walls which the city's occupiers, displaced Byzantine princes and expectant Ottoman sultans, had shored up as they made Nicaea their capital in waiting. Iznik clearly had a fabulous past; its present, however, was thoroughly provincial, with brightly painted cinder-block cottages, neatly parked tractors, pavement piles of firewood, and kitchen gardens abandoned to a thin fuzz of winter weeds and to scratching chickens.

What I noticed were the roofs. They were topped with the desiccated twiggery of old storks' nests, and braided with plumes of unfurling chimney smoke. The storks had long since left for Africa, spindly emblems of fortune and new life. They would return in the spring just as the year's traditional spate of new babies, conceived in the sappy nights of high summer, was getting under way. So it was that the storks brought the babies and, on account of their preference for nesting on rooftops, duly established the chimney as their delivery route; I liked to think that Nicholas had been here, if only to have taken note.

I walked past the ruins of the great church of St. Sophia, already all but destroyed by earthquake and fire when it was further reduced during the Turkish advance in 1922; what remained of it, a few arched walls of brick and a minaret stump, was hunkered down in a pit at the center of town. The streets were largely deserted, with a few hunched figures hurrying between warm interiors. I was alone by the time I reached wintry orchards and slipped through a stone gateway to find myself on the edge of the lake. I looked beyond a shabby tea pavilion to ice-skeined rushes and snow-covered hills. It was here that the Great Council of A.D. 325 had taken place.

Nicaea was well suited to host Constantine's great Christian convocation. Its attractive resort setting made it a prototype Davos, and in a region, as Pliny had discovered, that abounded with Christians by the second century. Those who had deserted the temples and neglected their sacrifices were sure to welcome the bishops. The city, moreover, suited Constantine by virtue of its name. Nicaea, Victory, recalled his military triumphs of the previous year, which had confirmed him as undisputed emperor.

The Council at Nicaea was the most significant ecclesiastical event since the missions of St. Paul and the Apostles. It served as Christianity's confirmation service. It was here that Easter's date was agreed and the Nicene Creed was formulated as a primary statement of faith. The triune godhead was also established, despite determined resistance from the influential followers of the heretic Arius.

The spring of that year had seen some three hundred bishops, legendarily 318, making for Nicaea. A handful journeyed from the west, from Rome, Dijon, Poitiers, Córdoba, and Calabria, but the majority were eastern. The roads of Anatolia were clogged with bishops and their retinues, a procession of carts and carriages from Jerusalem and Antioch, Caesarea and Patara. But not, on the basis of best evidence, from Myra. The bishop of Myra is conspicuously missing from the early surviving lists of delegates at Nicaea.

This absence might have been readily accepted; it was, after all, entirely explicable that Nicholas had not made the long journey. The little we can sense of Nicholas' life—the lack of sea voyages and his circumscribed territory—hardly suggests an enthusiastic itinerant. He was absent from the lists, then, for obvious reasons; this stay-at-home had been minded not to make the journey, perhaps because he felt that the time away was better spent tending to the material needs of his Myra flock. Or perhaps because this apparently private man had wished to avoid the exposure, as he had once attempted to avoid it in Patara, that an appearance at Nicaea would entail.

The reasons for his absence from the roster have, however, been interpreted differently over the centuries. "On that momentous occasion," as one contemporary writer has described the Council, Nicholas "was so withdrawn that he is not even mentioned in the account of the proceedings." It was clear, as Nicholas' cult grew, that some among his legions of devotees found it hard to accept that their saint had not attended at Nicaea, and sought alternative explanations. Nicholas' burgeoning renown brought new commitments: he *must* put in an appearance at the Council, one of the best-documented events of his lifetime, if only to anchor his very existence in history. What also drew him to Nicaea was an iconographic accident; his association with trios—the falsely imprisoned soldiers, the butchered boys, the impoverished daughters—commended Nicholas as the champion of Trinitarian orthodoxy in its time of need. Nicholas' devotees came to argue with increasing conviction that he had not been absent from Nicaea as much as accidentally omitted from the lists.

Their insistence paid off. Nicholas would get to Nicaea in A.D. 325; it just took him until the ninth century to do so. The writings of Symeon first put him there, doing battle with the heretics: "The admirable Nicholas strenuously reduced the casuistry of Arius, reducing to naught his every tenet." Nicholas not only attended the Council, it seemed; he also played a heroic role there. The momentum was such that Nicholas' name was established in the lists by the thirteenth century, the insertion long since accepted as the mere correction of a long-standing omission. By the fourteenth century, he had moved to center stage at Nicaea. His verbal jousting developed into a more robust defense of the Trinity, when he put paid to Arius' heresies by boxing him on the jaw. The Council punished Nicholas accordingly, singeing his beard, depriving him of his miter and mantle, and clapping him in prison. Higher authorities were soon, however, to signal their support for Nicholas, when his instruments of office were restored by two angels. In later versions, the saint even eased into the undisputed lead role at Nicaea. One narrative has it that Constantine himself described Nicholas as one of the "three pillars of the world" in the Council proceedings; in another tale, he was even visited in his prison cell by Christ and the Virgin Mary.

Embellishment proliferated. The chronicler Le Père de Bralion wrote in the 1640s of Nicholas' subsequent return to Myra, where the bishop discovered that Nicaea had awoken an appetite for travel. According to De Bralion, the saint was soon off to Rome, stopping en route at Bari to prophesy, My remains will rest here. So it was that this prophecy was retrospectively embedded into history some 750 years before the event it claimed to foresee, when it had actually been invented 550 years after the event had occurred. But even that flagrant fabrication would not prevent it being represented on the ceiling of the great Romanesque basilica where Nicholas' bones were, indeed, to lie.

I would catch up with Nicholas at Bari. But first it was time to get home for Christmas.

11

HOME, TO A GAPPY grimace. I elbowed open the front door to the sight of my six-year-old fishing with a finger along her gums, her prepared welcome—"Daddy! Presents!"—lost in a clogged mouthful of reddish saliva.

"My tooth's just come out," yelled Anna, holding up a bloody trophy. Usually, two-year-old Lizzie echoed her older sister's every utterance. On this occasion, however, she understood that communicating Anna's swallowed reminder of my preset parental function was the priority.

"Presents!" she shouted.

I had barely put down my cases before Anna was badgering me for a matchbox in which she might present her relic to the Tooth Fairy. Coin and gifts, then, were what impressed the girls when it came to their childhood deities; in this, they were no doubt typical. It had been the same with the saints of adulthood, the proven deliverers of substance—bumper crops, intact cargoes, healthy babies—tending to endure. This was to put Father Christmas and the Tooth Fairy in charge of the girls' pantheon. For the mermaids, ogres, nonspecific fairies, and Handsome Prince Charmings who specialized in arousing mere emotions in the young—wonder, rapture, thrilling fear—this was bad news. They were condemned to be passing fancies or were even, as in a recent pronouncement on unicorns, declared nonexistent by Anna.

Lizzie continued her clamor for presents as I scrabbled in the kitchen drawer. My mind fell back on the banal observations that serve to deflect incoming infantile interference: that the household wasn't producing empty matchboxes like it used to; that giving up smoking was to blame; that the contents of the matchboxes that had served the cause of previous teeth were now unfeasibly crammed into the one remaining box; and that the tooth fairies were in the irritating habit of regarding the boxes as part of the tooth deal rather than returning them to the kitchen drawer. I gave up the search and emptied the lone matchbox into the drawer alongside a shingle of cell batteries, fuses, foreign coins, radiator keys, and dog flatulence pills. We lined the matchbox with a plug of cotton wool before placing Anna's tooth inside.

"See what happens if you put it under your pillow tonight," I said. The procedural reminder did not satisfy Anna, who had lost several teeth lately. She considered that the Tooth Fairy deserved a letter as a regular visitant as much as for seasonal reasons. "I know they both come at night, but it's not really like Father Christmas," I explained gently. "You can't really ask tooth fairies for presents."

"Dad, I know that," sighed Anna. "I only want to say hello." She folded the finished note small and tucked it into the matchbox.

I had barely doled out the girls' regulation doses of Istanbul plastic—a tea set and box of dominoes—when the relentless issue of presents loomed once more. Christmas was very close. Almost all the windows of our Advent calendar had been levered open to reveal robins and lanterns, Santas, holly sprigs, and ribboned presents behind their hinged cardboard casements. On the sidewalks of our town, pine and spruce needles were scattered like lacquered nail clippings, conspicuously beneath the trunks of parked station wagons. In the fading December day, the Christmas lights, the street decorations, and the tinsel-filled windows of the shops had charged the sky with a luminous wash. In the appliance stores, a chime-backed blizzard had caused deep drifting over the landscapes of the television ads. The snow had also infiltrated the shop window displays, leaving a thin scattering of flakes as well as the odd rogue pine cone overshoes, scarves, and watches; the meteorological signature of Santa Claus, who for a few weeks had made the place his own.

I had gone into town on a last-minute Christmas shopping trip; what I got was a dizzying glimpse into Nicholas' distant future. It seemed I had always known Santa; even so, getting to know the man he had been before had revealed the full extent of his transformation. It was not the changes in his appearance and his name that struck me, so much as the apparent betrayal of what he meant—the soul of charity corrupted, and relaunched as the seasonal crony of the retailers.

The town was saturated in Santa. His presence in Bath made amateurs of those fallen tyrants in Baghdad, Tirana, and Damascus, with their hoardings, banknotes, televised addresses, and statues. It bore the hallmarks of an accomplished military occupation. An inflatable Santa had taken up position on the ironwork balcony of the Royal Hotel alongside a sign advertising Roast Turkey Dinner, with all trimmings, at £12.95. From there, he occupied an excellent vantage point over the shoppers arriving at the railway station. Others were shinning up office drainpipes or hanging from ropes as they headed for the rooftops. Another, a human one this time, had established his grotto outside the abbey.

It was in the shops, of course, that his personality cult was most powerfully concentrated. Where frescoes and icons served Nicholas in the basilicas, a giddying proliferation of forms—cards, wrapping paper, gift tags, china plates, and cups—dispensed Santa's image from these temples of consumption. Santa, sleigh, and reindeer, outlined in tubular flashing lights, hung from shop walls; at the baker's, his image rose from cakes in a relief of red icing. It was, however, as a graven image—anathema to the Orthodox—that Santa had truly taken off. The most popular figurine that massed the shelves was of a man with one leg stuffed down a brick chimney stack, a sack over his shoulder with a trumpet and puppy poking out. There were ceramic Santas whose voluminous stomachs had been scalloped out to leave cavities that were filled with chocolate balls wrapped in gold foil; Santas fashioned from felt cones and dressed in red duffel coats decorated with reindeer motifs; foil-wrapped chocolate Santas, and Santa candles and candle holders, Santa finger puppets and Christmas tree decorations, the last with fiber-optic whiskers. There were plastic Santas kitted out in parachutes and mountaineering gear; even a battery-powered Santa who played a sax and moved his hips to the tune of "Santa Claus Is Coming to Town."

Santa's image was on earrings and key rings, on flashing brooches and balloons, on pillowcases and sacks, hats and stockings. There were Santa tea towels, cushion covers, bibs and coasters, teapots, trouser braces, wine-bottle stoppers, stamps and phone cards. There were Santa storage cartons, the red lids lined with white fluffy trimming and bags fronted by squeaky red noses. There were musical rotating snow-globe Santas, Santa sweet dispensers, and Santa jelly lollypops. There were Santa-shaped dog chews, Santa wind spirals and thermometers. There were porch placards proclaiming "Santa, Please Stop Here," Naughty Noises Santas ("Pull my finger and stand back"), Mrs. Santa's Sexy Underwear Kits ("because Santa needs love too"), and cards fronted by voluptuous girls in scant red

tunics and high boots. In one shop, an all-year grotto of baubles, tree decorations, and figurines called December 25, Santa's reign never passed.
Even the high street's biggest icons, Winnie the Pooh and Homer Simpson,
bowed to Santa in his season by wearing red hats with white trims.

Was it possible that Nicholas had intended this? Putting himself up for
sale, his every image hung with a price tag? I wondered about the missing
centuries, and the chain of events that had brought him to this. Even so, I
recognized, in the reach he had achieved, telling parallels with his success
in the saint's art of attracting devotees. In Santa, it had manifested itself
as a commercial brilliance that extended far beyond merchandising: he
had laid claim to all presents. It was easy enough to buy a present that was
devoid of Santa iconography; almost impossible was to query Santa's delivery rights. Delivery cut Santa in. It guaranteed him the gratitude every
present yielded, deepening the devotion in which he was held. The children loved him. The parents, though they knew Santa had reduced them
to present-buying automatons, loved him for bringing joy to their children. They were his congregants, crowding the shops to acquire ever more
extravagant presents in his name. With these presents, they confirmed
their love for their children, and in turn reinforced Santa's hold on their
children's hearts.

What had been lost was any sense of the need that Nicholas had once
met. Vast flows of computer games, robots, dolls, cars, and doctor sets
were streaming from the shops toward uncertain futures; gratitude at the
unwrapping, and initially fevered use, certainly, but then a slackening of
interest with the passing of the shallow waves these presents rode. The
subsequent waves, each crested by the next new things, would condemn
these presents to increasingly rare outings and finally to disuse. Some
would be posted on e-Bay and sold to the highest bidder before the daf-
fodils were out, the rest relegated to the shadowed backs of wardrobes
and cupboards where old presents moldered in their private landfills.
They would be relieved of the weight of successive Christmases only when
they were eventually put out in black bags for disposal.

Anyway, I did my Christmas shopping and trudged up the hill in the dusk.

The girls were in the sitting room, playing with the wooden figures in
the Christmas crib. Mary, the Magi, and a cow had been turned pink by
Anna's marker pen. Christ, whose Christmas presence had been reduced
to the carols and the double doors on the Advent calendar, was meanwhile

suffering the final indignity: the invasion of his Nativity scene by a posse of Barbie dolls and a dinosaur. I found my wife, Ash, pondering suitable names for tooth fairies in the kitchen. When I emptied my pockets of keys and coins, I found the Santa magnet among them; I slapped it against the fridge.

Until the sixteenth century, the churches of England were havens of the saints. Their gilded statues flanked the altars and occupied the curtained niches where daily masses were held and burning candles maintained. These statues were often hung with rosaries and with votive objects, often recast from cherished silver talismans donated by pious parishioners. Stone statues adorned exterior gables and alcoves. Saints' images were painted on walls and rood screens, hung in gilt frames and worked in stained glass. They were carved on drinking bowls, pew ends, and lintels. They were represented on chalices and candelabra and embroidered on banners. And their feast days crowded the church calendar.

The Reformation had purged England of its saints. Radical Protestantism had erased the vast proportion of their original imagery; the passing of the centuries had helped. All that survived of them were the church dedications and the odd panel of stained glass, disfigured wall painting, or rain-pocked statue. Among these were barely a handful of pre-Reformation instances of "Three Daughters": a twelfth-century granite font at Winchester Cathedral and, until a fire destroyed it in the 1970s, a thirteenth-century glass medallion at the church of St. Peter and St. Paul in Upper Hardres, Kent.

The rarity of these English examples of "Three Daughters" was proof that the Puritans had been thorough in their work. Even so, it was evident that the story had traveled remarkably well. Symeon had described "Three Daughters" as "the most charitable and the best known" of all the Nicholas stories. The Golden Legend, a highly influential thirteenth-century telling of the great saints' lives, gave it particular prominence. In a world nursed on miracles, an insistently human act of generosity had prevailed. Its indubitable resonance seemed to mark a tacit acknowledgment, even among the credulous Byzantines, of the supernatural's limitations when faced with such evidence of what man himself could achieve.

Either that, or the fact that any story about a saint with available funds to disburse was always sure to prosper.

Prosper it certainly had, appearing in every available format across an ever expanding range: in frescoes and icons, on altars and panels, in illuminated breviaries, psalters, and prayer books, on fonts and church gables. It was painted and carved and, from the early twelfth century, even performed as a staple of the religious plays that had begun as dramatic embellishments of the recited lines; they went on to be staged in churches, squares, and parks. Many such representations of the story were surely lost to the hammers of the eighth-century iconoclasts and the Muslim Ottomans and, in the West, to the bonfires and diktats of the Reforming Protestants. Those that survived were carved on a durable font, perhaps, or concealed in a high window, circumstances particular enough to suggest they must have been a tiny minority of the overall number. "Three Daughters" was a defining image of active Christian virtue until the Reformation.

The earliest surviving, though unconfirmed, instance of "Three Daughters" was painted on a wall in Rome during the eighth or ninth century. This fresco was spared the attentions of the iconoclasts by the timely (and comparatively forgiving) natural dereliction which overcame the church that contained it, Santa Maria Antiqua. The primitive composition, only recently restored, merely shows three girls, their eyes dark with sorrow. Something of the same iconographic immaturity is evident in the "Three Daughters" carved on the baptismal font at Winchester Cathedral. The font, carved in black marble from Tournai in Belgium around 1150, shows the father kneeling to receive the offering from Nicholas that will save him.

The image first assumed its familiar compositional contours in the thirteenth century—the partitioning by which Nicholas' intended anonymity is conveyed, and the convention of the cut-away that simultaneously allows the viewer access to the interior of the house. At the Church of St. Nicholas Orphanos in Thessalonika, the saint stands outside and reaches up while the chamber, relieved of its front wall, reveals the family within. The composition is similar at Chartres Cathedral, where the story has been carved in stonework on one of the great recessed arches in the transept; Nicholas makes his clandestine gift from outside, while the father lies supine and his daughters stand by his bed. They seem in thrall to their plight, or perhaps to the luminous tragic beauty of their assemblage—so much as to seem unaware of the shit that the pigeons of the Eure Valley have splattered upon them since they were sculpted here in the early 1200s.

Notable populations of frescoes of "Three Daughters," largely from the fourteenth century, survive across mainland Greece and on the islands, particularly Crete, and in Macedonia and Bulgaria, in Serbia and Kosovo, in Romania, in Italy and Sicily and even distant Georgia. It is commemorated on millions of Russian icons and on the great stained-glass windows of northern France and Germany, notably at Auxerre, Troyes, Bourges, and Freibourg. There are stone sculptures in the most distant corners; one is carved into a thirteenth-century capital supporting the chancel arch of an island church off Estonia.

"Three Daughters" attracted many artists of the Trecento and the Renaissance. Frescoes were commissioned at the Church of San Saba in Rome and at the great basilica of St. Francis at Assisi during the early fourteenth century. The story also appeared on many predella panels during the Trecento, notably by Lippo Vanni, Agnolo Gaddi, and Paolo Veneziano. Ambrogio Lorenzetti included the scene in the predella he painted for the church of St. Procolo in Florence around 1332. In the early 1400s, "Three Daughters" inspired a particular rash of renderings. Gentile da Fabriano made it the subject of one of his predella panels in the high altarpiece commissioned by the Quaratesi family for the Florentine Church of St. Nicholas Above the Arno in 1425. The following year, it appeared on the predella of a Pisa altarpiece by the great Masaccio. Lorenzo di Bicci completed one for an altarpiece of the monastery of San Niccolo in Florence in 1433; Fra Angelico gave it particular prominence on a Perugia altarpiece in 1437; and Fra Filippo Lippi painted it around the same time in a Florentine chapel. Other Renaissance artists drawn to the story included Lorenzo di Pietro, Francesco Pesellino, and the Dutchman Gerard David, who made it the central panel of his triptych *Three Legends of St. Nicholas*.

The image in these representations has its variations, among which some prefigure the path of Nicholas' onward trajectory. They close the gap between the man he is and the man he will become, and provide glimpses of his future. Sometimes, as in the Gerard David picture, the girls are not awake and distressed but lie asleep in bed; they strikingly presage the manner of Christmas children with a joyful awakening ahead of them. Then there are the paintings of Fra Angelico, Pesellino, Lorenzetti, and others where the clandestine Nicholas is dressed in a red cape.

The Ramaća Fresco. (© Republicki Zavod za zastitu spomenika kulture, Belgrade)

Finally, there is the fresco at the Church of SS. Constantine and Helena, formerly St. Nicholas, in the village of Ramaća, Serbia. The fourteenth-century church, built by a priest and his son, stands in the wooded uplands of the Sumadija south of Belgrade. The fresco, dated to around 1392, is on the south wall of the narthex and is vertically arranged. At the bottom, reduced by his despair, the father huddles on the floor. He wraps his robes around himself as if against the cold and stares upward with an expression of pure pleading. Above him is the bed where his three daughters lie, their sleeping faces fixed in anguish. From the far side of the bed a wall rises to a low roof, again cut away to let us in on the action unfolding outside: the haloed Nicholas, dropping a dowry sack not through an open window but down a chimney pot.

Our daughter awoke us in the early hours.

"Mum," whispered Anna, "my fairy's called Charlotte." We congratulated the excited child and ushered her back to bed.

"Charlotte?" I mumbled to Ash, settling back. "Where did you dream that up?" The Tooth Fairy evidently remained in good shape. Even so, next year might well prove Anna's last chance to visit Father Christmas in Lapland.

12

Nicholas was beyond reach that afternoon. A close crowd of Russians had taken possession of his crypt. Mournful drifts of plainchant, punctuated by a series of compacted grunts, rose from the wide steps that descended to his shrine on either side of the choir. I could not get to him by going down, so I looked up, beyond the buttressing arches that spanned the great nave and the galleries above them, to the ceiling.

It was May, and I had rejoined Nicholas at his European landfall. Bari's twelfth-century Romanesque basilica, built to house his mortal remains, had a bastion exterior and plain ashlar inner walls, but the ceiling paintings were extravagantly rococo. Gilded scrolls and winged angels, cherubs' heads and swags of foliage framed florid images, largely of Nicholas' role at Nicaea, reminding me where I had last left him. Here was Nicholas striking Arius, suffering his beard to be singed, and being visited by Christ and the Virgin.

These 1660s paintings served a clear intention: to establish Nicholas as a leading presence at a historical event that he is unlikely to have even attended. Backing Nicholas' presence at Nicaea served Bari's own interests by lending substance to a subsequent episode that reflected divine credit upon the city: the saint's visit here. A ceiling centerpiece presented—as the natural sequence to Nicaea—Nicholas on a Bari quayside, among a crowd of grandees and stevedores, pointing fixedly at the earth, to prophesy: *My bones will rest here.*

So they had, but some 550 years before it was first prophesied that they should do so. I detected at Bari the first inklings of a political agenda. The invented prophecy was questionable, even by hagiography's dubious standards, in that its purpose was not to hymn the saint but to legitimize his "translation" to Bari, which the Byzantines and their Turkish successors pointedly regarded as theft. I remembered how at the Demre basilica the word STOLEN had been scrawled across a sign recounting the events of

1087. Not that such scheming should have surprised me; this, after all, was Catholic southern Italy.

Bari had changed Nicholas. He had put on ecclesiastical weight. He had a beautiful Norman basilica with a fine treasury and a crypt that was hung with icons given by Serbian tsars. Knots of priests passed in black canonicals. Shiny black saloon cars with tinted windows drew up outside the administrative offices lining the basilica courtyard. Within, church officials served Nicholas' wide-ranging interests, extending his reach, furthering his reputation, and selling his image from the busy gift shop. The contrast with Demre was striking. I had left the land where Nicholas was an exiled memory and stepped into the heart of his flourishing cult.

The basilica stood within Bari's old city, where high walls screened off the nearby Adriatic. These great fortifications enclosed narrow lanes which thrashed like a catch of eels, knotting themselves into alleyways that gave onto courtyards and promenades where sudden sunlight flooded. Lovers nosed past on mopeds; in the front rooms, beyond the open doors, women rolled pasta dough in the flickering dapple of daytime television. It was only when I looked up that I found Nicholas. Above front doors, on ledges or in alcoves illuminated by cerise bulbs, the patron of the city was repeatedly represented. Sometimes his painted image stood alongside the Virgin Mary's; the frame that contained them was propped on a wooden ledge from which a net pelmet hung, like an altar. Elsewhere, a hinged glass door enclosed the alcove where he stood, a gesso figurine about a foot tall and in yellow robes, the ensemble flanked by a pair of vases that held plastic roses. Sometimes, he appeared as a painted plate-size medallion cast in plaster. Nor did he restrict himself to private shrines; he had also colonized the old city's public spaces. He appeared on a fifteenth-century stone relief set in a high archway, and as a stone statuette shelved on a corner above the street, befouled by pigeons but venerated by telephone engineers to judge by the conspicuous private margin they had allowed him in the surrounding tangle of wires.

Bari belonged to Nicholas. But the bewildering range of painted and graven forms that he took here suggested something else: that his escape from Orthodoxy had also freed him from its iconographic confines. He could begin to express himself.

St. Nicholas carving, Bari Old City. (Author's photo)

Bari, even by the sundered standards of the late eleventh century, was a divided city. The port on Italy's southern heel was caught between the Catholic West and the Orthodox East, whose rites and liturgies had been diverging for centuries. The West was aghast that Orthodox clerics should marry; the East objected to the use of unleavened bread in the Latin Eucharist and to the insertion of the contentious "filioque"—"and the Son"—into their Creed. From 1054, when a visiting Roman retinue strode into the basilica of St. Sophia at Constantinople to excommunicate the city's patriarch himself, schism was official. The schism ran straight down Bari's main thoroughfare.

Bari and the surrounding province of Puglia had been Greek Byzantine for centuries, but also were home to substantial populations of Latin Lombards and Normans. Greek and Latin bishoprics stood side by side across the region, largely unharmoniously, though some Greek churches, for complex reasons of accommodation, actually adhered to the Latin rite, and vice versa. The Latin one, with the comparative proximity of Rome, had held the upper hand in Bari until the eighth century, when the Byzantines took the city. The Greek rite subsequently predominated, especially from

1043, when the patriarch of Constantinople imposed it across Puglia. But with the increase of Norman influence from the 1050s, the Latin church had begun to recover. In 1071, when the Normans captured the city after a three-year siege, the churches reverted to the Latin rite.

At once uncouth but devout, territorially insatiable but chivalrous, the Normans burst the seams of their northern French heartlands like an eleventh-century force of nature. They had initially discovered Bari, a major sally port for the East, as pilgrims; a band of them were first sighted in the region visiting the shrine of St. Michael, the archangel of the flaming sword, at Monte Gargano in southern Italy on their return from Jerusalem in 1016. The Normans liked what they saw of the area and, having detected a power vacuum as the consequence of Lombards and Greeks, Arabs and local chieftains fighting each other to a standstill, resolved to return with the wherewithal to make it theirs.

With the capture of Bari, the Normans ousted the Byzantines from their regional capital and seat of the catapan, or governor, and so won control of the southern Adriatic. The fall of Bari has made a relatively modest dent in history, eclipsed as it was by two events, one of which highlighted Norman ascendancy, the other Byzantine decline, to more spectacular effect: respectively, the Norman conquest of England five years earlier, and the battle of Manzikert within weeks of Bari's fall. The Byzantine empire, at once under attack on its eastern borders and its western ones, suffered a defeat by the Turks in distant Anatolia that would mark the beginning of the end, eventually leading (as Nicholas may even have divined) to Turkish possession of Constantinople. The more immediate effect of Manzikert was to leave swathes of Anatolia undefended against Turkish incursions. These all but simultaneous events at either end of the Byzantine empire—the Norman capture of Bari, and the battle that left the Turks free to threaten all Anatolia, and specifically Myra—would lead to events sixteen years later with lasting implications for Nicholas' future.

With their capture of Bari in 1071, the Normans determined to extend their influence in the eastern Mediterranean, continuing their campaign against Byzantine possessions with a series of ambitious forays in the Adriatic. But by 1085, with death and illness claiming their inspirational leaders, Bari's military initiatives had ground to a halt. Nor were the city's religious credentials in good shape. In 1066, Bari's archbishop, Andrew, had been on a visit to Constantinople when he converted, without warning, to

Judaism. He fled to Egypt and was not seen again. He never explained his conversion, though a certain Solomonic justice might have been divined in his refusal to choose, preferring absolute withdrawal from the warring Christian churches that claimed him. Christendom saw it rather as a defection to the faith whose congregants had killed the Messiah. The episode reflected badly on Bari. The new Norman proprietors, inheritors of this apostatic mess, determined to redeem the city. They sought by a single stroke to restore Bari's religious reputation and so demonstrate the extent of its reinvigorated reach. It was time to procure for the city a saint.

Bari already had a patron saint, Sabinus, but the onetime bishop of nearby Canosa was not the man to reestablish the city as a major force. What was needed was a replacement saint from the top drawer. A saint who could compare with Andrew, Timothy, and Luke, Constantinople's protectors, or with Mark, whose bones had been smuggled out of Alexandria and taken to Venice in A.D. 828. Or with Matthew, the most telling and recent parallel, who was brought to Salerno and reinterred there in a newly built basilica bearing his name in 1080, shortly after the city fell to the Normans.

Saints' bones were the most venerated of all Christian relics. The faintest association with a holy person or event bestowed a relic value on belongings of any sort. Proximity to the revered being enhanced the value of clothes, robes, and shrouds, but body parts were of a different devotional order. Cities, monasteries, ambitious hamlets, and shrines sought these divine bones, which functioned as protective talismans, tokens of spiritual authority and civic prestige, so much so that they often came to provide communities with their name and thus their very identity. They were also lucrative pilgrim magnets. An inconvenience was that ancient taboos surrounded the disinterment of the dead. The Romans had legislated against the practice. Inscriptions on gravestones and sarcophagi, especially in Anatolia, cursed those that would desecrate their contents. Under the fourth-century emperor Theodosius, it was forbidden to move the dead even a few feet. There was consequently a pragmatic emphasis on those parts that came adrift naturally or ritualistically in life's course: hair, teeth, nail clippings, even foreskins, umbilical cords, and vials of breath, as well as natural secretions such as mother's milk.

The relic collectors were not, however, to be denied. They cited the apparent endorsement of the practice by St. John in Revelation where he described, as part of Christ's vision, the souls of the saints enshrined beneath a church altar. There was also the example of the original desecration, though divinely achieved, of the tomb of Christ himself. Constantinople's Church of the Apostles ignored the strictures of Theodosius, securing for its reliquary the bones of St. Phocas, St. Paul the Confessor, John the Baptist, and the prophet Samuel. The soaring market meant that cases of disinterment were only a matter of time, especially in the earthquake-ruptured landscapes of Italy and Anatolia, where grave robbers were able to claim the manifest support of the forces of nature in their work. Even so, demand continued to outrun supply. The natural consequence was that relics began to be broken up as a means of maximizing their salable value. Crosses were reduced to tinder, shrouds were shredded, crowns divided into single thorns, bones splintered. And in a famous dictum—"In the divided body, the grace survives undivided"—Theodoret of Cyrus endorsed the practice. This splintery diaspora meant that intact saints were decidedly rare by 1087.

The practice had the greatest implications, of course, for the saints themselves. Disintegration had its advantages in that it helped extend the saint's range, but it did so thinly. The real concern was the reductive effect that the dispersal of relics might have upon the saint's power base, weakening the appeal of the original shrine. To expand was essential, but to do so excessively was to court oblivion by undermining one's very foundations. Nicholas was uncommon in that he had somehow found a way to flourish without being broken up. By 1087, only a finger—reported at a German monastery in the 1050s, probably fake—and a number of teeth had been documented as having strayed beyond Myra. And Nicholas had devised a means of supplying a stream of relics, with no implications as to his intactness, to spread word of him. From his shrine at Myra, his bones had developed the ability to produce a miraculous liquid which was variously known for its healing qualities as manna, ambrosia, or myrrh.

Nicholas' special ability, peculiar to a number of canny saints, seems to have been acquired over centuries. Certainly, pilgrims to Myra were commonly taking away vials of the substance by the tenth century. It had supposed qualities as a balm or ointment, though it was more likely preserved than applied, like comparable secreted relics such as the Virgin's milk. Nicholas' myrrh was not only highly prized but apparently inexhaustible. When Barbier de Montault visited Bari in 1875, he was able to look into the tomb, where he distinctly saw myrrh dripping from the bones. He described it as "[a] little heavy, like a drop of oil; transparent, limpid and almost without taste." It was available even today, though diluted, at Bari's basilica gift shop, where it was sold in wax-stoppered bottles, painted with scenes from the saint's life.

I remembered the shabby gift shop at Demre from my visit the previous winter: postcards, film past its sell-by date, local booklets on St. Nicholas with spines cracked by the sun, and the small hemp sacks that claimed to contain holy earth. The sacks were the basilica's best shot at establishing a replacement relic for the myrrh-seeping bones, which it had long lost; they traded on whatever ancient sanctity still attached to the place. Earth had long been held to have special qualities as a treatment, notably against wounds, plague, and reptile bite, in various Anatolian towns and eastern Mediterranean islands including Chios, Samos, and the Black Sea port of Sinop. But not Myra; I was impressed by the way that Demre's Turks had taken to the essential spirit of the relic trade, blithely peddling holy earth even as mechanical excavators removed it from the site with giant shovels.

Ridvan Bey, the architect in charge of the restoration at Demre, knew about Nicholas' myrrh. He directed me to another sarcophagus; this one lay in an alcove of the mausoleum where the Nicholas frescoes were being restored. The sarcophagus was marble and decorated in acanthus leaves. But its most significant feature was a round hole low in the side: a drain where run-off could be collected.

It had long been the eastern belief that water which was passed among saints' remains emerged sanctified by the contact. The practice was widespread in the early church, and the holed sarcophagus suggested it had occurred at Myra. I sensed an association of sorts between the practice and Nicholas' exudations of myrrh, the one explaining the other; this sarcophagus might even have been the saint's original tomb.

That Nicholas' miraculous seepage had come to be known as myrrh, or *murra* in the Greek, was strikingly interesting, especially since Myra itself may have been named after myrrh. Myrrh (*Commiphora myrrha*) correctly refers to a shrub which yields a bitter unguent that was primarily used for its astringent and antiseptic qualities as an embalming fluid. It was best known as the Magus Balthasar's darkly prophetic gift to the infant Jesus. It figured in Jesus' death not only as a sedative offered him upon the Cross but in the preparation of his corpse. Its qualities not only prevented putrefaction in corpses but also commended it to the living: the ancient Greeks took myrrh into battle to clean wounds against infection.

Commiphora myrrha is restricted to the Arabian Peninsula, but Myra may have been named on account of the fact that myrrh was often used as a generic term for a range of embalming incenses which were abundant in Lycia. Myra had a long tradition in the production of such incenses, as the Russian abbot Daniel noted in his account of his pilgrimages to the Holy Land in 1106. "The town of Makri and all the surrounding country, as far as Myra," he wrote, "produces black incense and gomphytis; it exudes from the tree in a viscous state and is collected with a sharp-edged piece of iron. . . . Another shrub, resembling the aspen, is called raha." This shrub, according to Daniel, attracted worms that reduced the bark to a powder. The powder was collected and mixed with the resin from the first tree before being boiled in a copper cauldron to produce the incense, which was sold to merchants in leather bottles.

I suggested to Ridvan Bey that Nicholas' miraculous myrrh-seeping might have been bound up with local funerary customs and rituals. He smiled and directed me to the nearest graveyard. It lay north of the town, among fields near the ancient amphitheater. In this scruffy place, frequented by geese, the raised graves were walled with concrete and topped with headstones that dated their dead in the old Arabic calendar. And every grave sported a sprig, some recently picked, others brown and brittle. They were branches of myrtle (*Myrtus communis*). Out in the villages, myrtle branches were even today piled over fresh graves. Myrtle deodorized the dead, just as myrrh had done. It also had similar antiseptic qualities. The local people still used myrtle oil, dabbing it on cuts. They sold bottles of it in Demre's shops. An ancient embalming culture, albeit in reduced circumstances, survived here. This gave new impetus to the theory I was shaping: that the name chosen for Nicholas' posthumous seepages tacitly acknowledged a distant misconception. That devotees at the sarcophagus had once mistaken, by accident or design, the myrrh-mingled run-off from water poured through the saint's embalmed remains for a holy elixir of Nicholas' own making. Had this established a local belief that would eventually supply the saint with centuries of limitless relics?

Vials of his myrrh may have first brought the miraculous Nicholas to the attention of the people of Bari. Certainly, they were all aware of him by the eleventh century, for Nicholas had succeeded beyond even his own expectations. He was regarded as the most effective of intercessors, particularly in everyday matters, the saint who could intervene against authority, guard against shipwreck, and even provide much-needed money. No saint was more popular. Anna Comnena, the Byzantine emperor's chronicler daughter, described him in the twelfth century, twice, as the greatest saint in the hierarchy, and once as the greatest of all bishops. Certainly, both leading camps within eleventh-century Bari had their own reasons to be drawn to him, the Greek citizenry because he was a link to the Byzantine world they had recently been severed from, and the Norman rulers because his acquisition would represent a telling affront to their traditional enemies in Constantinople.

What, finally, commended Nicholas to Bari was that his remains were both vulnerable and accessible. The Byzantines had lost control of Myra, which now lay on the front line between advancing Turks and retreating Christians. Relations between the two religions had been deteriorating for decades. Christians burned copies of the Koran in eastern Anatolia, and in 1087 a Pisan fleet attacked Muslim Mahdia in Tunisia. Three hundred Westerners were expelled from Jerusalem in 1056. Caliph Hakim ordered the destruction of the Church of the Holy Sepulchre in Jerusalem, and from his base at Smyrna a Turkish privateer by the name of Chakas launched raids against Byzantine settlements on the Anatolian coast. Nicholas' shrine, guarded by a few brave monks, was in peril of falling into Muslim hands.

Bari recognized a unique opportunity not only to win Nicholas for itself but to garland the act with honorable motive; it was not a theft, then, but nothing less than a rescue mission, in the face of Byzantine inaction, on behalf of all Christendom. Retrieving Nicholas would redeem Bari.

The massed knights of Europe would attempt a similar retrieval, on a far greater scale, when they headed east to reclaim the holy places of Christ in 1096. What Bari was in principle attempting with its bid for Nicholas was the Crusades in miniature, nine years early.

13

ON AN APRIL DAY in 1087, three ships appeared over the southern horizon and put in to Andriake. The fleet's chronicler, the first of many, would waste no time on the scene—the high prows, the lateen sails closing on a shoreline seamed pink with oleanders—but merely observed that the crews made fast in the "usual manner." The first chronicler of many, because the exploits of the party, from Bari, would attract international attention. And the usual manner, because the visitors were subtle enough, at least at this early stage in the operation, to betray no outward signs of what they were about to attempt: the most celebrated heist of the age.

The chronicler, a Bari clerk named Nicephorus, recounted how the ships' arrival at Antioch some days earlier had occasioned fevered discussion among the crews. The subject was not the price their grain cargoes might fetch, nor the local brothel rates, nor when they could expect to be back in Bari, but how they were to remove "the body of the most blessed Confessor of Christ, Nicholas" from his shrine at Myra. An explanatory rider might have been expected. Its absence supposes that Nicephorus saw nothing the least outlandish in the scheme, no doubt because the Bari fleet was not the only one intent on acquiring Nicholas that year. The only surprise was that no attempt had been made on Nicholas since Myra's recent abandonment in the face of the Turkish advance, which had left the saint largely unguarded: the most popular saint, at the height of relic fever, available for removal. Some sources hold that the Bari fleet encountered eleven ships in or around Antioch that spring whose crews all had designs on St. Nicholas. Nicephorus claimed that a fleet of Venetians—past masters in the art of *translatio*—had already equipped themselves for the job with "iron instruments." Another chronicler even observed that the Venetian crews hurried through their dinner to hasten their departure for Myra.

Such Venetian ambitions most likely decided the Bariots, for they knew

of no sharper spur. Bari and Venice, which had been eyeballing each other
from either end of the Adriatic for some time, had recently come to blows;
the Venetians, old allies of the Byzantines, had come off the better. They
had defeated the Norman fleet near Bari in 1081 and driven their garrisons
from Durazzo (Albanian Durrës) and Corfu in 1084, effectively extinguish-
ing any lingering Norman ambitions to take Constantinople itself. Beating
the Venetians to St. Nicholas would at least soothe Bari's smarting.

The Bariots wasted no time in Antioch. They sold at speed and stowed
the holds with whatever merchandise was to hand, largely careless of its
cargo value. They also embarked some passengers, clergymen, and pilgrims returning from the Holy Land, no doubt figuring that an ecclesiastical presence might prove useful, legitimizing even, in the imminent
venture. On arriving at Myra, they sent out scouts to check for roaming
Turks. Then, leaving a party of fifteen guards to watch the fleet, they put
ashore. They made their way down the road I traveled earlier in this narrative, though many centuries later and in another season, in the opposite
direction and, finally, in a rented car; sometimes, the gulf of history
seemed so brutally wide that I had to remind myself that we were all in
search of the same man.

The party found just four monks serving at the basilica, one more than
Charles Texier would find when he visited in 1836, though this was not to
imply a comparable dereliction in 1087. In fact, a dramatic recovery in pilgrim numbers had been evident on the Mediterranean sea routes since the
tenth century. With the removal of the Arab privateers' haunts from Italy,
southern France, and Crete, Greek and Italian merchantmen on the trading
routes to Syria and Egypt were once more offering safe passage to pilgrims.
Counts, abbots, bishops, and duchesses led large pilgrimages from A.D. 960
onward; 1033, the thousandth anniversary of Christ's death, sparked a particularly fevered period of pilgrimage. Harald Hardrada, a Danish
claimant to the English throne, made a pilgrimage in 1034; Duke Robert I,
William the Conqueror's father, made his way to Jerusalem the following
year. Armies of pilgrims, three thousand under the bishop of Cambrai in
1054 and some ten thousand under the archbishops of Cologne and Mainz
a decade later, headed east. Many called at Myra, where St. Nicholas was
approaching a giddying peak of popularity, so much so that his basilica underwent a major restoration in 1042.

By 1087, however, bands of marauding Turks had put most of Myra's populace to flight, leaving a lonely quartet to tend the basilica. This state of affairs lent weight to the Bariot argument that Nicholas was not best served at Myra. The argument had physical support in the shape of the forty-seven men who had arrived at the basilica gates, asking to see the saint's resting place; it was clear that the visitors' subtlety was not numerical in nature.

It was not the group's size, however, that first aroused the Myra monks' suspicions, nor the fact that so few of the visitors were clergy or pilgrims. Nor was it even that the majority were heavily armed, and not merely with swords (which were accounted usual, especially with Turks on the roam), but with more revealing implements; Nicephorus mentions only an "iron mallet," but we can reasonably assume a wider range of tomb-breaking tools including stone chisels, picks, and crowbars. Instead, it was the incessant questions that led the monks to challenge the visitors, for they were accustomed to a less enquiring breed of pilgrim. The Bariots instantly abandoned all pretense. Truly, they had come to remove the saint, they declared, and would thank the monks to direct them to the true location of his remains. They knew all about the Byzantines and their wily ways, and were determined not to play the textbook dupes, who invariably departed with the wrong set of bones in these circumstances.

In this, however, they had underestimated Nicholas' custodians. The monks had settled upon a more abstract defense, which was to absent themselves from the issue by invoking a higher will than theirs. They had, they insisted, already shown the Bariots the very place—though it hardly mattered. "The holy confessor of God," one monk explained, "will never let you touch him." The Bariots, as they were to demonstrate, could also play at this game. They riposted with the claim to know differently, explaining that the pope, recently in Bari, had commanded the translation on the instruction of the saint himself, who had appeared to His Holiness in a vision. And so to the parley. When the monks of Myra and the men of Bari locked horns that day, they were agreed on one central principle: that the will of Nicholas would decide the matter. Precisely as Chrysostom, the twenty-first-century bishop of Myra, had claimed—on matters ranging from the holding of mass at Demre to his own well-being under anesthetic—at the Patriarchate in Istanbul the previous winter.

For seven hundred years, Nicholas had been an active presence in Lycia, tirelessly fielding pilgrims' varied appeals and sending them on their way with vials of his elixir. When it came to his own interests, however, he had remained insistently invisible. It was as if he appreciated that nothing serves a saint like the impression of selflessness. By operating out of sight, he made it appear that he had no interest in, and exerted no influence over, his own progress. It was a classic saint's sleight of hand: why, if he flourished, it was purely owing to his devotees.

To this rule, however, Nicholas allowed himself one exception. He would not stand by when it came to interference with his bones, whether that meant their division or their wholesale relocation. Saints commonly insisted on controlling the location of their bones, and of the shrines that housed them, which they considered essential to their very integrity. They had an acute geographical sense of where their interests were best served—a profound dread of the backwater, of civic decline, of the distant, gimcrack shrines that upstart robber princes might remove them to. They habitually refused to be moved if the direction displeased them, causing paralysis among the bearers of their relics, or halting the oxen hitched to the wagon on which their sarcophagus was to be translated. St. Millan had stymied an attempt in 1053 by King Garcia of Navarre to remove his remains to Najera, near Burgos. He caused his coffin to weigh so heavily that the king's men were forced to leave it by the road, where the chastened king duly built an oratory to the saint. Nicholas already had a history in this regard. A Muslim fleet had tried to steal his relics back in A.D. 808, but the raid had failed when a storm rose to scatter the ships off Myra. The admiral should have known who ran matters locally, sea conditions included; which was the gist of the monks' robust message to this latest lot of interlopers.

This was not to prevent Myrites and Bariots from doing all in their power to influence events that day. These mortals were not able to locate the seam that divided human endeavor from saintly magic, but were aware that there must be a limit to Nicholas' miraculous powers. Otherwise, he would have relocated under his own volition at a time of his choosing. Besides, the real point of their efforts was to show Nicholas how much he meant to them. This led the monks to make a sudden dash to alert the remnant townsfolk, and the Bariots to block their way, tie them up, and set a guard at the basilica entrance.

Nicephorus was writing from the Bariot perspective; even so, he seems to have had a point when he interpreted the unfolding events as signs of a saint desperate to be gone. The city may have been Nicholas' base for three quarters of a millennium, supplying him with regular infusions of pilgrims, but pilgrimage's recent renaissance did not alter the fact that the Turks were coming. The Turks might not prevent the pilgrims from visiting the shrine—they knew a lucrative scam when they saw what they took to be one—but Nicholas had no intention of enduring infidel rule, especially when the majority of Myrites had already fled. Myra under the Turks, though it would be sure to bring Nicholas the curiosity of a modest constituency among those pragmatic Muslims who covered all bases by habitually seeking favors at Christian shrines, would condemn him to a long withering at the root, which was patently not part of the plan. It was time to leave, and to let the Bari men know his wishes.

The Bariots were considering how they might proceed when one of their clergymen accidentally knocked a vial of Nicholas' holy myrrh to the floor. It did not break but began to vibrate distinctly, which Nicephorus interpreted as a message from Nicholas, thus: "Why are you so slothful in performing your duty? It is my will that I leave here with you."

At this, one of the sailors threatened a monk with his sword, repeating their demand that the actual resting place be confirmed. The monk began confidently, by emphasizing that "many emperors and other potentates have done their best to carry out what you now plan; but they had no luck because the saint of God was unwilling." Then, without warning, he began to buckle. "Yet perhaps it may happen through you," he acknowledged, "because the Confessor of God himself last year warned us in a vision that his abode would be moved elsewhere." Nor had this been the first such rumble of dissatisfaction; it was all coming out now. There had been an earlier vision—the air was thick with them—in which Nicholas had informed the people of Myra that he was disappointed in them. Unless they returned to the city, he was prepared to consider offers from elsewhere. And they clearly hadn't returned, at least not enough of them to revive his commitment to the place.

One of the monks recovered sufficiently to make a last desperate appeal to Nicholas that he stay. "Though by his holy admonitions Nicholas holds us responsible," he declared, "we believe that by the will of God he will not this easily desert his own humble servants." Now, by helping or hindering, Nicholas must decide his own future. A Bari man by the name of Matthew picked up an iron mallet which he smashed against a marble floor slab. He soon revealed a "very white marble tomb" and broke it open, revealing the saint's remains immersed in a holy liquid. The liquid released a wave of "delightful perfume," which wafted beyond the basilica and as far as the waiting ships where the crewmen received its unmistakable message: Nicholas had consented to join them.

Matthew, overjoyed, clambered into the sarcophagus, where the relics were "swimming in an envelopment of all perfumes." He handed the bones to his colleagues, who arranged them in a covering of new silk before bearing them back to the ships amid Latin chants of praise. By the time they had boarded, a beseeching crowd of Myrites had gathered along the shoreline. Some waded into the sea, grabbing at the ships' rails and crying that Nicholas—or at least a part of him—be returned to them. But Nicholas was on his way. The people of Myra, the sailors pointed out, had had their fair share of the saint. They had at least retained the sarcophagus and the precious, though now finite, liquid it contained. There was also a miraculous icon which Nicholas, by an unspecified prompt, had commanded the Bariots to leave as consolation. As they set sail, with Nicholas' relics snugly settled in a ship's locker, dirges reached them from the shoreline.

They reached Patara the following day. Wind and tide were against them, however, and they had hardly covered another twenty-four miles when they were forced to put ashore. They found themselves at a place called Perdikca, or Partridges; yet another name for St. Nicholas Island and its adjacent bay, which was now known as Gemiler. These stops at his old haunts might have suggested a surrender to sentiment, the saintly equivalent of lingering in empty rooms after the removal lorry had pulled away, taking in the stories that the scuffed skirtings and stained carpets recalled, before he slammed the door on his Lycian past. In fact, he had serious business to attend to. The crew only realized that Nicholas himself had halted the translation when the seas fell calm as they put ashore. Was the saint having second thoughts? Or was it because some of their number had behaved in a manner that was bound to displease him, by pilfering from his holy relics once they were stowed on the ship? Taking turns to swear their innocence upon the Gospels duly flushed out the guilty sailors. They restored Nicholas' humor by returning his missing bones to the ship's locker before celebrating mass in one of the island basilicas I had visited in the winter. And when they put to sea, they did so under sails newly swollen by a favorable wind courtesy of a contented Nicholas. "They were thereby given to understand," wrote Nicephorus, "that the Confessor of God himself willed that his relics should never in any way be divided." But Nicholas was out in the world now.

On May 9, the ships arrived at the port of San Giorgio, four miles south of Bari. Nine hundred fifteen years later—but two days early, Italian festivals being what they are—I would be waiting for them among a shoreline crowd. An outdoor mass was in progress. The congregation had made space for itself among lines of RVs, all identical, but parked askew as if their angles might signify the independent spirits of their owners. The air smelled of frying onions. Radios rang out and swimming outfits flapped from tree-strung washing lines. The place where Nicholas had first put ashore in Europe was not only named after a rival saint but had since become a camping site. No matter; Bari would put things right.

San Giorgio is a little harbor founded on a grudging indent in the rocky shoreline, and it is inconceivable that it was ever anything else. Certainly, it hardly seemed an essential port of call for a fleet that had traversed the Aegean, Ionian, and Adriatic Seas, especially when Bari lay so near. So this stop had all the earmarks of a pause for effect, as a bride might halt before the church to check herself in a compact. At San Giorgio, they prepared Nicholas for his arrival by building a handsome casket for his relics. The first glimpse of Puglia had imbued Nicholas, it seemed, with an Italian sense of ceremony, or even the beginnings of a vain streak.

The mass at San Giorgio marked the beginning of the annual reenactment of Nicholas' arrival. Beyond the close-packed congregation, besuited men strolled, keeping errant soccer balls at bay, their nostrils pinched at the smells of German barbecues. Nicholas took the form of a large sixteenth-century portrait framed in ornate gilt. He was propped on a raised dais, against an altar that was draped in damask and topped with candles.

A small blue fishing *barca*, charged with the office of bringing Nicholas the final few miles to his new home, waited offshore. The owner had gone to such lengths, garlanding his craft with lilies, festooning the shrouds with plastic pennants and party balloons, and positioning a red velvet lectern amidships, that it had quite worn him out. He dozed in the stern, his head flung back over the gunwale so that his hooked nose bobbed like a hairy shark's fin above the gentle swell. Beyond him, out on the Adriatic, I could see the coast guard launch that usually patrolled to prevent less welcome arrivals from the East. Modern migration meant rolls of dollar bills and clandestine landings that often ended in interceptions and custody. The sea that the migrant Nicholas had crossed to a rapturous welcome had now closed. In its place was a barrier through which seeped desperate illegals from Albania and Turkey.

A robed bishop was delivering an oratory through a microphone. His repeated refrain soon acquired the force of a slogan: "il santo del oriente e occidente." Bari's lofty take on the translation, though others regarded it as a typically Italian grab, was that this Orthodox Byzantine had spanned the sundered Christian world by converting to Latin Catholicism. It was a persuasive line, at least to the benefiting church, and not without historical substance. Eleven years after Nicholas' arrival, the pope had convened a council of 183 bishops from both churches in a bid to end the schism of 1054. The eight-day council took place at Bari. The bishops gathered in what is now the crypt—the basilica above it had hardly been begun—directly before the tomb of St. Nicholas. The eastern saint, now reinstalled in the West, was the bishops' point of union. The Greeks, unsurprisingly, saw it as an abduction, reluctant as they were to concede that Nicholas had willingly defected.

These awkward issues were obscured by the strains of opera from a crackly speaker, which marked the end of the mass at San Giorgio, and by fireworks, which burst against a blue sky, not only waking the barca owner with a start, but leaving a retinal imprint that remained visible even when I closed my eyes to sleep that night. A uniformed guard of honor—bishops and priests, soldiers, coast guardsmen, naval cadets, carabinieri, and police—converged on Nicholas, bore him to the jetty, and saw him safely settled on the lectern.

I followed Nicholas' triumphant entry into Bari from the windows of the bus that ran along the scrubby seafront. By the time we had caught up, the saint had attracted a flotilla of leisure boats, fishing smacks, and canoes propelled by frantic paddles. He approached the Bari quayside to a cacophony of car horns, klaxons, and foghorns, which rose to a crescendo as his barca came alongside. The air was littered with screeching swifts, each celebrating its own arrival from the south, as I made my way through gathering crowds to the quayside where the barca was moored. Trucks customized as food stalls and painted like Gypsy caravans were parked along the front. They sold nuts and candy floss, raw mussels and sea urchins soused in lemon juice, panini filled with paprika sausage or hunks of fat-glazed pork sawn from pigs spit-roasted to a dark scarlet, disturbingly entire even unto their hairy singed ears. On the other side of the road, a less favored pitch, refugee hawkers sat beneath shredded calico canopies, selling screwdriver sets, pliers, and CDs. On the tarmac before them, automated puppies rose on their hind legs to pirouette with a sweetness that their beleaguered owners could not match.

Nicholas was still propped on his barca lectern, and I was able to get close enough to the portrait to see what Europe had made of him. For one thing, he was dark, a characteristic I'd also noticed in many of the old city's alcove figures and paintings. In the case of his great statue that stood in the nave of the basilica, he was positively Nubian. These representations, like the sixteenth-century portrait, postdated Nicholas' arrival by hundreds of years. It was as if something defensive lay beneath the joy that Nicholas' acquisition occasioned in Bari: the instinct to exaggerate the otherness of the outsider had been caught in the oils of the Bari artists and absorbed into St. Nicholas' local iconography. What that persistent darkness, apparently xenophobic, actually did was confer credit on both parties; that Nicholas was an outsider not only enhanced his excellent judgment in choosing to relocate to Bari but also reflected Bari's achievement in attracting him.

As for the rest, he was more recognizable in this particular portrait. He had the same luxuriant beard and high forehead and was yet to adopt those badges of Catholicism, the crosier and miter. He still wore the bishop's embroidered shoulder mantle, though the Orthodox omophorion would henceforth give way, with minor variations in style, to the Latin pallium. The hands remained in the established arrangement, except in one particular regard. Nicholas' left hand held the closed book upright so that the protruding boards ran parallel. And balanced upon them, as if on tracks, were two golden globes supporting a third so as to form a pyramid. I might have assumed Nicholas had taken up boules.

Holy stories, like the saints they referred to, had jostled to find favor with their audience. They naturally enjoyed differing levels of popularity. Some stood the test of time, increasing their standing with succeeding generations, while others could only watch their relevance drain away. Even so, under the protection of Orthodox iconography, the most withered tale continued to find a place on the margin of at least some biographical icons.

Conversely, those that had flourished remained as one of a number of episodes arranged with largely equal weighting around the central image of an equally unchanging Nicholas. An iconographic communism was at work, which failed to recognize or reward the variable resonances of these stories.

It was only when these stories reached the West, with its comparatively liberal artistic cultures, that the successful images were able to press for proportionate representation. What the West offered these episodes was what it promised the nighttime refugees who crammed rubber dinghies and fishing boats to evade the Adriatic coast guard off Bari: opportunity. New permitted forms, particularly sculptural, and a comparative freedom of expression meant that particular Nicholas stories could now go it alone on altars and wall panels. But the most telling change was right before my eyes. I was looking at evidence of a story so successful that it had achieved, at some point in the late fourteenth century, a symbolic short-hand form in the central image of the saint itself; the three globes represented the dowry bags. The story that had emerged in the West as the greatest of them all was now as essential a part of Nicholas as the Bible he had always carried. Thenceforth, he was almost always to be seen cradling the three globes on the book, as if the virtue that the episode enshrined was the prime lesson of its pages. "Three Daughters" was in Europe, and Europe approved.

14

NICHOLAS WAS CARRYING THE three globes the following morning when his effigy left its appointed place in the basilica to be carried through Bari.

It was the anniversary of Nicholas' translation. I had risen with the dawn and made my way through the old city, closing in on a rising murmur. A holy mass had packed the basilica. Crowds crammed the courtyard, and spilled into the adjacent Piazzetta of the 62 Sailors. They mingled with naval cadets, brass bands, and functionaries, and knots of men in ceremonial breeches, tights, tailcoats and cockaded bicornes. Pilgrim groups from Naples, Benevento, and Vasto wore uniform neckerchiefs and carried banners embroidered with images of the saint that proclaimed them as "Pellegrini S. Nicola," the braided edges invisible beneath pinned offerings of euro notes. Many bore staffs topped by crucified Christs and adorned with lily bunches, olive branches, pine cones, fatsia leaves, or feathers; the more practical had fitted their staffs with hooks where furled parasols were hung and secured with a band. Some pilgrims carried coiled ropes, with loops tied along their length, which they would distribute when the current of the procession threatened to sweep them away.

A peal of bells announced Nicholas. A roar of applause greeted him and the pale sky bloomed with arcing flowers. The Orthodox icon who had arrived as a Catholic portrait the previous day had undergone an overnight transformation, to emerge as a three-dimensional effigy; here was a man seeking a fuller idea of himself. Nicholas' statue stood eight feet high and was robed in yellow and vermilion and bedecked in chains of office. He wore a golden halo and carried a crosier in one hand; his ivory pallium was inset with stones and ornately worked crosses. He stood on a richly worked silver base, which rested upon the shoulders of twelve Bariots in

dark suits and sunglasses, menacing as Camorra pallbearers, at least until
a cloud of red rose petals from an upper window engulfed them. Nicholas
set off to receive the city's allegiance. His procession generated a riptide
that bore everything with it, pilgrims and petals, bicornes, pennants, and
French horns, and left me clinging to the door of a duty ambulance until
the pull had slackened.

I stepped inside the basilica and made for the side vestibule, which
housed the treasury. It was a trove of votive statues and crystal candlesticks, German chalices and Russian icons, Angevin crosses, incense burn-
ers and lamps, and enameled glass manna bottles. In one display case,
planks from the casket that bore Nicholas to Bari were bundled with a
purple ribbon. Crusader knights and pilgrims returning from the Holy
Land had donated other relics to the basilica, holy objects retrieved, like
the remains of Nicholas himself, from areas under Muslim control. Many
were now displayed in seventeenth-century reliquaries: armored limbs of
silver or gold that displayed, behind glass insets, the bone fragments of St.
Thomas and St. James and of St. Longino, the centurion who had pierced
Jesus' flank. On ornately worked stands were mounted relics that did not
lend themselves so readily to contextual extension: a thorn from the
Crown, a shred of sponge, a piece of the True Cross, Mary Magdalene's
tooth, and from the head of the Virgin a hair, which an optimistic sign described as missing.

Bari had proved, in the Nicholas way, an inspired move. The contents
of the treasury evoked the Christian tide that had swept through the city,
particularly during the twelfth and thirteenth centuries, leaving a reverent deposit of retrieved relics by way of nourishment. The city that had
lost its archbishop to Judaism had, with Nicholas' assistance, recovered
its Christian integrity to become a prime assembly point for the Crusading
armies just thirty years later. It was Europe's end point on the southern
route to the East. The first armies, from northern France and Germany,
had traveled through newly Christianized Hungary, but it was not long
before a second, more southerly wave began mustering at the Port of St.
Nicholas, to wit, Bari. The Norman leader Bohemond raised an army of
seven thousand knights and embarked from Bari in October. The army
under Count Hugh, son of the French king, followed suit. Robert of
Normandy and Stephen of Blois both readied their armies in Bari

(though they sailed from nearby Brindisi). It is not known what route was taken by the bands and brigades of the Count of Toulouse, Adhemar of Puy, and others, only that a contemporary chronicler wrote that "many took the shorter route through Pannonia [a Roman province largely in modern southern Hungary], but more still through the Portum Sancti Nicolae."

Bari rang with the clank of chain mail in the autumn of 1096 as thousands of Norman and Frankish warriors congregated on the city. They found billets, procured supplies and horses, negotiated with ship owners on the quaysides, and with wagoners, blacksmiths, and forage merchants. They prepared their arms, trained their men, and tore red cloaks into strips, which they attached to their smocks, back and front, in the form of crosses. And they prayed for the success of their holy venture.

Nicholas had been quick to establish premises in Bari, though it would be decades before his basilica was completed. The original church, largely constituting the present-day crypt, was consecrated by the pope in 1089 when he expressed "his excessive love for the blessed confessor Nicholas." The ribbon cut, Nicholas installed himself in his new premises, one eye on the door. He did not have long to wait.

Nicholas had clearly excelled, but not in the field of war. Christianity, hymning the power of the sword against the infidels in the East, had a new regard for soldiers. The pope might have honored Nicholas in 1089, but the real purpose of his visit to Bari had been to cement Rome's relationship with his former Norman enemies, whom he now courted for their warrior abilities. The faith was on a war footing, invoking soldier saints like James, conqueror of the Moors, and Gabriel, chief of the angelic guard, and unfurling the banner of George, who had appeared as a vision on a white charger to spur the Normans to victory over the Saracens at the battle of Cerami, Sicily, in 1063.

Nicholas had other pertinent assets. Being in Bari put him to hand, materially so, which could not be said of St. George who was moldering in a far-off Roman crypt. Battle, besides, remained a distant prospect, with a sea crossing and a long overland journey beforehand. And in each instance, Nicholas was strikingly well equipped to help. The Adriatic crossing to Durazzo was indisputably under the aegis of the seafarers'

saint; it was even rumored that William the Conqueror had invoked
Nicholas' protection on his Channel passage to conquer England. Then
there was what Nicholas could offer on the other shore. Some Crusaders
may have been familiar with southern Italy, but others were far from
home. Almost none of them had any notion of what lay ahead in the
lands of the Byzantines, whom they distrusted despite their supposed
common cause, and the Turks, whom they loathed and feared in equal
measure. Nicholas, until only recently Byzantine, was familiar with the
territories the Crusaders were to negotiate: the mountains of Macedonia, the plains of Thrace leading down to Constantinople, and the long
haul across the sere steppes of Anatolia. There were even churches bearing his name along the way; one of these reassuring beacons, just four
miles from the favored disembarkation point at Durazzo, was described
by Anna Comnena as dedicated "to the memory of Nicholas, greatest of
all bishops." In Bari, Nicholas was almost unique in knowing what lay
ahead. He had invaluable knowledge of the world beyond the Adriatic.
When the Crusaders knelt at his shrine for the last time, the laden flotillas tugging at their harbor warps, they did not seek absolution or redemption there but the saint's material services, as guide and dragoman
on the journey that lay ahead. As for George and Gabriel, their time
would come.

I followed those distant Crusaders into the crypt and found Russians
once more, though in manageable numbers this time. Black-mantled
priests with pendent crucifixes and ponytails bustled across the polished
marble floors that rose to a vaulted ceiling. They passed among thickets of
Byzantine columns of marble and oolite, the capitals carved with lions
and goats, with peacocks sipping at chalices and griffins attacking hares;
much of the masonry had been recycled from the three churches that were
demolished to make way for Nicholas' great shrine. A covey of nuns stood
in domed black headdresses. A woman whose T-shirt bore the message "I
Love Cash" stood before a bishop in rich vermilion robes who wrapped
her hands in his absolving stole.

The marble tomb lay beyond a high iron grille topped with uncompro-
mising spikes. It was flat-topped and doubled as an altar, hung with thuribles and the glow of suspended candles. At the front, there was a low arch
where Russians queued to kneel, each canting head and shoulders to find

himself in a dark interior, above a holy sump leading directly to the remnants of Nicholas.

The translation to Bari had been rapturously received in Russia as the work of a sacred snatch squad. "The city of Bari rejoices and with it, the whole universe exults in hymns and spiritual canticles," read one liturgical statement composed shortly after 1091. The translation was honored there with a special feast day.

Even so, there was among the Russians a recurrent desire to make Nicholas their own, just as the strategists among them coveted the territories of the saint's homeland. One Russian legend preferred to see the translation as a kind of insecure prison transfer during which Nicholas' soul took off for his spiritual home, Russia. The monks at Myra echoed wishful Russian thinking of a more material nature when they informed a nineteenth-century visitor that Nicholas' relics had actually been taken from Myra to St. Petersburg in a frigate during the 1820s. The truth was rather more prosaic; the Empress Alexandra Fyodorovna, wife of Tsar Nicholas I, had secured what were surely token relics of Nicholas on a visit to Bari. They were duly installed at St. Nicholas' Cathedral of the Sea, St. Petersburg, on December 5, 1847.

Even so, these varied attempts to bring Nicholas home seem to have been failures. Nicholas truly resided at Bari, whence they must make pilgrimages if they were to revere him in the fullest sense. It was a measure of Russian commitment to Bari's resident saint that they built their own church of St. Nicholas and adjacent pilgrims' hostel there in 1911. For its part, Bari did acknowledge the special relationship that Russia and the wider Orthodox world had with Nicholas when a vault in the basilica crypt was dedicated as an Orthodox chapel, complete with iconostasis, in 1966. The chapel commemorated the recent lifting of the anathemas the churches had originally served upon each other back in 1054. Even so, the gesture seemed tokenistic. The Russian veneration of Nicholas, as much in Muslim Demre as Catholic Bari, was tolerated but hardly welcomed. Even as they prepared for holy mass, delivering Bibles and posting signs that indicated the price of candles, the priests kept one eye on the crypt stairs in the manner of street hawkers who had come to regard it as the way of things that they would be interrupted.

Their tenure here might be temporary, but the rising chant of the Russian women moved me far more deeply than the brittle Latin incantations which I had heard in the nave. My thoughts drifted away to the last tsar, who had come to pray before the shrine of his saintly namesake in 1892, when he was still tsarevich. He had provided the crypt with a new floor of variegated marble. I had last seen the tsar's faded portrait on the walls of the podvoriye in Istanbul: bearded hauteur and braid epaulettes above a starched breast hung with ribboned crosses and stars, the whole divided by a diagonal turquoise sash. Something of his divinely appointed spirit seemed to share possession of those crumbling Istanbul tenements with the saint, just as their images shared the walls. Tsars and saints had always moved in the same celestial circles that hovered high above Russia. In the case of the two men called Nicholas, however, particular connections had bred.

A year before his visit to Bari, Nicholas had traveled to distant Vladivostok as chairman of the Trans-Siberian Railway to inaugurate the works there. At the site of the passenger station terminal, he laid an image of St. Nicholas, Russian patron of travelers. The saint, invoked to work wonders by driving the world's longest railway line to Moscow, had reached the Sea of Japan.

They had arrived at a pinnacle, but one skirted by the steepest slopes. The Bolsheviks would soon plot them precipitous descents. It was inevitable that they should have seen saint and tsar as imperialist accomplices, each offering succor to the other. The tsar would die in a Siberian basement along with his family and retinue in July 1918; the saint's image would be hunted down, and ripped from the walls of churches, homes, and railway stations to be destroyed.

It was posthumously, however, that these strange parallels grew compelling. In the 1970s, nine skeletons were found buried beside a remote stretch of road near Yekaterinburg, where the imperial family had been executed. It was not until 1991, with the thawing of the Soviet ideological permafrost, that DNA from the skeletons was positively tested against bones and blood samples known to have come from other members of the Romanov family. Seventy years after his murder, on July 17, 1998, the bones of Nicholas II were removed to St. Petersburg and placed in the crypt of the Cathedral of St. Peter and St. Paul. Two years later, he was made a saint. I was pondering how it had come about that two men called Nicholas, subsequently saints, had both been disinterred and ended up, at least partially, in cathedrals in St. Petersburg, when a Catholic priest in a white cassock descended the stairs with a finger to his lips to hiss, "Silenzio!" Tolerated, not welcomed.

I caught up with Nicholas at the Molo San Nicola. At this end of this harbor mole, another mass was in progress; another sea journey awaited the saint on a lavishly decorated fishing trawler. All narrative discipline seemed to have fled the *festa,* doubtless due to the conflicting inputs of church and the state's various organs—tourism, culture, coast guard, harbormaster—before being topped off by a final dictate from the mayor's office.

Nicholas did not seem to mind; nor did the Bariots. Crowds of black-swathed grandmothers and grizzled ancients, courting couples sharing cigarettes, and mothers with babies slung against their flanks had gathered on the mole to put to sea, to formally honor Nicholas and the sixty-two sailors, or to merely bob in a weed-tressed boat on a warm spring morning. The instruments of this watery pilgrimage were the local fishermen in their blue-oared dinghies. They massed at the landing stage, inviting boarders. It seemed, however, that the centuries had leached the ways of the sea from the Bariots; either that or the levy, five euros a head, had put them off. Only when most of the available craft had pulled away did there begin, in the Italian manner, an increasingly desperate jostle for the last few places. I was among those left behind to watch the flotilla gather round the effigy of St. Nicholas as the trawler was lit up in a daylight dance of smoke puffs and fireworks.

The pilgrims had left. Along the front, starlings and pigeons picked the ground for nuts and crumbs. On the seawalls, the wind caught empty bottles which lay flat, making them veer like compass needles. By the late afternoon, the flattened grass had begun to rise, erasing the shabby ground plans of the hawkers' stalls. The people of Bari gathered at the basilica for the culmination of the *festa.* They had dressed in suits and their shoes shone like boiling pitch; they might have been attending a court judgment or interviewing for an honorary position. The packed nave was heady with perfumes, pomades, deodorants, and colognes, a bouquet to rank with the divine fragrances that had spurred the Bari sailors at Myra. The basilica grew hot. Faces flushed. Solicitous husbands fanned their women-folk with open hymnals and blew cool air against their own cheeks from funneled mouths. Through the responses and the Creed, beads of sweat sagged on damp foreheads. Toward the end of the service, an eminent assortment of robes and suits rose from their seats to gather at the steps of the crypt. The congregation joined them at the shrine by means of a large monitor screen suspended in the chancel. Pixeled prelates clasped the hands of mandarins. Discreet sacristans maneuvered in the background. The screen murmur died away as a white-robed deacon approached the tomb carrying a glass bottle and a long-handled silver ladle, and the nave followed the crypt into silence.

The deacon crossed himself, gave his robes a graceful hitch and knelt before the tomb. He placed the bottle and ladle inside the arched entrance before bowing his head to follow. He wiggled his posterior to achieve an optimum position. On these adjustments all Bari waited. It was not long before the first whisperings passed among the crypt, transmitting an incipient unease to the nave. Nicholas had produced holy myrrh on each anniversary of his translation to Bari for more than nine hundred years. This transubstantiation of bone to elixir was evidence that the saint continued to look with favor upon his chosen city. Running dry could only mean one thing: that he had done with Bari as he had once done—and the precedent could not be denied—with Myra. The restlessness grew; a low murmur of anxiety arose from the congregation. In a growing need for information, attention shifted from the faces of the retinue to seek signs as near to the source as possible, which meant long moments when nothing in all Bari was more closely scrutinized than the deacon's bottom, an object that had acquired an unlikely oracular significance. Indeed, it was not long before its every movement invited a collective interpretation expressed in music-hall unison. A forward tip, indicating that the deacon was reaching out, triggered an expectant intake of breath throughout the basilica; an abrupt settling of the cheeks on the heels, marking an unsuccessful attempt, caused a tiny collective exhalation of disappointment. Soon enough, the congregation were ahead of the bottom; so much so that the unmistakable permanence of its latest repositioning readied them for the end. The deacon backed out of the tomb, rose to his feet, and turned, lifting the evidence high above his head like a virgin's bloodied nuptial sheet. There was a momentary pause before he shook the bottle to reveal the transparent liquid it contained. The basilica burst into applause.

The saint had stuck with Bari.

15

O UTSIDE ST. MARK'S BASILICA, where richly worked portals sucked in crowds as adjacent ones flushed them out, I planted my feet against the turbulence and looked up.

A recessed arch was dressed in a thirteenth-century mosaic above the portal of St. Alipio. The arch was flanked by plundered columns, which bore the weight of the mosaic; and the mosaic, as if to return this structural favor with a narrative one of its own, emphasized that the columns were not the only items stolen from the East to furnish Venice's great basilica. The episode the mosaic recounted had taken place in Alexandria, Egypt. The scene was split; the arch ceiling depicted a group of cowled Christians who supported a shrouded corpse lately removed from its tomb. The main scene occupied the rear wall of the recess: a party of turbaned and colorfully gowned Muslims variously recoiling from a large wicker basket, hands over mouth, arms outstretched, gazes averted.

The story recounted how Venice had acquired (in a richly acquisitive career) its most prized possession. A Venetian ship had called at Alexandria in A.D. 828. On board were three men resolved upon a singular plan: to remove the holy relics of St. Mark, which had lain in Alexandria since he was martyred there in A.D. 68. The caliph of Egypt had recently demolished the saint's church to provide building materials for an ostentatious palace, imperiling the adjacent tomb. The plan was as timely as it was audacious. To secure their prize, the Venetians would have to work "right cleverly," as the thirteenth-century historian Martino da Canale put it.

Right cleverness was something of a Venetian standard. With the cooperation of the guardian at St. Mark's tomb, the trio removed the saint to a large wicker basket and concealed him beneath layers of pork and cabbages. In the meantime, another body had been procured. It was dressed in the saint's original shroud and, in the way of artfully arranged teenagers' pillows, was settled in the tomb as a body double.

A good thing, too, for no sooner had the Venetians opened the tomb than a fragrance was released "so sweet that had all the spice shops of the world been in Alexandria it would not have been enough to scent it so." Clearly, the disturbing of tombs tended to trigger perfumed emissions; these might signal saintly enthusiasm but were hardly aids to secrecy. It so happened that the Alexandrians were familiar with the scent, not on account of previous attempts on Mark but because he also exuded as an annual occurrence on his feast day. Which was not near the day in question, lending the smell that wafted into Alexandrian nostrils the urgency of an olfactory burglar alarm. It could only mean, as Da Canale put it, that "Mark is moving."

The city authorities mobilized. Clerics descended on St. Mark's tomb in a flurry of robes, only to discover that the saint lay undisturbed. The persistent fragrance emphasized, however, that the alarm was genuine. Since it could not be countenanced that the saint had failed to control his own emissions, they might have examined the tomb more thoroughly. Instead, they advised their agents across the city to remain vigilant for the least sign of a moving Mark. But at the quayside, where a cargo awaited clearance for loading on a ship bound for Venice, the instructions hardly dented the bureaucratic lassitude. The officers threw open a basket lid but turned away at the sight of the contents. In a lapse that would condemn the city's customs service to lasting derision, they cleared the cargo without further investigation.

So it was that a consignment of pork, unclean in the view of Islam, has long taken credit for springing St. Mark from his Alexandrian plight. The fact was that a consignment consisting solely of pork would have been sure to raise the eyebrows of the doziest official, especially with a top-ranking saint at large. Where the Venetians were right clever, it struck me, was in the addition of the cabbages. What was beyond dispute was that the Venetians had established a pattern that would be repeated in its essentials by their rivals to the south 250 years later: smuggling a saint from under the noses of the Muslims and carrying him away across the Mediterranean in a merchant ship.

The two translations did differ in one telling regard. St. Mark saved his saviors' ship from disaster on the voyage to Venice. One night, when sleep crept over the watch, the saint awoke the master to warn him of surf breaking on an unobserved reef beyond the ship's bow. This behavior, though it all but amounted to trespass on Nicholas' territory, only deepened Venice's enthusiasm for St. Mark. The saint's myriad miraculous abilities extended even to maritime protection—a prime asset, as far as the citizens of that aqueous city were concerned. Time would tell, however, that St. Mark's vigilance had merely been an initial attempt to impress his new constituents rather than evidence of a dependable, developed expertise. The city did secure some talents in its search for maritime patronage. St. Elmo, also known as St. Erasmo, who was martyred by having his intestines wound from his body on a capstan, had his Venetian seafaring devotees and a lagoon island in his name. But a top-notch maritime specialist remained a priority.

Venice had originated in the fifth century as a swamp stronghold, an estuarine refuge which prompted marauding tribes to seek out more accessible prey. From these inauspicious beginnings, the city began to trade in salt and salted fish. Venice duly flourished, rapidly establishing itself as a global trade link. It was at Venice that the Byzantines, Lombards, and Franks learned to do business. In A.D. 810, torn between the claims of East and West, Venice was confirmed by treaty as a Byzantine possession, though a pointedly autonomous one.

The arrival amidst the pork and cabbages of St. Mark eighteen years later marked the beginning of Venice's romp to supremacy. The lagoon city, supported on thickets of pile-driven larch posts, now had religious foundations to compare. Where the great basilica would duly stand, a wooden church was built to house the saint's relics. Space was made for the new arrival by the unceremonious removal of the city's predecessor patron, Theodore, which Bari would also imitate in its dismissal of Sabinus.

Flushed with confidence, Venice set out to consolidate its grip on the trade route to the Levant. It built such a naval fleet that the city's supposed masters in Constantinople were cowed into granting it vastly improved trading rights across the Byzantine empire. In 1000, Venice decisively defeated the pirates who had harried it from its Dalmatian hideouts, establishing its grip on the Adriatic. The victory was commemorated at *il Sposalizio del Mar*, the Marriage of the Sea. Every Ascension Day, flotillas of canopied barges and scarlet-oared galleons congregated at the mouth of the lagoon to witness the sealing of the city's nuptials with the Adriatic. From his painted barge, the doge dropped a gold ring into the waters off the Lido, the great sandbank that encloses the Venetian lagoon. The ceremonial contract was confirmed with a mass at the monastery basilica that was founded at the north end of the Lido in 1044. The monastery, where the new doge was elected in 1071, was dedicated to St. Nicholas.

The dedication may suggest that the Venetians had grown serious in their intentions toward St. Nicholas by the time the monastery was founded. The Lido basilica might even have been built in anticipation of the sea saint's acquisition. Venice had a voracious appetite for relic saints and in the manner of powerful cities, tended to get what it wanted. The city had removed its former patron, St. Theodore, from Constantinople, and St. Isidore from Chios. St. Stephen, St. Zacharius (father of John the Baptist), St. Lucy, and the theologian St. Athanasius had all come Venice's way. The city's armies typically returned with notable relics, bringing back St. Nicetus, the martyred bishop of Zara (now Zadar, Croatia), during the tenth century. Venice had an arm of St. George and a finger of Mary Magdalene. The city used saints as a general protective balm or deployed them against particular civic complaints in the manner of medicines. The unfortunate St. Erasmo was often invoked, for his association with intestines, in the case of bowel complaints, a common hazard in miasmic Venice. And in 1485, when a plague epidemic struck the city, the Venetians were quick to secure the acquisition from Montpellier of St. Roch, tested cure for all things pestilential. It was as the sea specialist they had so long sought, and also on account of his growing name in trade circles, that the Venetians targeted St. Nicholas.

The current patron, besides, was plainly malfunctioning. St. Mark had not lived up to his early promise. He had allowed the Venetian church housing his relics to burn down in A.D. 976. This suggested an alarming pattern of undue carelessness; St. Mark, it was said, had originally been burned to death. It had also compromised the credibility of the saint, since the Venetians could not be persuaded, in the absence of his relics, that he had survived the church blaze. The authorities strove to reassure the people that St. Mark had not been immolated, merely mislaid in the course of the basilica's reconstruction. These fears had plainly not dissipated by 1094 when a general fast was called, and the people ordered to assemble in the basilica to pray. There occurred, according to the eighteenth-century historian Flaminio Corner, "a slight shaking of the marbles of a pillar . . . which, presently falling to the earth, exposed to the view of the rejoicing people the chest of bronze in which the bones of the Evangelist were laid."

It hardly seems to have been a stunning coup de théâtre. In fact, it was more a gimcrack conjuror's trick, a staged stunt of the sort that might have been pulled on the other side of the Adriatic in totalitarian Albania: a flagging despot with a shot liver and cardiac failure attempting the illusion of continued good health from a balcony, a waving hand and a smile for the people, the whole assisted by rouge, distance, and a supporting hand in the small of the back even as the forces of succession maneuvered in the shadows.

The attempted revival of St. Mark was best understood in the light of the Venetian attempt seven years earlier to secure a suitable replacement for him. Venice's maneuverings in the eastern Mediterranean in the spring of 1087 represented the business end of a saintly putsch; acquiring a successor to the absentee pyromaniac the authorities had tired of covering for. The attempted resuscitation of 1094 was the pragmatic response to their failure.

Nine hundred years later, it was obvious that St. Mark had recovered and fended off any attempted coup. As for Nicholas, he had at last arrived at Venice in 1100, and in a job lot of Myra bishops if an anonymous monk is to be believed. The monk at the Lido monastery recounted the story in a document entitled "The History of the Translation of the Great St. Nicholas, the Saintly Uncle Nicholas, and St. Theodore, from Myra to the Benedictine Monastery of St. Nicholas of the Lido." In 1099, the Venetians had equipped a fleet to reinforce the Crusader armies occupying Jerusalem. The Venetians had taken an avid though hardly principled interest in the Crusades; being clever, they would secure exclusive trading rights in both Sidon and Tyre during the early twelfth century.

The departing fleet, under the spiritual leadership of Bishop Henri, moored off the Lido, directly by the Monastery of St. Nicholas, and went ashore to seek the blessing of the saint they would duly return with. Byzantine obstruction caused the Venetians to winter off Rhodes, before continuing toward Palestine in May 1100. They followed the coast of Asia Minor, as was the custom, and had already passed Myra when Bishop Henri insisted that they turn back and drop anchor there.

Myra, according to the monk, had been all but destroyed by the Muslims. Most of its inhabitants had fled, and just four holy men stood guard at the basilica. They may even have been the same long-suffering quartet from 1087, no doubt by now thoroughly fed up with rapacious Italians.

When the Venetians asked for the resting place of St. Nicholas, the guardians showed them a broken tomb, the work of the Bari lot thirteen years earlier; it is to be imagined that a shopkeeper, about to be cleaned out once again, could not have flourished his empty till with more eloquent resignation. It was at this very moment that the Venetian play for the saint began to bear fruit. One of the monks ventured—that fatal weakness again—that the broken tomb had not necessarily been that of St. Nicholas. An unwise move: that the saint might still be available, and that rival Bari might have been saddled with a dud, excited the Venetians beyond reason. They set about the basilica, overturning altars and lifting marble floor slabs. When they found nothing, they turned on the guardians in the usual manner, torturing them to extract information.

One of the monks eventually broke, but only partially; he pointed out a tomb whose contents might satisfy the Venetians. It contained two other bishops who had preceded the great saint in his office at Myra: the saint's uncle, also Nicholas, and a certain Theodore. The Venetians bore these consolations back to the ships, but a few persisted with the search. They had not long continued when a remarkable fragrance engulfed them; so anxious, it seemed, were the relics to be translated to Venice that they had deployed their scent early, as a locating aid. The Venetians followed the scent to a tomb where their hammers soon revealed the great saint, conveniently identified by an ancient inscription.

The ecstatic Venetians embarked their precious trio of reliquaries and continued to the Holy Land. There, they lent modest assistance to the Frankish Crusaders, and doubtless secured some trading concessions, before making for home in the autumn. On their timely arrival back at Venice—on December 6—they delivered the three bishops to the Church of St. Nicholas on the Lido.

I boarded a vaporetto bound for the Lido with a final few passengers: a crowd of children and their mothers heading for the beaches, and an old man, flexing his ankles to some private tune so that his diamond-patterned socks moved like an accordion below a sallow sunken calf. As the Lido appeared through the haze, a sandbar so thin that the Adriatic beyond showed as breaking surf in the gaps between the holiday homes, the fabled domes, palaces, and campaniles at my back faded from view.

Venice impressed Nicholas, but it did not seduce him. Byron, Turner, and Ruskin might rhapsodize over the picturesque decay of moldering statuary and crumbling palazzos in subsequent centuries, but sainthood was an unsentimental business. Nicholas evaluated Venice's assets in the manner of a real estate agent: a uniquely positioned ascendant city, then, fast rivaling Constantinople as a trading port, and with excellent security, surrounded as it was by sandbanks and shifting shallows that made it all but impervious to attack from the sea. Venice, unlike Constantinople or Bari, had no need of walls. Nor would it be undone by silt, as Patara and Myra had been. In fact, the silt from the rivers around Venice—the Piave, the Brenta, and the Sile—contributed to the formation of the Lido. And without the sacred offshore bulwark where Nicholas established himself, controlling maritime access to the city, neither the lagoon nor Venice itself would have been possible.

Not that Nicholas was entirely oblivious to his past; and Venice, being Byzantine, might serve to reconcile the old empire to his Catholic defection. The translation of 1087, to Bari, had not finished him with the Byzantines, but it had certainly complicated their feelings for a saint who was no longer solely theirs. It had accelerated the process of Nicholas' own division, much as the schism of 1054 had done with the two churches. In his increasingly distinct Orthodox and Catholic manifestations, he had begun to split.

Any hopes of rapprochement were scuppered in 1204, when the armies of the Fourth Crusade arrived at the walls of Constantinople. They had voyaged by sea. Byzantine decline during the twelfth century had sealed off the land routes to the Holy Land. The Venetians, with the one navy capable of doing the job, were engaged by the Frankish Crusaders to transport and supply some 35,000 soldiers and knights. In a transparent admission of their intentions, the Venetians offered to throw in a further fifty galleys on the understanding that half of all the booty would be theirs. In June 1202, Nicholas' place in Crusader history repeated itself. Where the armies of the previous century had massed around St. Nicholas at Bari, so those of the Fourth Crusade were billeted in the shadow of the saint's basilica on the Lido; and once again the saint's relics, with the help of an anonymous monk, could claim to be present. His proximity gave the knights of the Fourth Crusade one good reason to seek the saint's blessing; the longer sea journey that lay ahead was another. Besides, they had time on their hands while their leaders strived to stump up funds to pay the Venetians.

The funds did not materialize. The Venetians offered to waive part of the payment if the Crusaders would divert to help them recover the rebellious Dalmatian city of Zara. The bankrupt Franks acquiesced in what would prove to be a crucial betrayal of principle: the deployment of Crusader forces against fellow Christians. When the Crusader armies reached Constantinople, they fell in with Prince Alexius, son of the recently deposed emperor. Impressed by the prince's claim and by his promises, the Crusaders flexed their muscles at the walls of the city; the emperor was subsequently restored and soon gave way to his son. Alexius IV soon found that his treasury was in no condition to pay the Crusaders, nor did he have the authority to force the Orthodox church to submit to Rome. He had made promises to the Crusaders that he could not enforce. In April 1204, Franks and Venetians who had set out to liberate the Holy Land now sought redress by attacking the great city of eastern Christendom. They soon breached the walls on the Golden Horn, and set about the city in a manner that mocked the least pretense of Christian unity. For three days, the soldiers were given free rein. In a matter of hours, the world's greatest art repository was ransacked. Prostitutes were paraded on the altars of St. Sophia. Carts were driven into the churches and laden with carvings and gold vessels, with silks, jewels, and robes, candlesticks and silver thuribles. When many of these objects were next displayed—agate cups and crystal lamps, enameled book covers, chalices and holy relics, porphyry and serpentine mosaics, and granite pillars—they adorned the walls and the treasury of St. Mark's in Venice.

The waterside monastery of St. Nicholas on the Lido had long since closed, but the adjacent basilica still operated, though it had been rebuilt—and never quite finished—in the seventeenth century. It was a buttressed edifice with a brick façade that had been left undressed, except for a marble portico topped by the bust of its founder, Doge Domenico Contarini. The church was empty, forlornly so after St. Mark's. But as my eyes adapted to the thin light, I could make out its centerpiece, a great Baroque altar. Its base was paneled in an ornate floral mosaic of inset Carrara marbles and Travertine alabasters in blacks and yellows, purples and antique reds. This was merely the beginning. From this comparative restraint, two spectacularly worked supports, each with its attendant cherubs, rose through a spill of scrolls and fruit to a high sarcophagus, which in turn was topped by three plinths, arranged in the apex of a medal rostrum. And here, carved in lignum vitae, stood the elevated statues of three bishops. With their miters, beards, and crosiers, the three were very similar in appearance; and in the case of Nicholas and his uncle, each holding the Gospels in his right hand, the likeness was uncanny. A Latin inscription on the back of the altar confirmed it as the last resting place of Myra's three bishops.

Unlike St. Mark's, where the countercurrents of the vast crowds had buffeted me, there was nobody at St. Nicholas' basilica. The same quiet that I had often experienced in parish churches back in England drew in noises from outside; waves, gulls, and the odd car that had found its way to the end of this lonely promontory. It was as if Venice's great plans for Nicholas had evaporated. No amount of Baroque finery could commend the city's claim to possession against that of Bari. The Bari translation had multiple chroniclers, arraying a formidable body of evidence against the flimsy single account of the Lido's anonymous monk. Besides, the Bari accounts predated the monk's, which suggested that the similarities between them were instances of Venetian plagiarism: the number of monks encountered at Myra, the means of persuasion, the trademark monkish wavering, the fragrant emissions. The Lido case was weak, and nothing spoke more eloquently of Venice's loss of nerve in its claim to Nicholas than the basilica's unfinished façade.

Later that day, when raindrops mottled the hot flagstones with a scattering of fast-evaporating coins, I went to discuss the relics with Dino Buso, who was padre at the Lido church in the 1980s. The relics, he explained, had been officially recognized, or authenticated, seven times over the centuries. In the majority of these *ricognizioni,* the process had entailed disturbing the relics. Had there, I wondered, been any kind of fragrance? "No," replied Padre Dino. "All that happens is somebody dies every time they open the boxes. Luckily, I was no longer at the church when they last opened them, in 1992."

In July of that year, professors, archaeologists, and clerics convened to examine the relics. They opened the great sarcophagus to discover a series of lead plaques, variously dated and inscribed in Latin with the details of previous *ricognizioni*. One described a repositioning of the relics in the choir of the basilica back in 1134, and another detailed the move to their current position in the rebuilt church in 1634. The sarcophagus contained three boxes, which were considerably smaller than conventional coffins. The boxes that belonged to the other bishops each contained a substantial number of bones. Theodore was very fractured; Uncle Nicholas was largely intact, with a fine skull. The Nicholas box, though it contained a fine ceramic vase and a coin hoard, had few bones by comparison.

"That was not so disappointing," explained Padre Dino. "Bari had examined their own bones back in the 1950s and assembled a plan of the skeleton which indicated that theirs was also incomplete, though far less so than ours. The Lido bones, though they are mostly fragments, did seem to supply the missing pieces to the Bari skeleton." The *ricognizione* committee concluded: "The Lido relics, supposedly the bones of St. Nicholas of Myra, composed of many white bone fragments, do correspond to the skeleton parts of the saint missing at Bari, unfortunately accidentally crushed and broken by a Bari sailor during their removal." Nicephorus' account of the Bari translation had suggested that the sailor Matthew's descent into the sarcophagus had been somewhat hasty. The Venetians had done well with the latest recognition. They had not attempted to question their old rival Bari's preeminence in the possession of St. Nicholas, but they had managed to assert their own real, if small, stake in the saint, and to base it on the clumsiness of a Bari sailor. They had been right clever.

The problem was that the two accompanying bishops played no part in the known history of St. Nicholas of Myra. Where they did appear, and insistently, was in the Life of that sorry namesake, St. Nicholas of Sion. Sion did have an uncle called Nicholas. An important influence in Sion's spiritual development, he had been an archimandrite at a nearby monastery (but was not at any stage bishop of Myra). Uncle Nicholas was buried at the mountain monastery of Sion where his nephew, and a certain St. Theodore, were also buried. It seems likely, furthermore, that the remains of the three bishops may have been moved to Myra after the dereliction of the mountain monastery. Was it possible, whatever the claim of the 1992 *ricognizione*, that the anonymous monk had confused his Nicholases, as many chroniclers had done, and that the Nicholas the

Venetians had brought home from Myra was actually Sion? And that Sion, a saint eternally hunched in the piggyback position, had yet again served the greater glory of his senior namesake by delivering him to Venice?

"San Nicola," murmured Padre Dino. "Il santo de la peripheria." Even here, with his power and prosperity, he somehow remained the saint of the dispossessed. "Remember the story of the Three Daughters," he added. I had not needed reminding. I had found them behind the altar of the Lido basilica, where the choir was paneled with carved wooden scenes from Nicholas' life. Giovanni da Crema had completed the work in 1635, representing the impoverished nobleman's house as empty and consigning the banished occupants to an alfresco despair. The daughters had sunk beneath a tree while the father slumped against a bough of his own to drown himself in a flagon of wine. Nicholas wore a low-brimmed hat, one that straddled the adjacent styles of cardinal and desperado, as he slipped his perfect gift through the window.

16

THE BYZANTINE NICHOLAS HAD traditionally resisted the least attempt on the integrity of his relics. He devoted himself to keeping them intact, or at least contained, much as he had preserved his earthly virginity. The time had come, however, to consider his position.

Nicholas' long confinement had certainly been good for his reputation. His sealed sarcophagus at Myra had served as a bastion against the fraudulent inventions of the relic peddlers, denying them any purchase on his name. The absence of genuine Nicholas bones known to be in circulation discouraged most attempts to pass off those of pigs, dogs, or nameless paupers as his holy relics. Nicholas' myrrh production had allowed him to defer a decision on his own dispersal long after the Orthodox theologians had reconciled their church to the division of saintly remains from the fifth century. All he might lose was the odd nail, bone splinter, or tooth, accidentally drawn off as the myrrh was decanted from the sarcophagus. This he accepted as natural wastage in a process whose miracle was to produce relics without any significant diminution of himself.

The translation to Bari had inevitable consequences, which may have forced Nicholas' hand. Emerging from the Myra shrine finally left him vulnerable to the unscrupulous. Peddlers, quick to recognize that Nicholas' newly hatched relics had the cachet of purity, exploited it with all the unseemly vigor of pimps touting a nun who had abandoned her vows to return to the world with a vengeance. It was as much for his long confinement as his general standing that Nicholas' relics were particularly sought after. Once he was out, there was little to protect him from being linked with bones of uncertain provenance. It was the price of translation. He might as well accept the inevitable sullying and concentrate on the undoubted advantages of fragmentation.

Confinement at Myra was not without its drawbacks. Myrrh, though a well-regarded relic, was a mere emanation; an actual piece of the saint commanded greater devotion. Myrrh's inexhaustibility suggested a lack of commitment; the same could not be said of bones. With bones, the saints gave a fragment of their finite selves. Where myrrh vials might decorate existing shrines, bones had the power to inspire new ones. Now was the time for a considered dismantling, one that would allow him to support his push into Europe from his twin Adriatic beachheads at Bari and Venice with new shrines and centers of devotion. By replacing myrrh with bones, he would bring a new intent to his expansion. With a partial breakup, Nicholas could command a far wider presence. He need not sacrifice his core, and all Christendom could be his.

This new thinking is reflected in the two Italian translations, especially given the findings of the 1992 *ricognizione* at Venice. To recap: a Bari sailor left behind some of Nicholas' bones in 1087, which were collected by the Venetians from Myra thirteen years later. A simple oversight on the part of the sailor, we might suppose, except that Nicholas had stopped the translation to Bari in its tracks two days later to prevent the division of his onboard relics by pilfering. Which is to suggest the intention on Nicholas' part that some of his bones were left behind at Myra. The Venetians might take some time to collect, but it was now apparent that Nicholas had begun dividing his relics at the earliest opportunity.

Nor were Nicholas' relics slow to disperse following their arrival at Bari. A Norman knight, William Pantulf, obtained, with "God's blessing on his endeavours," Nicholas relics from "those who had translated the body." William took "one tooth and two fragments of the marble urn"— pieces chipped from the sarcophagus—back to Noron in Normandy. There, the relics were deposited "amid great devotion of the monks and rejoicings of the laity" at the Church of St. Peter in June 1092. And in 1096, the duke of Puglia gave the count of Flanders a gift of relics which included bones of St. Nicholas; these were duly enshrined at the Abbey of Watten, near Calais.

Moreover, it was increasingly evident that, in an apparent defiance of mathematical law, shrine presences at Bari, Venice, and elsewhere had no discounting effect upon Myra. By December 6, 1100, when his bones reached the Lido, Nicholas had achieved the remarkable feat of having three functioning shrines in his name. In 1102, the pilgrim Saewulf sailed from Puglia for the Holy Land, visiting Myra en route. Myra, though the chroniclers liked to represent it as grief-stricken by its loss, had clearly continued to operate. What should have been a double blow to the shrine—the second, Venetian theft had taken place just two years before Saewulf's arrival if the Lido monk is to be believed—did not even merit a mention from the visitor. A day's journey from Rhodes, Saewulf wrote breezily, "brought us to Patara where blessed Nicholas the archbishop was born, and where we were driven in by a great storm late in the evening. . . . Then we came to the city of Myra where St. Nicholas ruled as the head of the archepiscopate. . . . Having worshipped at the holy tomb in honour of the saint, we came with a favourable wind." New crypts breathed fresh life into Nicholas.

Legend has it that Nicholas effected a further strategic sell-off of relics in 1101. He appeared in one of his customary visions to a French clerk at the Bari shrine, instructing the man to carry a Nicholas relic with him when he returned home to the town of Port, near Nancy. The clerk duly carried off a finger bone to Port, where it inspired the construction of a chapel dedicated to the saint. Port would develop into a major center of Nicholas devotion and inspire the great fifteenth-century church that stands there today.

Nicholas was thus doing to Bari, but on a managed scale, what he had already done to Myra: soliciting the theft of himself for his own strategic purposes. The man who had halted his own translation when a single bone was pilfered from the onboard reliquary was not refusing to countenance the distribution of his own assets—that was inevitable, now that he was taking on Europe—but insisting on retaining control of the process. Within fifteen years of his translation, he had used his own relics to establish himself as an expanding international brand, St. Nicholas of Myra and Bari, Venice and Port.

The Nicholas diaspora, with the saint's sanction, gathered pace. His relics turned up everywhere. Bari was set on cementing itself as the heart of St. Nicholas devotion; it offered fragments of the saint as inducements to acknowledgment of that same fact. They were samples, strategically distributed, to sell Bari and its patron saint. Many of them, which had initially found their way to churches in Constantinople, were redistributed across western Europe after the sack of the city during the Fourth Crusade. A Nicholas hand took up residence at the saint's eponymous church at Carcere, Rome, while an index finger found its way to a chapel on the Ostian Way nearby. Another finger reached out to Ventimiglia in Liguria.

Another arrived at Halberstadt, eastern Germany, in 1206 and yet another at Gembloux, Belgium, in 1215. There were teeth at Heisterbach, near Köln. Teeth and hair from Constantinople reached Corbie, northern France, in 1204. An arm fragment, also from Constantinople, found its way to a village near Soissons in Picardy. Unspecified Nicholas relics were recorded at nearby Laon in 1523. Benevento, near Naples, had Nicholas relics on its 1723 inventory, and a church in Aarhus, Norway, claimed authentic Nicholas relics. Erik the Good of Denmark dispatched a Nicholas relic, acquired as he passed through Constantinople in 1103, back to the Church of St. Nicholas in Slangerup, near Copenhagen. Latterly, bits of St. Nicholas would find their way into the treasury of the Austro-Hungarian empire; and a reliquary containing several more pieces, provenance unknown, would be handed over to the Turkish authorities in Antalya a few years after the occupation of the port by the Italians, in 1925.

Nicholas courted Europe. As well as establishing this literal physical presence in its holy places, he had also been extending his influence out in the world ever since sailors had first invoked his name against a rising wind or visited his chapel to seek safe passage. He was on the foredecks and in the holds, on the quaysides and in the dockyards. It was a natural consequence of his patronage of sailors that he should extend his reach, in particular regions, to associated occupations like stevedores, navigators, ferrymen, fishermen, and shipwrights. And as the cover he provided to sailors came to encompass ships' cargoes, he had long since found his way into the warehouses and storerooms. He had been delivering Egyptian porphyry and Anatolian timber, Greek olives and Russian hides for centuries; almost, it seemed, to cover the losses incurred by his original act of generosity. The hard work was paying off as he attracted those in the trade and carriage professions including grain merchants and wholesalers, coal carriers, barrelmakers, and brewers.

He snared others with his legion of legends, which cited actions, objects, and ethics commending him to particular professions. His intercession on behalf of the falsely accused attracted a whole raft of legal sorts, particularly in France, from solicitors and clerks of court to prisoners. His production of myrrh drew in not only perfumiers but embalmers, chemists, and apothecaries. In due course, Nicholas was to establish an unrivaled portfolio of trade patronages.

It might have been presumed that Venice would have finally satisfied

Nicholas; established as he was through the Mediterranean and deep in the European hinterland, the chances were he would have felt safe here by the fourteenth century. St. Mark might have dominated, but Nicholas had done excellently in Venice. He was honored host at the annual Marriage of the Sea and patron of the Venetian fleet and of several churches. Among these was the beautiful San Nicolò dei Mendicoli, which he had acquired in the twelfth century from St. Nicetus, whose name was sufficiently similar to expose his church to confiscation. In one important respect at least, Nicolo did precede Marco in the city: in the lineage of that most famous of Venetian trading families, the Polos, who had returned unrecognized from their thirteenth-century trading journeys to the East, sapphires in their ragged hems and Magi stories in their minds.

The city was home to the *scuole* or trade guilds. There were hundreds of such guilds—gold beaters and gunners, caskmakers and shoemakers, casemakers and bakers, fruiterers, wool merchants, linen drapers, sausage makers, bucket makers, winemakers, furriers, tailors, druggists, stone cutters, cloth weavers and dyers—which numbered among their members many potential Nicholas devotees. Nicholas was patron of the Scuola dei Mercanti in the city, and a sure presence on the annual trade flotillas that left for Romania and the Sea of Azov, for Trebizond and Cyprus, for Armenia, for Spain and Portugal, France and England.

What Nicholas had learned at Patara, Myra, and Constantinople, however, was that the future always lies elsewhere. Even Bari would remind him of this when its citizens sided against William of Sicily by throwing in their lot with an attempted Byzantine reoccupation. When William retook the city in 1156 he left just two buildings of any note standing: the cathedral and the basilica of St. Nicholas. "And so it came about," wrote Hugo Falcandus, "that of the mighty capital of Apulia, celebrated for its glory, powerful in its wealth, proud of the nobility of its citizens and admired for the beauty of its architecture by all who saw it, there now lies nothing but a heap of stones."

Venice suffered a more gradual decline during the fifteenth century. The city had fought a series of sapping wars with the Genoese and expended considerable energy on controlling the north Italian hinterland. With the fall of Constantinople to the Turks in 1453, Venice's carefully cultivated trading privileges were lost at a stroke. A far greater blow was landed, however, when the Portuguese explorer Bartholomew Diaz rounded the

Cape of Good Hope in 1488 and so discovered the sea route to the East. From that decisive moment, traffic was diverted from the Mediterranean to the Atlantic. Trading supremacy passed to the nations of the western seaboard—Portugal, Holland, and England. With the opening of the oceans, the land routes began their inexorable decline. It turned out that Venice had flourished in an incompletely revealed world, and the inland sea that she straddled was a puddle.

Nicholas felt the decline at his back and moved on. It was time to make Europe's western seaboard his.

17

NICHOLAS WAS DRESSED IN red when I next saw him, and snow was in the air, and even in his name had appeared the first indications of the man he was destined to become: Sinterklaas.

Six months had passed and winter had returned. Under a leaden November sky, Amsterdam's streets and barge-bound waterways had merged, concentrating all color in the brightly dressed crowds that had gathered for the annual arrival of their saint. Familes were packed tight around the Oosterdok, the eastern harbor basin where Sinterklaas would disembark, and also lined his procession route along Prins Henrikkade. Children had worked their way to the front of the crowds, wearing home-made hats that bore the message "I Love Sint," or Saint. This shorthand could only imply one thing, that Sinterklaas was the one saint here worthy of mention, let alone love. The only saint left in Holland.

The Reformation did for the saints in the Netherlands just as it had done for them in England fifty years earlier. Their cults were attacked, their images hunted down and destroyed, and the churches that once bore their venerated names were now known by simple descriptives: Oude or Nieuwe, Grote or Dom, Old or New, Great or Domed. Nicholas had evidently survived the purges and adapted to the low-church austerities of this Reformed land, but not without significant modification. I was about to witness another arrival by sea and attendant street procession, but this was a markedly different man from the one who had put ashore at Bari.

Dutch lore had Sinterklaas arriving by steamboat from Spain and in the company of a sidekick called Zwarte Piet, or Black Pete. He no longer came, then, as a divine force—a box of sacred bones delivered to the quayside; a revered effigy borne through the streets—but appeared as from a children's storybook, a player in a traveling pantomime troupe. Such was Protestantism. His tubby steamboat, which bore at the bow the name *Spanje,* Spain, seemed to have been lifted straight from its proper place, which was to bob among bathtime ducks, before being set down on the Herengracht Canel. She blew sonorous horn notes, and belched vaporous clouds from a brightly painted funnel as she passed beneath lifting bridges, which rose to bow behind her. From the bow of this cheerful craft, festooned by balloons and flags, Sinterklaas waved amid a crowd of evidently replicable Zwarte Piets; this carnival character wore a blacked-up face and curly wig, and was variously dressed in purple, yellow, and blue doublets, all velvet and braid, with frills and feathered cap.

Zwarte Piet was Moorish. He was supposed to have fallen in with Sinterklaas in Spain. He was quite as dark as Nicholas himself had once been in Bari—but plainly was no longer. It was as if the saint, judging his color an inconvenience as he ventured north, had transferred it to his sidekick, to leave himself pale as the people he was now approaching.

As for his other features, Nicholas' beard had achieved an unchecked luxuriance that it had never approached in his icons, frescoes, and statues, and had turned from gray to snowy white. He looked older, almost outside of age, and might have had something of the mildly crazed itinerant about him except that he was immaculately turned out. His robes, though they were bright red, remained recognizably those of a Catholic bishop. He wore a stole, admittedly decorated with the civic insignia of Amsterdam, but his miter was high and decorated front and back with a gold cross. Dutch reform had not stripped Nicholas of all his papist finery.

In other respects, however, his transformation had continued apace. For one thing, he would shortly leave the steamboat under his own volition for the saddle of a horse. He thereby abandoned revered portage to take the reins of his own transportation for the first time, which would turn out a mainstay arrangement in the centuries ahead. The other significant difference was that the physical transition begun in Bari—from icon to effigy—had now continued to its completion: Sinterklaas was human.

Being human had its drawbacks, especially on horseback, which explained why the aged Amsterdammer who played Sinterklaas had neither attempted to carry the three golden globes nor been burdened with a crosier, another essential element of his Amsterdam iconography; this was because he would soon be expected to receive children from their parents' outstretched arms. And in Amsterdam, dropping a child was worse than dropping a crosier.

Amsterdam's first church, known as the Oude Kerk since the late 1500s, had been dedicated to St. Nicholas around 1300. No relics of his are known to have made their way to the city; sheer force of influence established Nicholas here. He was an early presence in Amsterdam, which was barely a hamlet in 1200. Even so, the place bore striking resemblances to Venice: the same unlikely waterlogged situation; the same early trade in fish, cured herring in this case, which would launch the city as a trading behemoth. Nicholas, not for the first time, called it right, moving here in the knowledge that the city would one day wrest trading supremacy from its canaled southern counterpart.

Where Venice began with the Adriatic, so Amsterdam first collared the Baltic, which provided it with what would be known as the mother trade: the carriage and sale of grain, lumber, salt, wine, and beer. The city became a renowned center of shipbuilding. It then moved into high-value goods and services—the Indonesian spice trade, diamonds, finance. At the Amsterdam docks, a million cargoes—gunnysacks of pepper and spices, oak barrels of wine, bales of tobacco or Turkish mohair, bales of Leiden cloth, ceramics, smoking pipes, tapestries, fine furniture—bore the reliable Nicholas' whispered name: a vote of thanks for their safe arrival, a prayer on their dispatch.

The saint's association with commerce, though many of his trade patronages had long since lapsed, persisted in the Sinterklaas procession. The procession only dated from the 1930s; the brainchild of the city's chamber of commerce, it was intended to kick-start the shopping season. It occurred a few weeks before the exchange of gifts (a far older tradition), which had always taken place on St. Nicholas' Eve in Holland, though the Dutch Christmas had been fast developing a comparable consumer habit of late. The shameless parade included a van, a newly launched model, stickered with Sints and Piets around the legend "Introducing the New Business Edition." Students in uniform smocks were distributing orange cardboard miters on which the cross had lost out to a trademarked golden arch. Children clutched plastic crosiers stuffed with sweets, and signs on Sinterklaas' behalf thanked the sponsors for their support.

Nicholas stepped ashore at the old arsenal to a chorus of applause, and the crowds hammered out the refrain "Sinterklaas Is in the Town," which they had hitched to the tune of "When the Saints Go Marching In." Sinterklaas boarded his groomed white horse and made off along the waterfront, gathering up children. Zwarte Piets swerved among the bands, parade floats, and majorettes that trailed him. From the sacks slung on their shoulders they handed out sweets and peppernuts, the gingerbread buttons that had a long association with the Sinterklaas festivities. Soon, their street-strewn offerings had turned to crumbs. Amsterdammers gathered at gable windows to watch. The procession passed the Schreierstoren; from this tower, sailors' families had gathered to witness the departures of ships, including that of Henry Hudson who would set sail for America in 1609. The procession bore left at the Central Station past the Church of St. Nicholas. The church's façade, busy with arches, domes, and campaniles, had a high alcove where a statue stood, familiar with his gilded miter and crosier. Sinterklaas might have acknowledged it. But he had moved on, leaving Catholicism behind in the course of the Reformation, and he did not spare his former self a glance.

Amsterdam's Catholic Church of St. Nicholas was built in the 1880s, when the Roman church in Holland was finally permitted to emerge, chastened, from centuries of clandestine observance that the authorities had inflicted upon it for its own suppression of reformers under Spanish rule back in the sixteenth century. I eased myself from the crowd and stepped inside.

Protestant sentiment had been gaining momentum across northern Europe since the fourteenth century. By the sixteenth century, it was a powerful force for reform. It took objection to Catholicism's undue wealth and venality, its decadence, superstition, and hypocrisy. It derided the established use of indulgences—vouchers that could be earned or, more commonly, purchased, as a means of reducing one's allotted time in purgatory. It proposed to recast religious practice as a private communion with God, releasing man from obligation to the hierarchy of self-appointed intermediaries that cluttered the approach to the heavenly throne: on earth the pope and his cardinals, bishops, and priests, and in heaven the company of saints. Protestantism took particular exception to the saints, seeing them as proxy agents or brokers who grew fat by their position alone, extorting devotion in return for the divine influence that they claimed, often in specialist areas, with God.

The saints had come under fire before. In the eighth century, the iconoclasts had destroyed their icons and statues, but by way of objection to the
practice of human representation. Turks had attacked them in the Ottoman advance across Anatolia, but this was to be expected from a rival
faith. This time around, however, the saints themselves were at the heart
of a highly principled objection, and from within what might once have
been called the Christian family. The Protestants, unable to conceive of a
God who would suffer such a court of lackeys and stooges to profit by
keeping the people from him, regarded the saints as no better than divine
racketeers. They were first able to take concerted action in England, when
Henry VIII's break with Rome in the early 1530s over its refusal to sanction a divorce that might allow him a male heir gave free rein to a reforming, anti-Catholic, and hagiophobic tendency.

English iconoclasts had been breaking rood screens and church images
of saints, though not with official approval, since the 1520s. In 1533, London skeptics removed statues from their church niches and pricked them
with bodkins, needles or pins used to pierce holes in cloth, to see whether
they would bleed. It was not until 1534, however, that the state-sanctioned
campaign to unseat the saints began, with the publication of a church
primer that omitted the entire Litany of the Saints. Now, Protestant radi-
cals felt free to rail against the wasteful gilding of relics and the lighting
of church candles before saints' statues. They dismissed relics as pigs'
bones and urged people to redirect money spent on pilgrimages to alms
for the poor.

In 1536, a large number of the saints' days that filled the church calendar, and an especially high proportion of those that fell during the harvest
period, were abolished, ostensibly to improve agricultural production.
Among the banished were St. Swithin, St. Martin, St. Margaret, St. Mary
Magdalene, St. Laurence, and St. Augustine. People were now to work on
these days and not to fast on the previous evening. A 1537 publication
called the Bishop's Book, a new preaching protocol, stated that it was "utterly forbidden to make or have any similitude or image, to the intent to
bow down to it or worship it." A set of injunctions issued in 1538 exhorted
the people to charity, "and not to repose their trust . . . in wandering to
pilgrimages, offering of money candles or tapers to images or relics, or
kissing or licking the same." Saints' relics were now sought out and destroyed. Candles were forbidden to be lit before saints' statues. Preachers

derided the notion that saints could command particular intercessionary territories or patronages.

The dissolution of the monasteries began in 1536. Religious establishments were sacked and sold off cheap, along with their vast libraries of manuscripts. Illuminated pages containing the lives of the saints, sold by weight, were used to "scour candlesticks" and polish boots. Grocers, soapsellers, and fishmongers wrapped their wares in the vellum pages of gilded legendaries that spoke of desert fathers, holy martyrs, and confessors. Parchments were packaged up and "sent over the seas to the bookbinders, not in small numbers, but in times whole shipfuls."

In 1541, the ecclesiastical authorities proclaimed that all images were now to be removed from cathedrals and parish churches. They also turned their attention to December 6, abolishing the St. Nicholas Day celebrations. With the coronation of the new king in 1547, injunctions proliferated. Images were subsequently banned from private houses. Banners were forbidden. The paintings on church walls were whitewashed and covered with texts that inveighed against idolatry. Stained-glass windows were smashed or painted over. Church plate, vestments, chalices, church funds, and donations were all confiscated. Altars were removed. Bonfires of images and papist books burned throughout the land. And from the 1560s, the abolition began of religious plays, which told the stories of the saints, Nicholas notably. In a few decades, he and his like had fallen from their exalted positions and were driven out of England.

In the Low Countries, however, the saints retained the official protection of the Catholics, whose Spanish enforcers unleashed a brutal persecution of the Dutch Protestants. Those who dared to practice their private religion outside the offices of the church—by praying or reading the Bible at home—could expect to have their tongues sealed with branding irons so that their heresies might not be heard as they burned at the stake. Those who retained the power of speech were only permitted it so that they might recant by invoking the saints, notably the merciful Virgin, from the depths of their agony.

The Catholic authorities might have appreciated the irony that the saints they were protecting, and even invoking in their persecutions, had themselves suffered something similar at the hands of the Romans in the arenas of Anatolia some thirteen hundred years earlier. The effect then, as now, was akin to a brutal pruning that forced new shoots. The Dutch had little respect for what the church of Rome saw as the natural order. An innate Protestantism showed even in their man-made landscape: polders, in defiance of the sea, had been mechanically drained and turned into meadows. By the 1530s, Dutch dissent was rising. Pictures circulated of cardinals and bishops with cloven hoofs, and of enraged men hacking at statues with picks and axes. Crowds jeered the holy sacrament as it was paraded through the streets, even when it was to succor the bed-bound sick. One woman, when she was tried for heresy in 1527, dismissed the holy oil used for anointing the sick and dying as "good for a salad or for greasing boots." Cue an awkward shuffle of foreboding from the myrrh-seeping Nicholas.

By the 1560s, the authorities across the Low Countries had taken to killing Protestants in industrial quantities, herding them into winter rivers, or tearing them limb from limb and impaling their body parts on doors and walls. The persecution only stoked the dissent. When a Delft priest abandoned Catholicism mid-service, his congregation wasted no time in removing all images from the walls and carting a statue of St. George into the gardens. In 1566, all of Antwerp's forty-two churches were ransacked. Middleburg and Flushing followed. In Amsterdam, dissenters ran amok in the great Church of St. Nicholas; service books and priests' vestments were thrown from the doors, altars and organ smashed. Amsterdam finally fell to the Protestants in 1578. The Catholic clergy fled and their celestial accomplices were ripped from their frames, levered from their plinths, and whitewashed from the walls. Wooden statues were burned or smashed; a metal one of St. Nicholas was melted down to make coin. Nicholas, not only saint but also bishop, did not appear to stand a chance.

So what was he doing here, sporting his bishop's robes, on the streets of a city that had seen off his kind some four hundred years earlier?

Around the walls of the nave of the Catholic Church of St. Nicholas, a painted frieze ran, depicting episodes from the life of the saint. "Three Daughters" was prominent. Painted in the early twentieth century, the scene was bathed in moonlight and the daughters embraced with affecting emotion. Nicholas at the window wore a discreet brown cassock.

With its charitable tradition, Amsterdam might have been the place to explore the defining concern of "Three Daughters." It so happened, however, that the story and the city shared another theme, which hijacked my attention: prostitution. To walk the two hundred meters from this Nicholas church to the other one, now the Oude Kerk, was to encounter the daughters whom Nicholas had not reached. Or, to put it another way, there were neon signs advertising "private cabins," "hot pussy," and "real live fucking show" within yards of leaving either church. The girls stood in their windowed booths in bra and panties, or starched white nurses' uniforms. Some had a phone to the ear. Others scanned the crowds for business, instant allure illuminating their expressions at the first sight of what they took to be a genuine punter. Some had the painted faces of old pros squeezing a final season from the business before retirement. Others were beautiful.

I remembered how Nicholas was also encamped hard by the brothel at Karaköy in Istanbul. Then there was Venice, with its "whole streets of that sort of ladies of pleasure, who receive all comers," as a seventeenth-century visitor put it. It could be argued, of course, that Nicholas and prostitutes had one thing in common: whether you called it serving sailors, or snaring them, they were bound to frequent the same haunts. Besides, anybody who sought to save girls from prostitution was obliged to establish a presence among them.

Written accounts of "Three Daughters" make it clear what the girls were saved from by Nicholas' timely intervention. Symeon does not sound the habitual retreat into coy euphemism, but writes that "the nobleman determined to sell into prostitution at a price his three beautiful daughters to whoever were willing to buy." For Byzantine women, the threat of prostitution was not remote and mythical, like attracting the attentions of a cantankerous dragon, but very real. The selling for sex of children as a means of staving off penury was rife. Street prostitutes, fleeing from rural poverty, abounded in the cities. A better class of courtesan, attired in silk and gold cloth and liberally perfumed, performed at banquets and theater shows. Justinian's consort Theodora had previously worked in a Constantinople brothel, where she permitted clients to place ears of grain in her private parts that geese might then peck at them. Bordellos flourished across the empire, their doorway inscriptions exhorting clients to enter and enjoy.

Special hostels were established on the roads and in the ports of Anatolia to prevent pilgrims from falling prey to the prostitutes who worked the common inns. The same principle operated at the Christian youth hostel, in the heart of the red-light district, where I stayed. We were a mixture of Christians and cheapskates; certainly, it was the dormitory tariff that had attracted me. While the budget visitors were out spending the money they had saved on accommodation, the Christians stayed in to watch a movie. It was an American evangelical offering intent on smuggling in its moral message—no premarital sex at any cost—by wrapping it in a rumbustious soundtrack. It was not, it seemed, a sell that met much resistance. A girl in the audience wore a T-shirt that read "I'm keeping my cherry," a widely held sentiment, to judge by the murmurs of assent that punctuated the movie's message-laden moments.

Things were different, however, in the male dormitory. I was awoken on several occasions by involuntary utterances of dream-state pleasure during which a whole series of cherries was clearly being surrendered. A private room next time, I resolved, as I pondered celibacy's renunciation of the very force that made us. Celibacy was, of course, the line that Nicholas had taken as a young man, avoiding the company and conversation of women. Did the fact that he had established his Amsterdam territory alongside the city's hookers reflect an accommodation of sorts?

I was reminded of Harold Davidson, the Norfolk rector who had set out to save London's prostitutes in the 1930s; he took up performing with lions (unsuccessfully; he was eaten by one in Skegness) after being defrocked for taking an unseemly interest in the girls he sought to save. William Gladstone, Victorian statesman, had founded an association in London to reclaim fallen women, which assisted those who had been driven into the sex trade by want. The association offered sanctuary and helped arrange medical aid, alternative employment, marriage, and emigration. A similar organization, the Midnight Mission, was founded in New York in 1867, with "men of years, benevolence and social standing" trawling the streets for girls to invite back to the refuge.

Gladstone's involvement in the cause deepened significantly from the 1850s. Over the years, he met at least ninety prostitutes, whom he encountered when walking London's nighttime streets. Gladstone's concern for London's prostitutes was sincere, but he also acknowledged that he was in the grip of more complex motivations. There is no suggestion that he engaged in sex with prostitutes; but this Victorian, suffering from the intense self-denying sexual hypocrisy of the age, was certainly aroused by the encounters. He even scourged himself with whips to subdue the sexual feelings that such meetings had provoked. What Gladstone had stumbled upon, though it caused him torment, was what it feels like to be fully human.

By Amsterdam, Nicholas was learning the self-same lesson.

18

A THIRD ST. NICHOLAS church stood halfway between the first two, though more discreetly. Where the Oude Kerk and the Church of St. Nicholas had been built as conspicuous Catholic monuments to fourteenth-century supremacy and nineteenth-century reemergence respectively, this one was invisible from the street.

I entered a terraced canalside house on Vorburgerwaal, home to a stocking merchant in the mid-seventeenth century. Its narrow, high façade was crammed with windows, as if the interior craved daylight, and was topped by a comparatively restrained gable. Where other gables were ornamented with dolphins, shells, and cornucopia, this one had made do with a decorative scroll above either eave. The house, now a museum, exemplified period Dutch style: sturdy oak furniture, hangings, paneled walls, and tiled floors in dimly lit interiors that Vermeer might have conjured.

On the fifth floor, however, the house gave way without warning to a church. Interior walls, which proliferated on the lower floors, spawning endless parlors and sitting rooms, had melted away to leave the entire level open. The two floors above had also been dispensed with, exposing a spacious roof pitch, except against the walls where they continued to support balustraded galleries that overlooked the pews. Saints' statuettes sheltered in niches, and a life-sized statue of St. Nicholas perched on a mezzanine. An enormous eighteenth-century depiction of Christ's baptism, flanked by marble and gilt pillars, by cherubs and trumpeting angels, rose from the altar to the height of the upper gallery. The muted gable made sense now, as guarded as the exterior of a speakeasy, a gambling den, or, in less liberal cities than Amsterdam, a brothel.

In 1579, a year after the overthrow of the Catholics, Amsterdam and the northern provinces had united as the Netherlands. The Protestant authorities promised religious tolerance, but public observance of the Roman rites aroused deep antipathy. Catholicism went into hiding, building itself secret churches across the Netherlands: fifteen in Utrecht, eleven in Haarlem, and at least twenty in Amsterdam. The stocking maker's house on Vorburgerwaal was converted to contain a church dedicated to St. Nicholas in the early 1660s.

Protestantism had driven Nicholas from the old churches and confined him to his Amsterdam attic. Three hundred years later, and just a mile to the north, the Frank family and some friends would seek refuge from Nazi bestiality in an attic of their own. In July 1942, they took to the back annex of the family warehouse on Prinsengracht, where they were supplied by sympathizers through a door hidden behind a bookcase. The comparison is odious—the theoretical Nicholas could never know the unimaginable horror that threatened the Franks and finally engulfed them upon their betrayal by Dutch collaborators in 1944—but it is pointedly insistent. When the Franks went into hiding, they were placing their hopes in the innate Dutch respect for the sanctity of the home. It was Nicholas' own familiarity with the Dutch home, which he had been insinuating himself into for centuries, that would protect him from the zealots of his age.

The panoply of saints had been rigorously suppressed since 1578. But Nicholas, to the irritation of the Calvinist authorities, proved uniquely resilient to the purges. They might have removed his every last statue and painting from the public churches and chapels, but they had not reckoned with the fact that Nicholas was well established beyond the obvious places of worship. He had recognized the limitations of great churches in his name—at Amsterdam and Utrecht, at Ghent and Brussels—for all the devotional imagery they contained. Establishing his saint's day as widely as possible across his range was one thing; but springing it from the pious confines of the churches to root it in the streets, and in the homes that gave onto them, offered him greater security.

The feast of St. Nicholas was observed in Utrecht as early as 1163. It spread across the Low Countries, Germany and Austria, France, Switzerland, and England and duly established itself across much of northern and central Europe east to Romania. It took an insistently popular form: an English Catholic called Henry Machyn described the feast in London during the 1550s, when processions headed by individuals dressed as St. Nicholas "went abroad in most parts of London singing after the old fashion," and were "received among good people into their houses, and had much good cheere as ever they had, in many places."

To some households, the saint came with a different purpose. The sixteenth-century Swiss writer Hospinian wrote how "it was the custom for parents, on the vigil of St. Nicholas, to convey secretly presents of various kinds to their little sons and daughters who were taught to believe that they owed them to the kindness of St. Nicholas and his train, who, going up and down among the towns and the villages, came in at the windows, though they were shut, and distributed them. This custom originated from the legendary account of that saint having given portions to three daughters of a poor citizen whose necessities had driven him to an intention of prostituting them."

Hospinian's German contemporary Thomas Naogeorgus confirmed the practice:

> Saint Nicholas money used to give
> To Maidens secretly,
> Who, that he still may use
> His wonted liberalitie
> The mothers all their children on the eve
> Do cause to fast
> And when they every one at night
> In senselesse sleepe are cast
> Both Apples, Nuttes, and peares they bring,
> And other things besides
> As caps, and shooes, and petticotes,
> Which secretly they hide,
> And in the morning found, they say
> That this Saint Nicholas brought.

The custom of gift-giving in imitation of "Three Daughters" probably took its inspiration from the saints' plays which had often taken as their subjects the stories of St. Nicholas. They evolved in the tenth century as dramatic adjuncts to feast-day liturgies but soon became popularized and duly moved outside the church's orbit. That process had seen "Three Daughters" move beyond word and image to theatrical representation; now, the narrative took another giant step forward by establishing itself among the cherished rituals of the home.

The imitation was not strictly faithful; a wide variety of elements attached to the ritual beyond its gift-giving core. In many places, the saint in full pontificals called at houses on St. Nicholas' Eve to enquire about the behavior of the children. The children tried endearing themselves to him by filling a shoe with straw and carrots, which they left out as an offering to the white horse Nicholas had taken to riding at some stage in his progress north. Nicholas was often accompanied on these visits by a helper. These assistants had pronounced regional variations; what they had in common—unlike Zwarte Piet in Holland, lately softened by the sanitizing constraints of commercial sponsorship—was a decidedly more fearsome form than the benign old saint. In Austria, he was the monstrous horned Klaubauf or Krampus; Père Fouettard, or the Whipping Father, in France; and the fur-clad Pelznickle in Germany. These figures sometimes visited on the absent saint's behalf or even combined his characteristics with their own in disturbing composites. Whatever their form, these old disciplinarians served as reminders that the night's gifts were strictly conditional: only well-behaved children who knew their catechism could expect to receive them. Their fierce aspect was a finger raised in warning that children must earn their annual indulgence from St. Nicholas. The diligent were sure to find that he had filled their shoes with nuts, apples, and oranges; the undeserving, however, could expect the dreaded twig, which symbolized a birching from the saint's mean sidekick.

The saint's feast flourished, particularly in Holland, where it was duly established as the most cherished of all holidays. Several Dutch artists painted the feast, notably Jan Steen, who returned to the scene several times during the mid-seventeenth century. One such work, *The Feast of St. Nicholas*, hangs in Amsterdam's Rijksmuseum. The painting depicts a domestic interior that might have come straight from the lower floors of the house on Vorburgerwaal, a room dominated by thick drapes and a dark wooden chimney hood protruding from the ceiling and hung with a tasseled pelmet. What saves this interior from austerity is the cast of ten and their joyful clutter: grandparents, parents, servant maid, and a mob of children surrounded by gingerbread and honey cakes, waffles, scattered walnuts, an apple in which a coin has been embedded, and an orange. Add a tree and the flicker of a television and the scene would recall a modern Christmas.

Much of the painting's drama focuses on shoes. One, retrieved by the servant girl, is laden with presents; another lies discarded. A third shoe belongs to a boy, reduced to tears by the birch twig it has yielded and by

Jan Steen, *The Feast of St Nicholas*. (Courtesy of the Rijksmuseum, Amsterdam)

the fact that his siblings have fared much better. In the foreground, a glee-ful toddler clutches a laden bucket of toys in one arm and a doll in the other. And in the arms of the father is a baby girl clasping a gingerbread figure of St. Nicholas.

So much for the suppression of Nicholas' image. Expulsion from the churches had not finished it off but only encouraged the alternative, secu-lar forms, into which it had long since diversified, to flourish. Toymakers did a brisk trade in St. Nicholas dolls over the feast. The bakers of the Low Countries had been preparing gingerbread cakes and honey tarts in the saint's molded form, complete with crosier, miter, and bags of gold, since the thirteenth century. Nicholas had ensured the preservation of his image by embedding it in popular culture; coating it in sugar, marzipan, and licorice surely helped. Even so, the authorities were foolish enough to pursue the saint into the kitchen. Following ordinances in Delft in 1607 and Arnhem in 1622, Utrecht outlawed the "baking of likenesses in bread or cake" in 1655. And on December 4, 1663, around the time that Nicholas' last few spared images were taking to the attic at Vorburger-waal, Amsterdam's magistracy passed a statute condemning as idolatrous the sale from the stalls along the Vijzeldam of St. Nicholas dolls, and censured the feast-day trade in cookies, cakes, and candles bearing his impress or shape.

It was no accident that the satirical Jan Steen should have been drawn to paint *The Feast of St. Nicholas* around the time of the Amsterdam gingerbread statutes. He intended the painting not only as an expression of affection but also as an active defense of a much-loved institution. It's a canny work, which places in the hands of babes objects the authorities had seen fit to proscribe. Steen need not have worried. The statutes of 1663 caused an insurrection of eleven-year-olds in Amsterdam who ridiculed the authorities by marching for their rights to bear gingerbread cakes of St. Nicholas. The children are bearing them still.

Nicholas had developed another key attribute by Steen's time, one that the father in *The Feast of St. Nicholas* points out to the daughter in his arms. Hospinian had written in the 1500s how St. Nicholas magicked his way in at the windows, "though they were shut." After centuries of service, windows had begun to present the saint with a problem. They were no longer his sole preserve. They had begun to attract heavier and heavier traffic, and that largely illicit; lovers, housebreakers, vagabonds, and witches in life, literature, and lore alike entered by the window. What Nicholas needed, if his intentions were not to be mistaken, was an entrance route he could once more call his own.

Back in Byzantine Myra, where cooking tended to take place outside and rudimentary stoves or braziers were used for winter warmth, chimneys had not existed. In colder European climates, open indoor hearths served the same function. In some cases, conical hoods made of wicker, wattle and daub, or plank provided some relief from the smoke by feeding it into the roof space, where openings in the eaves or gables allowed it to escape. The modern chimney seems to have emerged during the thirteenth century, among the chillier lands that Nicholas encountered in his historical drift to the north, where it was discovered that an enclosed stone flue not only contained the smoke but also helped create a draft to expel it. Among the earliest recorded recognizable chimneys were those reported as having fallen in an earthquake at Venice in 1347, and those built by a lord at Padua in 1368. St. Nicholas had discovered them by 1392, as the fresco at Ramaća in Serbia demonstrates. What this architectural advance had provided him with was a pioneer route, an untrodden trail, which would take his gifts, and subsequently himself, to the symbolic heart of the home—a route that would at once signal his distinct intentions and deliver a reminder of his supernatural abilities.

So it is that the father in the painting indicates to his daughter, who will one day repeat it to her own child, how St. Nicholas arrived during the night.

19

THE SHIP WAKES OF the sixteenth century, though they faded like vapor trails, churned a vast clockwise circle upon the North Atlantic as pioneering Europeans set about exploring North America. They had learned to approach the unfamiliar coastline from the south, reserving the more direct northerly route for the return journey, when favorable winds would drive them homeward across the berg-strewn high latitudes. By continuing the return leg in a clockwise direction, they would arrive at Genoa, Oporto, or Cádiz, Bristol, or Amsterdam. These were the ports they had left many months earlier; steering southwest with the trade winds, they had put the winter behind them as they closed upon the Canaries. At the West Indies they picked up the Gulf Stream, which bore them northeast, past Cape Fear and Chesapeake Bay, to pick at new discoveries along the seaboard of the New World.

Nicholas, courtesy of his Catholic devotees, had already planted feet on various landmarks that fringed this hoop-shaped sea route long before the *Unity* of the Dutch West India Company left Amsterdam for the Hudson River on January 25, 1624. There was the Portuguese island of São Nicolau, which lay among the Cape Verde group, and St. Nicholas Mole, a port on Haiti's northwestern corner which Christopher Columbus named after stepping ashore there on the eve of the saint's feast day in 1492. Columbus also gave Nicholas' name to the neighboring cape, and to the St. Nicholas Channel north of nearby Cuba. And an hour later on the clock face, at about nine, the Spaniards had named a Floridian port St. Nicholas Ferry.

With the failure of the Catholics to establish supremacy in North America, these Nicholas presences largely stalled. The Haitian port lapsed into obscurity and St. Nicholas Ferry was duly renamed Jacksonville. It was now time to try again, at shortly after ten o'clock, in the island-strewn harbor at the mouth of the Hudson River. But the world was transformed. Nicholas must now depend upon Protestants to get him there.

The great harbor had been discovered by Giovanni da Verrazano in 1524, but its river did not acquire a European name until Henry Hudson, working out of Amsterdam, earned the right to fix his to it by sailing up it in 1609. There had been a Dutch trading presence on the Hudson River ever since. Even so, Europe had barely removed the New World from its box when, one spring day fifteen years later, the *Unity* worked its way through the narrows that the Verrazano Bridge now spans. A jigsaw jostle of land and water greeted the settlers, with sandy beaches fringing a low shoreline that occasionally roused itself to oyster middens and to modest bluffs that would one day be flattered to be known as "heights." The waters were vigorous with the thrash of salmon and shad, and the air was clogged with mosquitoes and pigeons. Except for the trails and seasonal campsites of the Lenape natives, the place seemed virgin. The Manhattan skyline was crammed with the crowns of hickory, walnut, and enormous oaks; riotous wild roses, vines, plums, strawberries, and whortleberries had long since reclaimed the itinerant Lenape's abandoned vegetable plots. The woods were well watered and abounded with venison and with acorns for foraging pigs: the sort of details that passengers on the *Unity* were sure to have noticed. They had not come, like those before them, to barter glass beads and knives for beaver and otter furs before making for home. Manhattan's first European settlers, they were here for good.

It was on such a ship, New York lore would have it, that St. Nicholas also was borne to Manhattan. Not Nicholas' bones, which were all but done with traveling, but the idea of him as the presiding spirit of the city's founding settlement, New Amsterdam. It was evidently an appealing notion. In 1809, exactly two centuries after Hudson had made the river his own, the New York writer Washington Irving attributed the role to St. Nicholas in his *History of New York*, imagining the feted arrival of the saint in the great harbor, on a ship bearing a figurehead in "the goodly image of St. Nicholas," "with a low-brimmed hat, a huge pair of Flemish trunk hose, and a pipe that reached to the end of the bowsprit."

This was no minor modification. Even in his Amsterdam manifestation, Nicholas had been readily recognizable as the thirteen-hundred-year-old bishop of Myra. Three months aboard the *Unity* would seem, however, to have turned Nicholas profane, for he not only ditched his bishop's robes for fancy civvies but took up the Virginia weed as well. The truth was that Irving did not intend this dramatic conversion to be taken entirely seriously. He had published his *History* under the pseudonym Dietrich Knickerbocker. The surname was a popular term for New Yorkers of Dutch origin; it referred to the popular Dutch custom of baking dough balls for use as children's marbles. An apparently serious history of London might as well have been ascribed to one Charlie Cockney. The truth regarding St. Nicholas' arrival in New Amsterdam, as Irving would no doubt have conceded—but never was invited to, for succeeding generations of historians seemed to take his genial, occasionally surreal, and hugely influential burlesque at its word—was always going to be more complicated.

Nobody appreciated this better than Nicholas, who had been adept enough to identify, assess, and evade every peril for over a thousand years—the advance of Islam; the decline of the various cities he had made his own and of the pilgrimage routes that nourished him; and the pogroms of the iconoclasts. Even when the world seemed his, Nicholas remained in a state of heightened alert. He had no faith in security of tenure, regarding his bastions of devotion as temporary safe houses that he must be prepared to abandon at shortest notice. This self-same vigilance had kept him on the move and helped ensure against obscurity or erasure. But Nicholas had never faced a threat to compare with Protestantism.

Protestantism took profound objection to the saints; the hated saints, who made midgets of men and sapped them with the devotions they demanded. The particular problem for Nicholas was that the Protestant faith claimed the very region that the saint had settled upon (once he had appreciated that the future assuredly lay with the mercantile powers of Europe's western seaboard, notably England and Holland) as his own power base. Those nations would indeed flourish, but Nicholas was destined to play peripheral roles there. He would leave, as was his wont, a shadow presence behind; in Amsterdam and across the Netherlands, he would cower in attics, awaiting the annual token of pantomime affection that his saint's day warranted, while the evidence of his former influence in England would barely extend beyond the churches that continued to bear his name. As for himself, he was left with no choice but to move on in search of new devotees. The problem was, he had pushed himself to Europe's margins, where only the ocean lay; which was what brought him to the Amsterdam quayside to seek passage to the New World.

Those same waterfronts had witnessed the annual arrival of Sinter-

klaas, all balloons and celebratory foghorns, a few weeks before. But no
pageant commemorated the departure I now imagined there, the forced
evacuation, early in the seventeenth century, of a saint who had lost the
Dutch churches and could not know how long he might keep his place in
their homes. Nicholas' flight was undocumented, but would find its parallels in the banishments of his own people three centuries later: the last
White Russian armies pushed back to Sevastopol in 1920 and the Rum
Greeks crowding the Smyrna waterfront in the autumn of 1922. Like
them, the Dutch saint feared that his very survival depended on a passage out.

The Protestants viewed their old dependence upon Nicholas and his
like with contempt; in his fall from grace, Nicholas had surely burned
whatever boats might have carried him to the New World. He must immediately banish the least idea of traveling in the style he'd grown accustomed to; never again would he know the revered luxury he had
experienced on Columbus' voyages in the 1490s and on the translation
to Bari. It did not help, of course, that 1087 was commemorated every
May in Italy and Russia—as cruel a reminder of his glory days as forc-
ing an athlete, lately an amputee, to watch recordings of former victori-
ous breast-tapings. The delivery of Nicholas to Bari had been the entire
glorious point of the voyage there; it was a measure of how far he had
fallen that the primary concern of the *Unity* passengers was to put an
ocean between themselves and their Catholic persecutors, Nicholas included.

Passages were freely available, to humans at least, on the early ships to
the New World. It was not until the famines and pogroms of the nineteenth century that the desperate and the persecuted largely awoke to the
allure of America and crammed aboard ships bound for New York. In the
early seventeenth century, the distant land did not look so attractive, especially not from the bustling quaysides of the Netherlands, which could
fairly claim at that time to be the most civilized, liberal, and prosperous
nation on earth. The Dutch West India Company, though it might offer
inducements, struggled to invest its evocations of a pioneering life across
the ocean with much appeal. The company had more luck with Protestant
Walloons fleeing Catholic persecution in Luxembourg and the Namur,
Hainault, and Liège regions of what is now southern Belgium. The *Unity*
sailed with a handful of Walloon and Dutch families, along with a few

unattached individuals who brought the total tally of men in the party to forty.

One of the Walloons, Catelyn Trico, from Valenciennes, was just eighteen when she sailed for the New World, and just four days married to one George Rapalje. Catelyn would give birth to her—and the new settlement's—first child, Sara, in June 1625. Many years later, when she was in her eighties, Catelyn recalled that the four other single women among the settlers had chosen husbands from the men available, and wed them at sea—a spare detail, which evokes a party of staunch, self-reliant, and clear-sighted souls. The future the settlers had resolved upon was largely dependent on their own fortitude and endurance; but it was a future, at least, beyond the reach of diabolical cardinals, and of the saints that their racks and wheels served.

These people were, according to Catelyn Trico, "all of the Reformed religion"; which was to declare them sworn enemies of the saints, and of saints' representation in any form. There might even have been among them those who had wielded axes over church statues or warmed their hands before bonfires of bubbling images. Nicholas could abandon the least prospect of making the crossing in material form—on a popish medallion slung around a settler's neck, say, or on a painted image lovingly secured to a bulwark. Nor was there the least possibility, pace Irving, that the Dutch West India Company would have permitted a figurehead of the saint on the prow of a ship that was to play a historic role in establishing an avowedly Reformed settlement in the New World. It is to be imagined that the mildest audible invocation of a saint on board the *Unity* would have been greeted with stern disapproval. Nicholas would secretly shin up the anchor chain, then, rather than board by the gangplank if he were to make this crossing; secreting himself, in modern terms, in the shadowy depths of an aluminum cargo container. His only option, though it must have galled the very ocean's onetime patron, was to stow away. To reach the New World, he must somehow depend on the *Unity*'s passengers giving him secret space in their hearts.

These people had turned their backs on the saints—it was true—but to significantly varying degrees. Some of the saints, especially those who demanded devotions as part of the ritual round, they were able to dismiss as mere racketeers; the saints at the top of the hierarchy often attracted the deepest resentment among Protestants, with Dutch reformers dismissing the Virgin Mary as a "simple woman" and even an "empty flourbag." Other saints, though they were removed with equal ease from the alcoves and walls of the churches, clung more tenaciously to the mind. Saintly support was a habit of many centuries. To adopt the twin tenets of Protestantism, self-reliance and direct communion with God, demanded a courage that was particularly tested in times of peril. Protestantism, like parachuting, required a considerable leap of faith. Managing without the saints who had buffered people against their great trials, soothing their fears and pains, proved more difficult. Even the most strictly Reformed might invoke St. Margaret of Antioch, patron of childbirth, from the depths of labor, or St. Roch when plague threatened. Even the severest hagiophobe might cry out to the saints of the fields when famine threatened the harvest, or appeal to St. Erasmus in the racking pains of appendicitis.

The same was true of the sea. Protestantism might have cleared it of the monsters of popish superstition, but the Reformation was unable to shrink the ocean in its measurelessness, or to rid it of storm, shipwreck, piracy. The world the *Unity* was headed for was unimaginably remote. Hardened explorers and cod fishermen were the only Europeans to have seen it; many of those boarding the *Unity* had not even been to sea before. Then there were the privations they could expect before even beginning their new lives in America: discomfort and illness, notably dysentery and typhoid, all endured amid the squalor of mildewed confinement between decks. The crossing might have been specifically designed to test Reformed zeal to its limits. Was this how St. Nicholas was smuggled aboard—on the whispered breath of an apprehensive teenager who checked herself from making the sign of the cross as the *Unity* let go her mooring lines that January morning and swung her bow toward the Zuider Zee? And did this sustain Nicholas on the voyage so that his name, privately muttered, accompanied sighs of relief as the settlers were put ashore months later in a new-leaf hickory dapple among their tools, their barrels, their canvases and sacks of seed?

Almost four centuries later, St. Nicholas has a great many New York churches to his name; of all the saints, only the Virgin Mary has more. His is the Russian Orthodox cathedral, with its brick and tiled façades and its five onion domes crowned with crosses, which rises above the Upper East Side on wintry mornings like a vision of St. Petersburg. The Antiochian Orthodox Cathedral in Brooklyn is his. He has Albanian Orthodox, Romanian Orthodox, and Russian Orthodox churches in Queens; Ukrainian Catholic and Roman Catholic ones in Brooklyn; a German Catholic one on the Upper East Side; a Russian Carpatho–Russian Orthodox Greek Catholic church on the Lower East Side; and Greek Orthodox churches in Flushing, Brooklyn, and Staten Island.

The fact of these churches, superficially digested, may cause them to be offered as evidence of Nicholas' long association with the city, fruit of the first ax blows of those indomitable Dutch and Walloon settlers whom the stowaway saint had started a new life alongside back in 1624. In fact, the earliest of the churches, the German Catholic church on East Second Street, was not founded until the 1830s; the rest followed in the twentieth century.

The churches actually stand witness to the arrival of the saint's mostly Orthodox devotees from southern and eastern Europe and the Slavic countries, a consequence of the social and political upheavals that had led to Smyrna, Sevastopol, and the like. The saint's original constituents had finally caught up with him in the New World; arriving, it might be imagined, to administer a reviving dose of devotion to the saint who had shown them the way there.

The truth was that the emigrants were too late; to all intents and purposes, their new churches honored a saint that the city had never known. Nicholas and his Orthodox original had been fracturing ever since the eleventh century; recent events had accelerated the process. Circumstance had long since forced Nicholas to adapt so radically that this devotional staple of the migrants' old lives was unrecognizable in their new ones. Every step along Nicholas' journey had entailed change, but nowhere more than New York. New York was where he started, in the classic migrant's manner, all over again.

Washington Irving claimed that there had been a much earlier St. Nicholas Church—a chapel, with an image of the saint elevated before it, in the middle of what is now Bowling Green. Irving peddled the notion that Nicholas had had it easy, playing a prominent role in the founding of New Amsterdam. It was Nicholas who had appeared—that miraculous Byzantine facility of his—to indicate where New Amsterdam's fort would be constructed: at Manhattan's southwestern corner, where the Customs House now stands.

The truth was that receiving the dedication of Manhattan's first church was beyond Nicholas; the abolition of saints' names from church dedications was as integral to Dutch reform as the removal of the physical images the churches contained. The settlement's actual first church, far from being a chapel—the word had offensive Catholic associations—was termed a congregational hall. It was incorporated into a horse mill—as "a spacious room sufficient to accommodate a large congregation"—that one François Molemaecker was busy building near the East River in 1626. It did apparently carry bells, which the more strictly reformed might have abhorred as popish, except that these bells had been carried from Catholic Puerto Rico with the Dutch West India Company's capture of that city from the Spaniards in 1625; that lent them the rather more satisfying peal of Reformist triumphalism.

Arrival in the New World marked the beginning of Nicholas' problems. From the moment he stepped ashore, he was obliged to seek a purpose beyond the familiar confines of the church. He might have begun by counting his blessings: that he had not ended up among the Puritans to the north. The Massachusetts legislature passed a law in 1651 punishing the observance of Christmas, which it considered "a great dishonour to God," with a five-shilling fine. New Amsterdam, compared to this, was a paradigm of multi-faith toleration where prisoners were provided with tax-free alcohol and the new church, built from quarry stone and oak shingles in 1642, was funded by subscriptions pledged during a boozy wedding feast. Calvinism held sway, but religious minorities including Quakers and Jews, Anglicans and Baptists, Presbyterians and Lutherans were tolerated. There were even Catholics, with "two images on the mantelpiece, one of the blessed Virgin" sighted in a house near the port in 1643. This was to allow Nicholas, though starved of devotion, leave at least to remain. He achieved a low-key subsistence, perhaps as a mere memory among the settlement's Dutch and English populations. He may even have inspired, if only by strength of habit, sporadic skeletal celebrations on his saint's day—the offering of oranges, perhaps, to the children in the city's more tolerant homes. But it was hardly a living.

America, of course, had never promised it would be easy. For many of the new migrants, America meant adapting old skills or putting their backs to new ones as they acquainted themselves with the new land, with its differently modulated seasons and differently textured soils, and learned to handle unfamiliar weaves and grains. Many found themselves recommencing at the foot of an unfamiliar profession's dauntingly sheer face; working in the docks, at the shambles or the lumber yards, or going into service—in the modern vernacular, waiting tables—until hard work and the right attitude revealed the way to an opportunity. The question was what that opportunity might be in the case of an old saint who had long since stumbled from grace.

The seventeenth and eighteenth centuries proved unremittingly hard for Nicholas. Every December 5, if only for a day, a few old Dutch families retained him, but the welcome they gave him among the knickknacks, the oranges, and the gingerbread felt like a dying observance. Latterly, either side of the Revolution, he was brushed down and given part-time work as a symbol of New York's Dutch origins. The Dutch community, in danger of being ethnically submerged, deployed Nicholas as a dike against the aggressive advances fronted by the flourishing patron saints of the British and Irish. Dutch patriots, claiming direct descent from the very first settlers, celebrated St. Nicholas' Day with banquets and established societies in his name. But Nicholas, trained in the ways of stealth, had never been much of a rabble-rouser. Besides, St. George and St. Andrew could call on supporters in greater numbers; and St. Patrick more fervent ones. When the nineteenth century dawned over Manhattan, the dangerously marginalized Nicholas was in dire need of renewed purpose.

New York was outperforming Boston and Philadelphia by 1800. Between the 1790s and 1807, imports through America's great port rose fourfold and exports tenfold. So rapidly were the Manhattan waterfronts transformed, with new quaysides, warehouses, and the expanding premises of factors, importers, and commission merchants, that the wealthy abandoned their residences around the Battery and moved uptown, dragging the city's hub with them. Here the retailers began, filling the gap left by the importers and artisans as they discontinued the practice of selling direct from their ships' cargo holds along the dockside and from their ateliers respectively. Stores sprang up along Broadway and Maiden Lane and on Chatham Street, as Park Row was then known. Windows began to display luxury imported wares such as silks, linens, and cashmeres, stationery and books, muskets and violins, coffee and confectionery. And manufactured toys.

Children had relied largely upon their imaginations when it came to entertaining themselves in eighteenth-century America. They might have
made do with toys fashioned by parents or siblings: rag dolls, roughly
carved wooden animals and hoops. Certainly, manufactured toys barely
existed in any volume until the nineteenth century, when a better appreciation of their role in education gave a considerable boost to the trade.
Commercially made toys began to be imported from Europe, notably
from Nuremberg, in rapidly increasing quantities. In 1808, a New York
shop advertised "four hundred and fifty kinds of Christmas presents and
New-year's gifts, consisting of toys, childrens and school books, Christmas pieces, Drawing Books, Paint, Lead Pencils, Conversations and Toy
Cards, Pocket Books, Penknives, &c."

Imagine that Nicholas found his way to that shop. It was 1808, just a
year before Washington Irving's *History* would depict Nicholas "drawing
forth magnificent presents from his breeches pockets," but there was little
to suggest a transformation was imminent. Disenfranchised and down-at-
heel, his beard unkempt, Nicholas might have resembled a Bowery hobo
on the aimless walk he embarked on one winter's day. He passed among
the taverns, boardinghouses, and brothels down by the East River piers
where he paused to watch the brigs clustered along the quays. But it was
no longer any business of his—the loading of cotton bales, puncheons of
rum, and barrels of potash, and the landing of tea chests and rice sacks—
and he moved on. He passed depots and auction houses before turning up
Catherine Street. He admired the grand houses on Oliver Street, with their
handsome fanlights and marble steps, and the cherry trees that fronted
them, spindly with winter. He then turned into Chatham Street and
walked south until the building site of City Hall loomed from the common to his right. And so to bustling Broadway, and the storefront that
caught his eye.

Here were dolls made from porcelain and leather, and miniature
japanned violins and pianofortes, flutes and drums, and wooden muskets
and swords, and carved horsemen and drummers and lancers, and clay
churns and pails, wheelbarrows and tubs, and jointed snakes, and rocking
horses, and dolls' wooden bedsteads, tables, chairs, and cradles, and
leather whips, papier-mâché animals, writing slates, whistles, puppets and
marionettes, ivory rattles, music boxes, splendid chessmen, skipping ropes,
cups and balls, building blocks, wooden alphabets, magic lanterns, tea

sets, flags, masks, and accordions, rattles, arks, dominoes, magnetic fishes, jigsaw puzzles, penknives, and sugar mice.

Toys: the perfect children's gift. And what were children's gifts if not his very own area from his European days? An area where nobody could match him for delivery expertise. The window reminded Nicholas what he was good at.

20

M Y FLIGHT SQUEEZED INTO JFK shortly before a blizzard closed the airport. The aircraft trundled to a halt in a fenced corner usually reserved for planes that distant coups (fighting around the palm-fringed airport) had deprived of their home bases, or that the authorities had impounded after final requests to settle outstanding landing charges were ignored. Ahead of us, a queue of airliners showed as a chain of buttery lozenges: cabin lights, each signifying a row of humans who must precede us in the queues they would duly constitute at the airport's immigration desks. On that dark December night, reaching the terminal seemed like a grand ambition.

Passengers dozed or read. Others gazed from the windows where flakes buzzed around the lights, and the clean geometrics of planes, runways, and airport buildings were fast turning shaggy beneath the accumulating snow. Others considered how they might most effectively divide their time—the time they might finally have—between Bloomingdale's, Macy's, and FAO Schwarz.

A century ago, persecution and poverty had driven Europeans to New York. Now an anemic dollar did the trick. Even as desperate Chinese and Pakistanis stowed away in shipping containers or took to the undercarriage cavities of airliners, comfortable Londoners came here to shop for Christmas. Crossing the ocean for objects that their recipients might choose to return, or might have chosen to return, except that the ocean remained in the way, seemed to mix the epic and the banal in a curiously apposite way. It also spoke of the complexities of modern shopping. It was as well to be reminded, if only to fill the time on the snow-carpeted tarmac, that gifts were not meant to be complex; they were instinctive expressions of sympathy, respect, admiration, affection, and love which preceded even language.

Gifts duly came to be associated with established rituals. To the pagan

gods, they were given as sacrifices. The Romans nourished their human re-
lationships with symbolic *strenae*: presents such as gold for prosperity,
honey for sweetness, and candles for light. They also gave clay tablets inscribed with seasonal messages; prototype Christmas cards. The Persians
gave eggs as symbols of fertility, and the Celts exchanged holy mistletoe.
Gift-giving, in search of the cycle's natural punctuation point, tended to
gravitate toward the turn of the year. The Roman Saturnalia festival celebrated the grain god's revival from the depths of winter and ran from December 17 to December 24, after which Kalends marked the year's end.
Libanius, a fourth-century Greek sophist, described Kalends as a time of
profuse extravagance and generosity: "A stream of presents pours itself
out on all sides. . . . As the thousand flowers which burst forth everywhere
are the adornment of Spring, so are the thousand presents poured out on
all sides."

It was from these distant models that gift-giving cultures had descended, evolving into distinct, cherished regional traditions. What
these gifts kept in common was that they necessarily remained homegrown or handmade. Preserves, pastries, or needlework were usual gifts;
their exchange was largely symbolic and seasonal in nature. It was not
until the nineteenth century, with the mechanization of manufacturing
processes, that a burgeoning moneyed class began to have increasing access to a wide range of commercially produced goods. The symbolic gift
began to lose ground to the material one as the prosperous finally began
to recognize the potential extent of human need; and the custom of gift-
giving, with its sudden economic blossoming, became a manor worth
fighting for.

Gift-giving traditions in Manhattan closely reflected Old World
customs at the very beginning of the nineteenth century; they were yet
to cohere into distinctly North American forms. The New York Dutch
and some among their Low Country neighbors, notably the Walloons,
had retained a loyalty of sorts to Nicholas and December 6. Others,
particularly the Protestant English and north Germans, had terminated
Nicholas' gift-giving privileges with the Reformation. It was customary
among the English that gifts were given over the twelve days of Christmas, but particularly at the new year. The Germans, a growing presence
in Manhattan and Pennsylvania since the 1680s, had done away with

St. Nicholas' feast day in 1545 under the influence of Martin Luther. An early-seventeenth-century pastor in Germany made the reformers' case by denouncing St. Nicholas' role as "a bad custom because it points children to the saint while yet we know that not St. Nicholas but the holy Christ child gives us all good things for body and soul, and He alone it is whom we ought to call upon." The Germans shifted their gift-giving to Christmas and installed in St. Nicholas' old role the replacement that the new date insisted upon: Christkind, or the Christ child.

The Christ child had long been a pointedly literal focus of German church ritual. It had been common since the fourteenth century for congregations in parts of Germany and Austria to rock cradles as a means of providing symbolic contact with the infant Christ. In the sixteenth century, life-sized effigies of the swathed child were passed around German churches. At Crimmitschau in Saxony, a boy dressed as Christ was lowered from the church roof singing a Lutheran hymn; the tradition was abandoned when one such Christ plummeted to serious injury.

Luther's Christkind, fat with new function, flourished in Germany, Austria, Switzerland, and the French borderlands of Alsace. A supposedly pliant construct, it demonstrated a headstrong life of its own the moment attempts were made to impersonate him. It was largely owing to the practical problems inherent in representing the infant Christ that it morphed into an angelic figure wearing a gold crown lit with candles. When Christkind appeared in person, it was usually as a flaxen-haired child: the baby Christ, then, but played by a child old enough to be relied on to carry out its ritual responsibilities as it was bidden, in the German way, even if this meant gravitational accidents in the likes of Crimmitschau.

The Italians had comprised a small Manhattan community ever since 150 of them, Protestants fleeing the Inquisition, arrived in 1657. Italy's gift-giver was Befana, a big-nosed crone who wore patched clothes and broken shoes and carried a broomstick; the eponymous witch of the Epiphany. In the western church, the feast of Epiphany on January 6 primarily commemorates the Adoration of the infant Christ by the Magi. Befana had a particular association with the Magi, whom the Polos had spoken of on their return home from the East. Nicholas might have known of her from

Venice, or she might even have been familiar to him since his early days in Constantinople where the Magi's relics were supposedly translated in A.D. 490.

With their symbolic offerings to Christ—gold for a king, frankincense for a man of god, myrrh for one who would die—Caspar, Melchior, and Balthasar might themselves have been established in Italy as the presiding spirits of Epiphany gift-giving. They certainly succeeded in doing so in Spain and elsewhere, where they flourish to this day; but in Italy, they were stymied by the old woman whom they had happened to meet on their pilgrimage to Jerusalem. Befana met the manifest messianic exaggerations of these wide-eyed strangers with a scrupulous disregard; she insisted on finishing the housework before entertaining their madcap proposal that she join them. She finally put aside her broom, which has since become the witch's standard, only to discover that the Magi had continued without her. In Befana's story, destiny is foiled by domestic drudgery; she is Cinderella in reverse. She was named for an event at which she was pointedly absent; she has been consoled by her presence at subsequent Italian Epiphanies, providing children with gifts in a perpetual commemorative echo.

A popular variation contends that Befana did reach Bethlehem, but under her own promptings. She set off in search of her child, who had been abducted by Herod's murder gangs on Holy Innocents' Day, December 28. Arriving at Bethlehem, the confused Befana took the child she came across in a manger for her own. She laid her child's belongings, which she had carried with her, before the manger in an act of repossession. But the infant Jesus mistook the baby clothes for an offering (and one more usefully practical than the presumptuous abstractions of the Magi), and so made his own gift to Befana: that she who had lost her own child in the murderous hunt for Himself might find solace on that one night in bringing gifts to the children.

The Italians took to Befana, though she had her dark side. Where St. Nicholas expressed his through cantankerous sidekicks, Befana mixed a decided waspishness with her generosity. When Tuscans rang earthenware bells and blew glass trumpets on the eve of Epiphany, they were as much to ward Befana off as to honor her appearance; and the children uttered incantations to save them from her power even as they thrilled to her arrival.

The Epiphany witch of Russian lore is similarly malicious. Babushka, or Grandmother, supposedly gave the Magi the wrong directions to Bethlehem. So it was that the perpetual provision of children's Epiphany gifts was not a privilege but was more in the nature of a sentence to community service. As the hours passed in a fuggy airliner cabin, I felt this sardonic Slavic assessment of gift-giving gaining ground among my fellow passengers.

The dawn of the nineteenth century thus saw three distinct characters jockeying for position as Manhattan's dominant gift-giver. It was odd, this interest, like a share surge in an apparently indifferent stock, or bids flurrying around an unremarkable auction lot. With little more than the exchange of a few cookies, oranges, and stockings, and the odd homemade toy, on a variety of dates, gift-giving hardly seemed to merit so much attention. Which only went to show that Nicholas, Christkind, and Befana were an astute, even prescient, trio: prospectors who could sense the motherlode beneath their feet.

As to the advantage, it was only clear that the competitors had strengths and weaknesses in their respective claims. Personal appeal counted in the battle for gift-giving, but the date each operated from was also a factor. First, because he had been longest in Manhattan, there was Nicholas. He was an established gift-giver, with a surviving tradition across much of northern Europe. His core American constituency was the original Manhattan Dutch, but this was a thinning population by 1800. He might, perhaps, be able to count on some nostalgic support among the German and English communities whose cultures had once honored him. Of special concern was his date, which could claim no relevance beyond the fact that it was his feast day. It also lay somewhat remote from the dates the other contenders operated from, which clustered closer to the Christmas period; indeed, Nicholas' feast day was in danger of being eclipsed by the Thanksgiving holiday, which was busy establishing itself in late November.

Prominent among the competition was the Christ child, operating from Christ's birthday: an intimidating partnership. It reminded Nicholas of his days on the pilgrimage route to the Holy Land, his own shrine at Myra a mere distraction compared with the great sites of Christ's Nativity and Passion. Even so, Christ's experience was in abstract redemption rather than material gift-giving. Besides, this Christkind was merely a sort of Christ, a fabricated crypto-Christ, who had only been giving, and that on Luther's instructions, since 1545.

This left the witch, whose greatest strength, given the paucity of support on the ground, was Epiphany, an excellent operational base. It had the Magi connection but its prime significance in the Orthodox Church was that it also commemorated Christ's baptism in the River Jordan. The early Christians had even regarded that significant dip—Christ's spiritual rebirth—as of greater moment than his actual nativity. They had begun observing Epiphany from A.D. 250, a full century before December 25 was first recognized. Eponymous Befana had staked everything on the date she had made her own.

It was an invisible fourth contender, however, that represented the greatest challenge to Nicholas. Its backers were the dominant English, who gave presents on New Year's Day in the established custom back home, and did so without the offices of a mythical deliverer. By the nineteenth century, the tradition had acquired an influential momentum among Manhattan's social elite. Gifts were the lubricant of New Year visits and parties, with the exchange of silks and cashmeres, books and jewelry, all accompanied by cakes and "a glass of cherry-bounce or raspberry brandy." So it was that gift-giving's formative years, the first three decades of the nineteenth century, took place among the elegant townhouses to the west of Broadway opposite City Hall Park, and in the stores on Broadway, Pine Street, and Chatham Street. It was there that the promoter and publisher John Pintard saw an "endless variety of European toys that attract the admiration and empty the pockets of parents, friends and children" in December 1830. Here, among the influential neighborhoods where the Roosevelts and Aspinwalls and the fur-trade tycoon John Jacob Astor had their homes, was where Nicholas must make an impression.

The problem was not one of geography. Space, as Nicholas had repeatedly proved, was no bar to him. He had moved himself all the way from Myra to Manhattan. The problem was time. English influence in the city was fast causing gift-giving to fix upon a date that lay between Christkind and Befana—and was positively remote from Nicholas. There was only one thing for it; Nicholas must abandon December 6.

He who had conquered the atlas must now vanquish the calendar; he must adjust his position in it by the best part of a month and do so before competing new traditions beat him to all the available ritual vacancies. If he wanted gift-giving, he must make the leap to New Year.

Nicholas had been associated with December 6 for well over a thousand years, which surely fixed him to the date by long and cherished tradition, the rustiest of unyielding rivets. This was to reckon without immigrant pragmatism; the natural dilutions and divergences that reshape traditions and customs in the proximity of other cultures. The New York Dutch had long since resigned themselves to the fact that the English, having stolen their settlement back in the seventeenth century, now outnumbered them by far. Dutch and English had long since become neighbors, and often enjoyed convivial relations. The relocation to New Year seems to have proved straightforward, as an 1827 account implies. "The Old Dutch settlers," it explained, "transferred the observance from the Eve of St. Nicholas, who you know is the especial patron of little children, to that of New Year." It seemed that Nicholas' day, far from being a liability that would make him founder far from the seasonal action, could simply be abandoned for a more buoyant date. Just as their fall had made an irrelevance of the saints, so their dates no longer mattered. Nicholas was free to roam the calendar for new opportunities. The ones who suffered by their dates were Christkind and Befana, bound to them by their very names, like spiders condemned to await the thrum of their webs.

With his newfound calendar freedom, Nicholas soon found his way to New Year. To those prosperous drawing rooms between Broadway and the shores of the Hudson River, with their brocaded couches, Turkish rugs, and ormolu clocks, Dutch families delivered him in person. He came as the gifts the Dutch brought to these social gatherings; freshly baked *koekjes,* or cookies—cinnamon *speculaas* and almond-filled *amandelkoek*—tapped steaming from their fruitwood molds. These cakes took the form of a figure who wore long stockings and a miter, with a crosier in his hands. Toys peeped from his sugar-speckled pockets, and upon a scroll attached to one of his buckled shoes "St. Nicholas" was written. Others bore the image in relief of the "noted St. Nicholas, vulgarly called Santeclaus," as an

St. Nicholas cookie mold. (Courtesy of Historic Hudson Valley, Tarrytown, New York)

anonymous New York writer wrote in 1808. The writer recalled the days of his grandfather back in the mid-1700s when he considered that "those notable cakes" were first invented. With these gifts, the Dutch not only reminded their English neighbors that they had been here first, but also provided Nicholas with his vital entrée to these gift-laden interiors.

The Nicholas cookies seem to have been influential. They may even have been instrumental in attracting to Nicholas' cause a coterie of highly placed New Yorkers who would transform the saint's fortunes. One member of this powerful mercantile and literary clique, since dubbed the Knickerbocracy for their supposedly Dutch or Huguenot origins, was John Pintard, who helped establish Washington's Birthday and July 4 as important dates in the American calendar. Pintard perhaps had the New Year gingerbread designs in mind when he commissioned a woodcut of St. Nicholas, which was distributed among the members of the New-York Historical Society when it met on December 6, 1810. The woodcut showed St. Nicholas holding a money purse in one hand and a "Birchen Rod"—vestige of the old disciplinarian—in his other. In the background, a pair of "Blue Yarn" stockings hung over the fireplace, one filled with "toys, oranges, sugar plums and Oley cooks." All the elements in the woodcut had their origins in the old Dutch feast except that the wooden shoes had since evolved into stockings as gift receptacles: a practical adaptation in a clogless world, perhaps, though the custom claimed far older roots. The use of stockings supposedly originated in parts of Italy and France where St. Nicholas was venerated as the protector of virgins, which was doubtless due to "Three Daughters." There, convent girls hung out their stockings on St. Nicholas Eve and found them filled with "sweet-meats" and "other trifles of that kind" by morning.

The influence of the woodcut on the fortunes of Nicholas was as nothing to that of the *History* that Washington Irving, a friend of Pintard, had published the year before. On October 26, 1809, New York's *Evening Post* had carried an advertisement:

> Left his lodgings some time since, and has not since been heard of, a small elderly gentleman, dressed in an old black coat and cocked hat, by the name of KNICKERBOCKER. As there are some reasons for believing he is not entirely in his right mind and as great anxiety is entertained about him, any information concerning him left either at the Columbian Hotel, Mulberry Street, or at the Office of this paper will be thankfully received.

Two weeks later, the proprietor of the Columbian Hotel then announced that he had discovered "a very curious kind of written book" in Knickerbocker's room, and threatened to sell the manuscript unless the outstanding room bill was settled forthwith. On November 28, the availability of Dietrich Knickerbocker's *History of New York from the Beginning of the World to the End of the Dutch Dynasty* was announced. Irving's book was a runaway success, finding rapt champions in Dickens, Coleridge, and Sir Walter Scott. It provided an early prototype for American literature and served Manhattan with a long overdue past, though a pointedly skewed one. It also supplied Nicholas' new venture with a lavish launch pad.

Irving's spoof not only served to promote St. Nicholas but also gave several pointers to his future development. He wrote how "the good St. Nicholas would often make his appearance, in his beloved city, of a holly-day afternoon, riding jollily among the tree-tops, or over the roofs of the houses, now and then drawing forth magnificent presents from his breeches pockets, and dropping them down the chimneys of his favorites." The gifts and chimneys were well-established elements from the European tradition, but the power of flight was a new one. It might have been a borrowing, naïvely rendered, from St. Nicholas in his Byzantine phase, when his vision ranged without limit. More likely, given the saint's form in these matters, was that he had acquired his aviation skills from a rival, much as he had lifted his nautical abilities from Nicholas of Sion.

Nicholas had a striking amount in common with the Epiphany witch. Indeed, Befana served her southerly, Italian territories much as Nicholas served his northern European ones: fruit and candies for the good children, coal or twigs for the badly behaved, and the same use of the chimney to deliver. Original copyrights in these respects might be argued, lost as they are in the mythological mists; but in the case of flying, it was clear that Nicholas did not develop until his American reinvention the ability that Befana had been demonstrating for centuries. He learned quickly. Irving would add a typically Dutch wagon to Nicholas' airborne entourage in subsequent editions of the *History*. Some years would pass, however, before another Knickerbocker confirmed the transportation arrangements in full.

Just as the *History*'s success confounded Irving, so his friend Clement Clarke Moore was only intending to amuse his own children when he wrote—though his authorship has since been contested—"An Account of a Visit from St. Nicholas" in 1822. This charming ditty was a far cry from Irving's complex work, but it certainly continued the process of developing St. Nicholas' new role and establishing him in it. In the poem, the saint comes at night, arrives in a sleigh pulled by flying reindeer, and fills stockings before leaving by the chimney. The poem also continues Irving's deconsecration of Nicholas, making him a "right jolly old elf" with "a broad face, and a little round belly," "the beard on his chin . . . as white as the snow," "his cheeks . . . like roses, his nose like a cherry," "the stump of a pipe . . . held tight in his teeth." The following

December, the poem found its way into the pages of the *Sentinel* in Troy, New York. The uniquely prolific publishing history on which it then embarked would fuel Nicholas through the early decades of his reinvention.

Moore's poem was largely whimsical, which only enhanced the contentious punch packed in its first line. " 'Twas the night before Christmas": a one-line proposal that St. Nicholas abandon New Year's for Christmas, and this only a few years after Nicholas had relocated there from December 6. The move that Moore proposed was radical; what the new date stood for could not be more different from the date Nicholas currently occupied. Christmas Day and New Year's Day, along with their respective eves, represented the holiday's extremes of meaning. Where Christmas was largely reserved for Christian veneration, New Year's meant pagan festivity and license. The two principles had been battling for the soul of the annual winter holiday ever since Christianity first set about subverting the pagan festival back in the time of Nicholas; from their bastions, they glared at each other across the week that separated them. The reality of the situation, at least in the early nineteenth century, was that the two principles' territories overlapped to create a complex holiday mood where religious observance and festivity coexisted, often uneasily.

Moore believed that festivity and feasting as well as Christian veneration, the whole bound by gift-giving, could be reconciled in a more pluralist Christmas festival. The suggestion upset not only New Year's champions but also those religious conservatives who believed that pagan gift-giving had no business sullying the Christian Nativity observances. The poem landed a significant blow in what would prove a protracted battle between the dates, but it was not decisive. For decades to come, many subsequent versions of Moore's poem would begin " *'Twas the night before New Year.*" Some New Yorkers continued referring to "New Year gifts" as late as 1847.

The day eventually came when the whole raft of New Year customs—the trees, the stockings, the nighttime gifts, and the visit of Nicholas—had slipped seven days back in the calendar. The defection to Christmas was wholesale. The immensity of St. Nicholas' achievement was now clear. Beating Christkind and Befana to gift-giving was certainly an achievement;

but this move from New Year's Day to a day that plainly belonged to another was sure to embroil Nicholas in a far greater contest, one for the very meaning of Christmas. He was squaring up to the church that had once banished him.

Things were moving fast. It was no surprise that Nicholas' name should have shown the first signs of change. Irving and Moore had been scrupulous, but slippage had been evident as early as 1773, when the pages of New York's *Rivington's Gazetteer* made reference to the "anniversary of St. Nicholas, otherwise called St. a Claus"; a first phonetic stab at the guttural Dutch "Sinterklaas." In the years that followed, the name appeared in endless forms—Santaclaw, Sancteclaus, Sanctus Klass, Sandy Claus, and Sinti Klass. And, in a singular usage that would spread beyond its German origins—as if victory had bestowed upon him the title of the one he had vanquished—he would also be known as Kriss Kringle. It seemed that, in that curious corrupted Christkind, Nicholas now had designs on Christ himself.

I had made a point of visiting Salisbury Cathedral a few days before leaving for New York, driving past sodden fields until England's highest spire rose above the river valley. I soon spotted what I was looking for, an ancient effigy embedded among the floor flagstones of the nave. The centuries had worn away the soft beige sandstone. Even so, it remained plain that this figure was that of a bishop, complete with robes, miter, and crosier.

It was only three feet long, hardly bigger than a Dutch gingerbread. Legend has it that the effigy honored a boy bishop, a Nicholas tradition that was established across Europe, from Spain to Switzerland, by the thirteenth century. According to the tradition, which commemorated St. Nicholas' famously precocious election to the Myra bishopric, a scholar or chorister was chosen to officiate as bishop from December 6 to December 28, the Feast of the Holy Innocents. For three weeks, he was dressed in vestments bordered with pearl, silver, and gilt, and attended by boy canons. He blessed the people, held various ceremonies, preached sermons, collected alms, and even led his retinue on visitations to local religious houses. The Salisbury boy was supposedly accorded his prominent resting place after dying in seasonal office.

The tradition had a practical function, which was to give vent to the instinct for revelry that had characterized the holiday season since pagan times. Even so, its moderating aspirations regularly failed as the bishops' reigns exploded into orgies of drunkenness, philandering, and violence. The boys had, as one commentator ominously put it, "the priviledge to breake open their Masters' cellar-dore." At Salisbury, the procession of the newly elected bishop to the altar often degenerated into an uncontrolled throng that resulted in "certain grave injuries." Worse still, a servant was "mortally wounded by the Vicar" on the evening of December 27, 1448. It was no surprise, then, that Henry VIII was quick to reform these "superstitious and childish observances" in 1541 as part of his wider assault on the Catholic church. "Children," he proclaimed disapprovingly, "be strangely decked and appareled to counterfeit priests, bishops, and women, and so be led with songs and dances from house to house, blessing the people and gathering of money; and boys do sing masse and preach in the pulpit, with such other unfitting and inconvenient usages, rather to the derision than any true glory of God."

The custom enjoyed a brief revival under Catholic Queen Mary— Henry Machyn recorded it in his diary during the 1550s—before it was outlawed for good under Queen Elizabeth. England's Protestant monarchs might have thought to have finished off Nicholas, but what they had actually done was to force upon him a secular future; an identical process had caused Nicholas' image, driven from the churches of Holland, to seek refuge in cakes and dolls.

The wilder holiday indulgences continued unabated, and nowhere more markedly than in early New York. Foolish ceremonials, masquerades, folk plays, nonsensical skits, and the firing of guns proved the bane of the city's eighteenth-century gentry. Mobs in fancy dress forced their way into smart homes to perform rude cameos. Gangs of urban rowdies dressed as Negroes, fur trappers, Indians, and Falstaffs roamed the streets during the 1820s. It was into this world, a Christmas season lived uneasily between street and home, that the recast Nicholas began to emerge. He clung to one fact from his European past: that people had impersonated

him for centuries. The question was whether he could attract imperson-
ators in his new guise.

Impersonation was a vital hurdle. It meant breaking free from the
cookie mold to spread his influence in the new sphere. The process of
springing "St. Claas" (as John Pintard knew him) from the confines of the
two-dimensional image was a gradual one. A pioneering attempt at a
more substantial physical form was made in 1832 when John Pintard—a
true champion of Nicholas—fashioned a kind of effigy of the saint and
fitted it with a "small white mask." As the family waited, Pintard caused
the masked head to appear at the other end of the room; widespread panic
ensued. In the way of prototypes, however, it had been far more successful
than it initially appeared, spawning a burgeoning tradition of family imper-
sonators who wore masks of wax-coated cloth with eyeholes and attached
whiskers. Santa—the name had begun to settle now—was on his way to securing Manhattan. "St. Claas," wrote John Pintard in 1831, "is too firmly
riveted in this city ever to be forgotten."

I did not reach Manhattan until the early hours. When I awoke, it had
stopped snowing. The whitened canyons of the city were topped by a
bright blue morning. The high-rise boilers belched smoke and steam,
which the keen wind whipped away; the buildings resembled a fleet of
freighters jostling against the stream to keep station. People were digging
out their cars from beneath eaves of snow and clearing storefronts with
wide shovels. The snow plows had left high banks of broken glittery crust
between the sidewalks and the avenues; cars and pedestrians poured down
their respective sides, their gray exhausts and silvery breaths streaming
skyward.

I stepped out and walked north, heading toward the East Side around
Sixtieth Street, where many of my fellow airline passengers were sure to
concentrate; Saks and Tiffany's, Bergdorf Goodman and Bloomingdale's.
And FAO Schwarz. I stepped inside the toy store. There were puzzles and
puppets, just as there had been in that store window two centuries before;
and farm animals, chess sets, playhouses, and cast-iron horse-drawn carriages. But there were also things which were not dreamed of in 1808: go-
carts and scooters, radio-controlled planes and moving polar bears,

talking watches and karaoke machines, DVD players in the form of toy cars, battery-powered attack submarines and helium-filled airships, skateboards, foldable bikes and miniature jukeboxes. Spider-Man, Batman, and Darth Vader, and a child-sized Mercedes 500SL.

What chance did Christ have?

21

NICHOLAS FACED AN EXACTING overhaul of his identity—appearance, personality, and even purpose—if he was to push ahead with his ambitions. All his name needed, however, was a tweak, no great hardship for a man who had already been comprehensively modified, into Nicola and Nikolai, Mikulas and Nicolao, Nigul and Klaus, by every language encountered along the journey. He particularly liked the latest variation. A mild corruption of his familiar Dutch title, Sinterklaas, its abrasive consonants and spiky vowels buffed to an American drawl, it was adequately different for the relaunch but sufficiently unchanged to retain an echo of the former self he was loath to relinquish. A managed evolution was what the man now known as Santa Claus was attempting as the nineteenth century gathered momentum.

Appearance was another matter. It was plain, wherever Santa was headed, that episcopal robes and stole, miter and crosier would not be traveling with him. The figure that Washington Irving and Clement Clarke Moore, Santa's literary midwives, had eased into the world was no longer a servant of the church. Their influential overlapping prototypes had clearly set out to defrock him, even though they continued to refer to him as St. Nicholas. Irving gave Nicholas, or at least his figurehead, an all-season sartorial style: a low-brimmed hat, with Flemish trunk hose or breeches. Moore's prescriptions demanded something more practical, a durable and warm outfit for descending chimneys in the depths of a New York winter. He dressed Santa in warm furs; these, as the poem noted, were grimed with soot, which lent their wearer a peddler's shabby appearance. To their evocations Irving and Moore both added a pipe. They also kept the beard but freed it from ecclesiastical constraint so that it grew increasingly unkempt.

With these disparate prompts "Santa Claus, or, St. Nicholas," as an influential 1841 New York woodcut described him, began feeling his way toward a new dress code. In the woodcut, he was dressed in a sensible

SANTA CLAUS, OR, ST. NICHOLAS, IN THE ACT OF DESCENDING BROTHER JONATHAN'S CHIMNEY ON NEW-YEAR'S EVE

The 1841 woodcut. (Courtesy American Antiquarian Society)

padded pea jacket as he began a chimney descent from a snowy rooftop. More decorative was his hat, which rose to harlequins' peaks fore and aft.

Theatrical contrast was evident from Santa's earliest manifestations, sometimes achieving heights of vaudeville flamboyance. The life-sized model of the "mysterious chimney friend 'Chriscringle'" that drew great crowds to Parkinson's Confectionery in Philadelphia in the same year as the woodcut was dressed in "striped pants and stockings, and flying doublet; a tasseled cap on his head." In an 1848 illustration, which had him in a thick knee-length coat over waistcoat and breeches, with a warm astrakhan pushed low on his head, Santa's practical side was back to the fore.

Santa's sartorial uncertainty was most tellingly demonstrated by the intrepid souls who pioneered his live impersonation. At the decorative extreme was one who appeared at a New York ball in the mid-nineteenth century wrapped in "an ample cloak of scarlet and gold." Another, "Sinti Klass," was sighted in Albany in 1848, wearing a tricorn hat and silver-buckled shoes and smoking a long pipe tied with orange ribbons. But in 1864 a woman wrote from Michigan how she had "often heard Santa Claus described, but never saw the old fellow in person"—until that year.

Her Santa wore a plain coat of buffalo hide in the manner of the common huckster, just as Clement Clarke Moore had evoked him, but with a surreal twist when viewed from behind; of "presents fastened on his coat-tail."

It must have been a singular sight; clearly, they did things differently in Michigan. Back in New York, Santa had long since worked out how to carry his presents. True, there had been earlier uncertainties on this score, notably from Washington Irving, whose Santa had drawn gifts from "his breeches pockets." The problem was all but resolved by the time of Moore's poem which described Santa's "bundle of toys he had flung on his back." By the 1841 woodcut, the "bundle" on Santa's back had visibly clarified into a sack that contained among other toys a sword, windmill, racquet, and horse—an arrangement that would serve him, except in odd-ball Michigan, to the present day.

The sack was a telling detail, for delivering defined Nicholas; and the nature of his cargo went to the heart of the man. It was in this regard that Santa had strayed furthest, it seemed, from his roots. In the days of his December 6 distributions, the fruits and cookies had served as symbolic evocations of his original act of charity. It was in the regrettable way of things that token knickknacks should have given way to sacks of expensive toys for the affluent, straining the old association with purses of gold beyond repair. Where Nicholas had found his very meaning in serving the needy, the emerging Santa favored the better addresses, as Susan Warner observed in her influential 1854 children's story *Carl Krinken: His Christmas Stocking*: "It may be noted as a fact," she wrote, "that the Christmas of poor children has but little of his [Santa's] care . . . in general, Santa Claus strikes at higher game—gilt books, and sugar plums, and fur tippets and new hoods, and crying babies and rocking horses and guns, and drums, and trumpets—and what have poor children to do with these?" It was not Nicholas' generosity that Santa had mislaid so much as his moral judgment; his largesse had gone astray.

It was hard to believe that a man who had served as a charitable model through the ages would abandon relief drops to indulge wealthy children. Instances of practical aid had characterized St. Nicholas—not only dowries, but timely interventions to prevent executions, prison visits to the falsely accused, sea rescues, the delivery of a grain cargo to the famine-struck citizens of Myra—and all those examples of material assistance in Russia which had caused him to be known as Ugodnik, the Helper. The words from St. Matthew's gospel—"I was hungry, and ye gave me meat: I was thirsty, and ye gave me drink: I was a stranger, and ye took me in: naked, and ye clothed me: I was sick, and ye visited me: I was in prison, and ye came unto me"—might have been written for Nicholas. His great strongholds, as if in thrall to the saint's influence, laid a singular stress upon charitable provision. Under his patronage, the Byzantines developed renowned public hospitals and poorhouses, old peoples' homes and orphanages. The Venetians had their numerous *scuole,* the trade guilds, which devoted energy and resources to charitable work. Dutch standards of social provision were admired throughout the world. The Amsterdam madhouse was visited by an Englishman in 1662 who commented on its separate cubicles and interior garden as "being so stately that one would take it to be the house of some lord." Great social prestige was attached to the administration of charity. The Amsterdam civic authorities commissioned a series of paintings in 1626 that represented their officers registering eligible paupers, distributing bread and clothing, and visiting a poor family at home; self-congratulatory in intention though these images were, it was Nicholas they truly acknowledged.

"Three Daughters" had enjoyed a specific exemplary influence. In *Piers Plowman,* the fourteenth-century English poet Langland enjoined rich merchants to give their wealth to, among other causes, "help maidens to marry or make them nuns." The provision of dowries for orphaned girls was a particular focus of charitable work across Christendom; dowries not only saved poor virgins from poverty but, in a direct lift from Nicholas, also protected their virtue from prostitution. In medieval Spain, charitable funds were often raised by guilds or confraternities formed by local aristocrats and merchants. One testament, dated 1389, commanded a cousin "to look for four poor virgins in Zamora for God and for the souls of my father and mother and brothers" by finding them husbands and supplying dowries donated from his estate. One such Zamora confraternity, which took it upon itself to dower young women, was called the Cofradia de San Nicolas. The claims of the various applicants were considered; the winner was duly married to a suitable husband on St. Nicholas Day in the local church. "Three Daughters" had continued to work as an effective example for centuries; then Santa Claus unceremoniously junked it by relocating from charity into luxury goods.

The truth was, Nicholas had always had another side, and to this Santa had remained perfectly constant. The Patara dowries were unconditionally given, but Nicholas was at once a man of the marketplace who understood that strikingly different rules obtained in commercial circles. To dispense money, one first had to make it. The works of the Venetian *scuole,* the Amsterdam authorities, and the Spanish confraternities—the orphanages, public hospitals, and schools, the poorhouses and dowries— were funded by wealth that derived from trade. And attaining prosperity in trade required settlement on every delivery: the price must be met. Without trade, there would have been no gold to redeem the three girls of Patara.

Nicholas had known that this was low-lying moral ground, complexly contoured and prone to exploitation, ever since fifteenth-century Lombard pawnbrokers adopted the three globes, that unsullied motif of his charity, to signal their rather more conditional provision of funds from the façades of their seedy City of London premises. It was equally characteristic that the most prominent nineteenth-century New York building to bear Nicholas' name was not a church or a mission building, an almshouse or an orphanage but the city's six-hundred-room St. Nicholas Hotel, built during the 1850s on Broadway, with walnut wainscoting and frescoed ceilings, gas-lit chandeliers and central heating, the most luxurious hostelry of the age.

From these dubious associations Santa discerned what should first be his duty; to restore to himself something of the influence Nicholas had once wielded. He had taken his devotional percentage on every cargo, human and material, safely delivered to the Old World's quaysides, and grown prosperous on the votive offerings that collected in his waterfront chapels. Banishment from the docks of the New World meant he must start from scratch, reapplying that delivery know-how with a ruthless commercial focus. And so to the 1841 woodcut, which demonstrated its iconographic mileage when it was customized by a shop in Albany the following Christmas. The woodcut's new caption read: "Santa-Claus in the act of descending a chimney to fill the children's stockings, after supplying himself with Fancy Articles, Stationery, Cutlery, Perfumery, Games, Toys &c at Pease's Great Variety Store, No 50 Broadway, Albany." The image itself had been reworked in a single significant regard. On the base of Santa's sack the words "From Pease's 50 Broadway" had been stenciled. Santa had just signed up to his first endorsement.

By the mid-nineteenth century, Santa had begun to acquire an unstoppable momentum. His became a staple image in the New York–based magazine *Harper's Weekly*, which had a circulation of over 200,000 copies by 1860, largely because it was one of the first American magazines to include illustrations. It was typically fortuitous that these illustrations, as influential as the first daguerreotypes twenty years before, should so regularly have been of Santa, a favorite subject of the German émigré cartoonist Thomas Nast, who drew him for numerous Christmas issues of *Harper's* between 1862 and 1886.

In 1863, Nast dressed his *Harper's* Santa in the Stars and Stripes as he distributed presents to Union soldiers; Nicholas, not one for missing out on history's moments, left his mark on the Civil War. That Santa took to the outfit seems to indicate that he was still to settle upon a uniform of his own; one reason he remained open to sartorial suggestion was that *Harper's* was published in black and white. Popular perception tended to dress Santa in a wide-ranging palette. No particular color scheme predominated, though Nast had his own ideas, envisaging the furs in which he usually portrayed Santa as tan-colored.

That all changed in 1869, when a book edition of Nast's Santa illustrations was published using a newly developed color printing process. The new processes did not think much of brown, preferring show-off tones, so Nast put Santa in red. The color was clearly established by 1913, when a letter to *The New York Times* asked: "What anarchist started the notion that Santa Claus should wear red? One would think, as a resident of the North Pole, he should wear the white fur of polar bears." The same newspaper was able to describe Santa Claus' general look as "almost exactly standardized" by 1927, with "red garments," a "hood and white whiskers," "the pack full of toys, ruddy cheeks and nose, bushy eyebrows and a jolly, paunchy effect." A century after his initial emergence, Santa had finally settled upon an outfit, at once efficiently insulated and flamboyant, which confirmed the original instincts of both Irving and Moore.

Nast also reinforced another Santa trait that the two writers had noted; an outward joviality that had never been evident in the saint. There was also the rapidly expanding girth; it was clear that Nicholas had taken to his new role with relish. This was no surprise, for riding the wave of the burgeoning American Christmas was an exhilarating business. Santa made the elaborately dressed windows of the high street his own before going live in the stores; Macy's of New York had the first living in-store Santa in 1862, while the first to actively engage with the visiting children was credited to a Brockton, Massachusetts, store in 1890. Then there were the Norman Rockwell Christmas-edition covers on the weekly *Saturday Evening Post* from 1916, iconic images that would go on to enjoy afterlives as reproductions on everything from poster prints and Christmas baubles to drinking glasses. The Thanksgiving parades were not long in following. The Macy's Thanksgiving Day Parade, first held in 1924, began with live animals borrowed from the Central Park Zoo but would in due course make its name with huge helium balloons of Felix the Cat, Mickey Mouse, Superman, Snoopy, and the like. These were no more than warm-up acts for the main event, the triumphal entry into the city of Santa Claus on a sleigh drawn by eight reindeer, attended by elves and toy soldiers, and watched on street and screen by many millions of Americans. The year 1937 saw the opening in New York of a Santa school whose students were trained in showmanship, toys, and child psychology. And in 1946 one of the world's first theme parks opened as Santa Claus Land in the town of Santa Claus, Indiana, which had been named back in 1852 in the judicious belief that it would at least keep the postmaster in work.

Santa had proved an enormous success among Americans; it was striking how closely he had mirrored the achievements of St. Nicholas though their worlds lay centuries apart. The truth was that *Harper's* and hagiographies, parades and saints' plays, Coke ads and frescoes served the same purpose in those different worlds. Santa and saint had always been interested in the same thing, which was to spread their names among the widest audiences. It was true that they had come to be associated with different values, but they still shared an essential notion of generosity that was the core of their appeal to children and their parents alike. The old ascetic gods had eased the woes of this life by promising a better one beyond, an arrangement Nicholas and Santa effortlessly improved upon by filling the one life with goodies on an annual basis. The difference between the two was that Santa was able to provide a great deal more than was his saintly forebear. His world thronged with presents that went way beyond fruits, nuts, and gingerbread. He was able not only to awaken a new appetite but to feed it. It was Santa's great good fortune, and the source of his runaway success, that the gifts had just gotten a whole lot better.

Santa had built on these advances back in 1931, when he entered a strategic partnership with Coca-Cola. The drinks giant had a problem with its product; Coke, though widely admired for its thirst-quenching properties, tended to suffer a sales fall-off through the winter season. It also had a problem with the law, which forbade it from advertising directly to the under-twelves who were of particular interest to the company. On both counts—winter and children—there was only one person to turn to.

Coke's Santa ads, illustrated by Haddon Sundblom, have achieved iconic status. In them, Santa appears among all the elements of his cult—prancing reindeer, sleeping children, presents, fireside stockings, children's letters—along with the notable addition of portly fridges. These stand open, revealing yellow-lit interiors stocked with ribbed Coke bottles. Santa does the drinking, as per the contract, but there is no doubt what the awestruck child in his arms would be doing if he weren't in such a restrictive advertisement.

It was clear that Coke benefited from Santa's enormous popularity. As for Santa, the deal put Coca-Cola's global resources—and far-flung billboards—at his disposal. He had the world in his sights; Coke would get him there. The condition was that he drink their product along the way. To no real harm; what was wrong with an American partnership set on conquering the world?

22

I T WAS TIME TO head north.

Anna and Lizzie had never prepared so thoroughly. They had written the letters to Father Christmas as the holiday company had requested, and they had entrusted the letters' safe delivery to their parents. They had traced the route of their journey on the old family globe. They had said long goodbyes to their friends—they would be away *two nights*—and they had packed. They now stood in the airport terminal, glowing under fleeces, woolly hats, gloves, and scarves, which they would not remove for fear of jinxing a journey that they scarcely dared to believe in.

"You'll be quite hot on the plane," cautioned the elf in the red-tasseled hat at the check-in desk.

"She's right, you know," said Ash. At our knees two swathed heads shook in determined unison.

The man my daughters were on their way to see had been bursting his American seams ever since the late nineteenth century. He began looking for opportunities abroad, in the old manner. It was no surprise that England, the world power busy exporting itself across the seas, should have caught his practiced eye. Two centuries after the American turkey had led the way across the Atlantic, Santa set off for his own assault upon the English Christmas.

Nineteenth-century England had been experiencing a major Christmas revival. The 1840s saw the publication of Charles Dickens' influential *A Christmas Carol*, as well as the appearance of Christmas trees and cards. Gifts, in recognition of the festival's growing importance, were abandoning January 1 in droves for December 25. The English Christmas was vital to Santa's renaissance, and he would take particular personal satisfaction in acquiring it. When he took ship to Liverpool, London, and Bristol, where the dockside churches still bore his name, he had reconquest on his mind. The English, largely because the strong but Dutch echo of Santa's old name in his new one was inaudible to them, were slow to recognize the new arrival as a reversioning of their old saint, and blind to the awkward irony of his return three centuries after they had banished him.

Santa Claus first declared his English intentions by appearing on the card in a horse race, etymological testing ground if ever there was one, at Epsom in May 1861. Santa Claus ran in the Heathcote Plate, finishing outside the places, a performance that gave no hint of his subsequent progress on a wider stage. In the 1880s, one William Brockie, near Durham, Northumberland, wrote how he had heard mention of a puzzling Christmas phenomenon that he guessed to be a corruption of Santa Cruz, the Holy Cross. A painting in the Royal Academy's summer exhibition of 1879 made more sense to its viewer, who described it as showing "two little girls coming, half in awe, half in hope, to examine their shoes left overnight in the Christmas chimney corner for the gifts of Santa Claus." Mr. Edwin Lees claimed in the same year to have "only lately been told" of a custom gaining ground in the English counties of Herefordshire, Worcestershire, and Devonshire:

"On Christmas Eve, when the inmates of a house in the country retire to bed, all those desirous of a present place a stocking outside the door of their bedroom, with the expectation that some mythical being called Santiclaus will fill the stocking or place something within it before morning. . . . [T]he giggling girls in the morning, when bringing down their presents, affect to say that Santiclaus visited and filled the stockings in the night. From what region of the earth or air this benevolent Santiclaus takes flight, I have not been able to ascertain."

The English instead took Santa for a mutation of their eponymous personification of the season, the tankard-hoisting master of ceremonies who had presided over the Christmas festival there for centuries. The jolly Christmas, sere and bearded, gave no gifts but did tend to expect them. He was in the habit of offering greetings at people's doors, where he would receive food and drink for his troubles. Often crowned with holly leaves, he hosted the festivities and feastings laid on by the great houses and colleges. In a carol of the mid-fifteenth century he was referred to as Sir Christmas; he subsequently attracted the titles of Mister, Captain, and Prince. Ben Jonson made him the main character of a court entertainment, *Christmas His Masque*, in 1616, when he wore a high-crowned hat and long beard and carried a thick club and a drum. It was around this time that the corpulent spirit of the English season arrived, despite a Puritan clamp-down on his activities, at his final name: Father Christmas.

Under the Victorians, Father Christmas reemerged, bleary-eyed, to continue the seasonal party, much as an indulged grandfather might revive from his afternoon snooze at the party-favor-strewn dinner table, straighten his crumpled party hat, wipe brussels sprout traces from his chin, and resume the annual descent into his cups. He was a harmless tradition but a vulnerable one, frankly in no condition to defend his corner against the American who lay in wait. Santa Claus, having acquired match fitness in the course of fighting his way to Christmas preeminence in the States, recognized an English pushover when he saw one. The force was with the new arrival, who was soon to absorb the cheery sot of the season much as he had digested Nicholas of Sion, Kriss Kringle, and others who stood in his way. The whole process was effected with an effortless stealth. With a canny deference to local sensibilities, Santa adopted Father Christmas' name and even his costume, the fur-trimmed cowled gown, so that his brilliant Christmas coup went largely unnoticed by the English.

Back in America, Santa had arrived at the point in his expansion where proper premises were called for. In the early days, he had been content to arrive around Christmas from a nebulous elsewhere—sometimes from Spain, as the Dutch had it—or alternatively to be billeted in the city of his emergence. A Cincinnati newspaper in 1844 announced that "the sterling old Dutchman, Santa Claus, has just arrived from the renowned regions of the Manhattoes, with his usual budget of Nick-Nacks for the Christmas Times." Now he was in need of a dedicated center of operations. The truth was that the transcendent Santa could not be accommodated indefinitely by a city hardening into metropolitan fact. The northward push of New York's grids of streets from the 1830s soon transformed the sylvan groves and fields that Irving and Moore had known into rows of brownstones and slum tenements where noxious liquor dens, pawnbrokers, and flophouses sprouted. Hoboes, prostitutes and bootblacks, fortune tellers and Chinese vendors walked the streets. A New York residency insisted, besides, upon a real address, which meant convoluted explanations. Furthermore, a particular affection for one city over others, given the rivalries they cherished, might regionalize his appeal. The place he sought must be neutral, incapable of causing offense; it must be liable to inspire, with an aptitude for the fantastical; and it must suit his season, which meant Santa

must look north. Nowhere north was then more topical (nor was anywhere ever more north) than the North Pole.

Explorers had been picking at the complex and largely ice-bound to-
pography of Canada's fragmented north for hundreds of years. John
Davis and William Baffin had sailed for the fabled Northwest Passage in
1587 and 1616 respectively, putting their names to the frozen seas, islands,
and straits that lay beyond Greenland. The fur traders of the Hudson Bay
Company had voyaged overland to the northernmost edge of the American continent in the 1700s, tracking the shores of the polar ocean. In
search of a route to China, they could not know that they would also pre-
pare the way for Santa's relocation.

The high latitudes, that staple of Georgian art and literature, were already pressing like pack ice against the imagination when the British government in 1818 repeated its offer of £20,000 for the discovery of the
Northwest Passage. The great prize kick-started an age of Arctic exploration just at the time that Santa Claus was emerging and himself pushing
north into New England and beyond: the two cold-climate ideas were destined for entanglement.

Santa's original city was the terminus for a number of the expeditions
in pursuit of the prize. In 1825, the explorer John Franklin arrived in New
York at the start of his overland journey down the Great Bear River to the
delta of the Mackenzie River, close to Canada's northern border with
Alaska. He described his reception by the New Yorkers as "kind in the extreme" and put that down to "the lively interest they took in our enter-
prise." On his return in the summer of 1827, Franklin was enthusiastically
received by New York's scientific institutions. The city corporation showed
its appreciation of his achievement by presenting him with a reminder of
its own, a medal struck to commemorate the opening in 1825 of the New
York State–funded Erie Canal. The canal, which opened up the U.S. interior by connecting the Great Lakes with the navigable Hudson at Albany,
ran close to the coach route that Franklin had taken to and from Canada.
Years later, when Franklin and his men were lost in the frozen north during 1845, many of the forty expeditions raised to discover their fate set out
from New York and were funded by interests in the city, notably the two
expeditions sponsored by the financier Henry Grinnell in the early 1850s.

The Arctic regions spawned epithets during the nineteenth century:
Ultima Thule; the barren grounds; the frozen north. The North Pole was

particularly popular. Explorers heading on a general Arctic bearing were commonly described as having gone "out to the North Pole." A pair of Eskimos were exhibited at Tavistock, Devon, in 1837 as having "just arrived from the North Pole." The usage reflected the fact that the point at 90 degrees north remained so far beyond human reach as to be unimaginable. The term's correct geographical application was so rare that it was all but shelved in favor of an Arctic generalization, as inaccurate as it was evocative, for which there was considerably more call. The term would gain added currency (even as its actual meaning was further confused) when James Clark Ross located the North Magnetic Pole, the shifting point on the earth's surface where the magnetic field is directly vertical, on the west side of the Gulf of Boothia near Baffin Island in 1831.

It was characteristic of the age that the entire point of the expeditions should have become by the by; what interested the public was not the discovery of the Northwest Passage but the opportunity to wallow in the romantic aesthetics of the Arctic experience. The largely stolid explorer accounts by Franklin, Ross, William Parry, and others were consequently alchemized by the poetry of Samuel Taylor Coleridge, the Gothic romances of Mary Shelley and others, and the melodramas of Wilkie Collins as an alluring evocation of the frozen Sublime; landscapes beyond scale, translucent glaciers and growling bergs, the unearthly Arctic light, the frost-nibbled noses of the heroic explorers, the nourishment in old leather, the howl of the dogs, and the sheer plummeting weight of cold upon the mercury.

All this, then, was the North Pole. This evocative abstraction, protected from geographical actuality by its inaccessibility for much of the nineteenth century, was free to serve fancier flights; it remained the natural home of myth and fantasy. Hans Christian Andersen was drawn to it; the ice palace of his snow queen in the eponymous story, published in 1845, was situated "high up towards the North Pole." It was no surprise that Santa should have followed her lead.

The relocation had taken place by 1866, when Thomas Nast's Christmas image in *Harper's* included a winter scene captioned "Santa Claussville, N.P."; the initialized form confirms that the term "North Pole" was in wide circulation and may imply that Santa's residence there was not entirely unfamiliar even then. It was fleshed out in 1869 when the text for the color edition of Nast's illustrations was supplied by a children's poem called "Santa Claus and His Works." The poem's author, George P. Webster, wrote that

"Santa Claus's Route," *Harper's Weekly*, December 19, 1885. (© 2000 HarpWeek)

Santa's house during the long summer months was "near the North Pole, in the ice and the snow." "I told you his home was up north by the Pole," he duly continued before revealing the debt he owed Hans Christian Andersen: "in a palace of ice lives this happy old soul." Nast extended the North Pole residence, providing it with a toy workshop in his illustrations for *Harper's* from the late 1870s. Among Nast's drawings was a girl mailing a letter to "St. Claus, North Pole" in 1879. Another, in 1885, depicted two children tracing Santa's Christmas Eve migration route on a map from the North Pole to the United States; humankind would finally make this journey in reverse when Robert Peary crowned a succession of failed attempts by planting the American flag at the North Pole in April 1909.

Peary's achievement was a triumph of endurance and logistical organization. It was more admired, however, in American exploring circles than by the figure who had installed himself at the North Pole forty years earlier; on Santa, it had a thoroughly unsettling effect. For one thing, it finally did for the place in its free-ranging sense, which explorers closing on 90 degrees north had threatened to do for decades, by insisting on the restoration of its literal meaning. Sir Arthur Conan Doyle made the point to Peary in a speech he gave at a lunch in the explorer's honor, hosted by the Royal Societies Club in London the following year. "It was the grievance that explorers were continually encroaching on the domain of the romance writer," he declared amid much laughter. "There had been a time when the world was full of blank spaces, and in which a man of imagination might be able to give free scope to his fancy." Conan Doyle might have been speaking on behalf of Santa, who was stranded in a spot that could no longer be freely evoked but was thenceforth, as Peary had discovered, "very much the same as any other part of the frozen Arctic sea in appearance," a desolate and featureless expanse of scoured ice where only the wind blew.

This was not Santa Land. In the absence of evidence to the contrary, Santa had long since been settling himself among the more comfortable accoutrements—snowdrifts and trees, sleighs and reindeer—allowed under the comparatively liberal regime of the North Pole's former sense. The scenes in which he was represented provided a factually accurate, if undoubtedly Arcadian, reflection of settlement on the Arctic's semitemperate margins rather than at the uninhabitable pole. It was not a discrepancy that would pass unchallenged. The Finns were among those who had designs on Santa. They felt that the North Pole in its general Arctic denotation gave their nation as good a claim to territorial rights over him as anywhere else in the high latitudes. When they went public, on Finnish government radio in 1927, they pointed out that Finnish Lapland could provide, among other things, the pasturing for Santa's lichen-hungry reindeer that the North Pole patently could not. This alternative setting, obviously more appropriate, led the British and others, though not the Americans, to adopt Lapland as the home of Santa Claus. Indeed, it seems from the letter found by postal clerks in Glasgow in December 1927, and addressed to "Santa Claus, Lapland, North Pole," that the shift was already taking place. (The letter was found to be from a little girl in the Midlands who had asked Santa to please send an annual; Glasgow's gallant postal clerks saw to it.) These were the historical meanderings that had brought Anna and Lizzie, with some practical help from their parents, to the airport, where a flight to Ivalo in northern Finland awaited them.

It was not until we were over the North Sea that the girls began shedding their layers; the temperature in the cabin had finally overcome their reluctance to abandon sartorial solidarity with Santa. Anna took to scanning the window, where clear skies over Norway revealed the first snowscapes. Lizzie eyed a little girl across the aisle.

"We're on our way to see Father Christmas," she told her.

"So are we," the little girl countered.

"So are we," several others chorused. The realization that Father Christmas was to be shared among the entire flight silenced Lizzie before she rallied:

"What did you ask him for?"

A Barbie doll, came one reply. A PlayStation, came another. A new bike. Stickers. A coloring book. A guinea pig. A tiara.

Lizzie informed the plane that she had asked for chocolate coins. She knew no more perfect gift existed.

The setting sun flared and guttered over the Gulf of Bothnia. The snow fields of Finland, checkered with dark stands of pine, turned pink in the last light. The plane banked to face the long lit strip that ran between the ice-latticed forest. The cabin lights illuminated the rising runway, which threw a frosted swirl of ice particles into the plane's tumbled air stream.

We were putting on our coats when her vigil at the window brought a squeal from Anna. On the tarmac, led by a man in fur boots, stood a reindeer. The creature shook its head so that snowflakes danced around its antlers like summer midges. It then stood still, and a planeload of Brits fell momentarily silent. In that tiny silence something strange and unworldly seemed to be contained, until it was put to flight by "Jingle Bells," which burst from the plane's sound system. The spell was broken; what stood before us was *Rangifer tarandus,* a prolific herd ruminant with a range across much of sub-Arctic Siberia and Lapland, Canada, and Alaska. The species was notable for several facts: that its antlers were uniquely present in both sexes; that it favored continued movement (though not at this particular moment) as a means of enhancing the headwind to keep the blizzards of biting creatures at bay through the summer, and to seek shelter in the trees or to forage for lichens beneath the snow with the onset of winter; and, finally, that its impressive splayed hooves not only equipped it with a snow-shoe mobility across deep drifts but also developed a winter concavity to provide it with traction on icy ground.

Washington Irving had installed his all-season St. Nicholas in a horse-drawn wagon. It was not long afterward, however, that Santa turned insistently wintry; the haulage shift was almost instantaneous. The earliest reindeer reference, complete with sleigh illustration, appeared in the anonymous *The Children's Friend*, which was published in New York in 1821:

> Old Santeclaus with much delight
> His reindeer drives this frosty night.

The new arrangement was confirmed in greater detail the following year, when Clement Clarke Moore specified an octet of named reindeer in "A Visit from St. Nicholas."

John Franklin was acquainting himself in the ways of actual reindeer, commonly caribou, just as they began their legendary relationship with Santa. It was October 1820, and Franklin, on his first expedition to the Canadian Northwest, knew caribou chiefly by the meat and fur their hunted carcasses yielded the native Indians. He now began taking a naturalist's interest. On a short walk near the Coppermine River he saw "upward of two thousand" reindeer. He observed the gradual whitening of their coats in readiness for winter and noted how they always traveled against the wind. Franklin also mentioned a "much larger kind" of reindeer which was found in "woody parts of the country"; this was the woodland caribou, whose range was much farther south, into Ohio and New Hampshire, until the weight of human settlement pushed them north during the nineteenth century. The town of Lyndon, Maine, was renamed Caribou in 1877 on account of the sheer volume of the local herds. To the explorer from England, the reindeer might have been exotic, but New Yorkers would have known the animal as a staple of their upcountry cousins across much of New England.

It was tempting to imagine this same familiarity might have commended the reindeer to Santa as his choice of draft animal. It was certainly the case that sleighs took over from wagons and carriages with the first significant snowfalls across the American north, but reindeer did not step up to the traces. The "rein" in their name actually comes from the old Icelandic and has no connection with the English word and the domestication it implies. Reindeer domestication was actually restricted to the European and Russian Arctic, where the Saami and other peoples had used them for hundreds of years to haul tents and supplies, food and firewood. If local usage had been the deciding factor, Santa could have chosen from two draft animals of the American winter: to the north, the formidable Inuit huskies that would haul Robert Peary to the Pole; and farther south, in the settled areas, dependable old horses.

Lura Beam described the horse sleds of her 1890s childhood in her memoir *A Maine Hamlet*. She rode on her grandfather's blue sled into the winter woods, where he chopped birches for the stoves while she was put to work peeling their bark for canoes. In her description of her sleigh-driving grandfather, trace elements of Santa can even be detected: "In winter when he drove his sleigh over the snow, he wore a sealskin cap and a very heavy overcoat. A buffalo-fur robe lined with red flannel was tucked around him. A long, knitted scarf, shaded from rose to garnet, a piece of Grandmother's knitting, flew out behind him."

Nor were sleighs confined to rural districts, as an 1820s description of New York's Broadway indicates: "Painted sleighs, with scarlet cloth and buffalo skins, are dashing along in all directions at a prodigious speed; some with two horses abreast; others with four in hand. . . . The horses have a string of bells round; and in these fine moonlight nights I hear them dashing away long after midnight." Sleigh parties to dinners and dances at taverns outside the city were very popular among young adults.

In his account of traveling through the United States in 1818, John Duncan described the New York sleigh as "an open carriage on two runners, shod with iron, exactly like a pair of large skates. They skim along so smoothly that a horse will manage eight or nine miles an hour with great ease. As there is no rattling of wheels, to warn pedestrians of their approach, the horse carries, by law, a row of bells round his neck." Santa's sleigh bells were the traffic siren of their day. "Jingle Bells" celebrates the joys of horse-drawn sleighing and was written by a Boston minister in 1857 on the occasion of Thanksgiving; but it is evidence of the strength of the reindeer's claim that they have effectively taken possession of what has become a Christmas ditty, despite their and Santa's total absence from the lyrics.

The honored American sleigh heritages of horse and husky did not prevent them being passed over in favor of a creature that had never hauled except in far-off lands. It was clear that something else had commended the reindeer to that anonymous writer who first suggested them in 1821. I thought of the planeload of silenced tourists. The reindeer had a mythical quality, and one that clearly predated his association with Santa. The Saami and others had long revered the creature on which they depended for their survival; its furs provided warm clothes and bedding, its flesh nourishment, and it was also their transportation. They believed that the dead returned as reindeer. The reindeer had another quality, however, one that even suggested a higher, if wayward, consciousness; a tendency to seek out mind-altering substances. Reindeer have been commonly observed uncovering and ingesting fly agaric. This highly hallucinogenic and potentially poisonous fungus, with its red and white Santa livery, delivers a predictably severe disorientation but one which, studies suggest, the reindeer seems inclined to repeat. *Rangifer tarandus* is a hardy hauler adapted to winter extremes and crucially capable of finding its own nourishment; but what may have clinched the deal for Santa was that it was not entirely indisposed to the sort of trips he had in mind.

The more mundane explanation is that the writer was drawn to Europe's sleigh-puller as an aging device, in acknowledgment of Santa's pre-American origins. All that could be known was that the reindeer on the tarmac, as the holiday rep explained, had become perfectly accustomed to flash cameras.

We woke to the first thin inroads of light revealing the resort we had glimpsed during the darkness of the previous afternoon. Wooden chalets lined the snow tracks, their gables hung with icicle spikes. Beyond lay the forest where the upper branches were dipped in frozen icing and the trunks embedded deep in drifts. We dressed in the thermal suits the holiday company had provided and stepped outside. A thermometer read −20 Celsius; the snow compressed beneath our boots with a moistureless crump, and the inhaled air left a claggy lollypop coating in the mouth. In the nacreous light I watched the girls' faces crumple against the cold; but their eyes shone.

The sun had touched the horizon but would not rise above it; this was not daybreak, so much as the endless night at its shallowest. Over the next few hours we went husky sledding. We dropped fishing lines through holes in the ice of frozen lakes. We stood around birchwood fires in huts. We drank tea and rubbed warmth back into the girls' hands. We turned blocks of ice into rudimentary sculptures. We ate bowls of salmon stew. We tried making a snowman, but were foiled by the powdery snow. And all the time the girls waited. Dark had returned by the time the man came for us; he found us in a pile of spilled limbs at the foot of a toboggan slope. He gestured to a snowmobile and we wrapped ourselves in the furs that lay on the seats. Then he gunned the engine and drove into the black forest. A skein of frosted branches passed above our heads, and in the vast starlit chill the runners rasped over the snow, throwing up a glittering dust; I remembered that I had wished for this on the journey to Santa's Kingdom the year before. The machine carried us through the trees into a great darkness, which was finally pricked by a distant light. Beyond the light, others duly unfurled; flaming torches edged a winding track that led at length to a clearing. In the middle stood a hut with brightly lit windows and a smoke plume drifting from the chimney. A single reindeer was tethered to a tree; it had dug a hole with its nose where it foraged for lichen or perhaps for wilder nourishment. As we clambered from the snowmobile, the door of the hut swung slowly open to reveal a figure and I slipped an envelope to the driver, as I had been instructed.

"*It's Father Christmas,*" said Lizzie. We crunched through the snow to the hut, where Father Christmas invited us in with a sweep of his arm. We took in the rough-cut timbers hung with lanterns; the wood stove; the neatly made bed. Father Christmas gestured to the bench beside the candle-lit table before settling in the chair opposite. The bearded old man in red robes who sat before Anna and Lizzie was holding something in his hand. He began to speak in a thick Scandinavian accent.

"Now, girls," he said. "Let's see what you have asked for." He read out loud and had not got far—Anna's books, board games, and felt-tips, and Lizzie's skipping rope, tapes, and chocolate coins—when it dawned on Anna.

"That's your letter," she whispered, nudging Lizzie. "He got our letters."

"Chocolate coins," said Lizzie, in case that much was unclear.

Father Christmas finished the letters and folded them in his pocket, which he patted flat. "Now I know what you want for Christmas," he said. "And here's a little present in the meantime." He handed the girls each a toy reindeer. And then it was time to go; the driver was looking over his shoulder as he gunned the engine of the snowmobile.

"He had our letters!" shouted an exultant Anna as we left the hut behind. "He was the real one." Santa's Kingdom was exorcised; with what might have been her last chance, Anna had reached her true north. As for Lizzie, she wondered where she now stood in relation to the chocolate coins.

23

ON OUR RETURN FROM the airport there was an American voice among the messages on the answering machine.

"Ho ho ho," declared its prerecorded tones, "this is Santa from the North Pole and your name is on my list to receive a holiday at the magical kingdom of Disney, the beaches of Daytona, and the unbelievable sunsets of Fort Lauderdale. Santa will also give the first ten callers a special gift of a free cruise to the Bahamas! Call toll-free to receive your holiday and your free cruise. Your claim code is Santa."

"Who was that?" asked Ash. But the girls had trailed into the room, still radiant from their recent encounter in a starlit pine forest.

"Oh, just some phone pest offering supposedly free holidays," I replied, hurriedly pressing the Delete button. My choice of cover was instinctive; the unsolicited pitch had long since replaced the wrong number when it came to explaining away awkward calls. Not that the evasion was anything but innocent, as innocent as the innocence of my daughters which it was aimed at prolonging. Besides, it happened to be entirely accurate. Things had been going wrong with Santa, as he was increasingly known in England, for some decades now.

Lapland might have been a haven of Santa devotion, but it was set against a gathering backlash against the man, largely triggered by intrusions of the sort that the phone message typified in miniature. Using magazines, newspapers, TV, the Internet, and now the answering machine as his vehicles, he infiltrated every home in the weeks before Christmas to tout a bewildering range of products and services, which often extended far beyond the season's usual gift-giving frontiers; what lay beyond the Santa spiel, it transpired, was the offer of a time-share in a Florida condo. In coffee bars, in the playground at the end of the school day and down by the allotment could be heard the aggrieved whispers of parents, the antimaterialist and the merely broke, bemoaning the sheer volume of presents Santa seemed to have promised their children. The appetite Santa had awoken was dulled; it was even whispered that people had begun to sicken of Santa.

Widespread parental concern was reinforced by institutional unrest on an international scale back in 2002, when churches across German-speaking central Europe declared against the Weinhachtsmann, the Christmas Man, as he was known there. An organized insurrection broke out, with the distribution across parts of Germany, Austria, and Switzerland of stickers declaring Santa-Free Zones. The stalls of Vienna's outdoor markets were plastered with posters where Santa was bisected by a diagonal red bar. Volunteers persuaded shopkeepers to remove Santa Claus imagery in favor of the Christ child and of angels. The Conference of Bishops in neighboring Slovakia and the Czech Republic joined the movement with the oratorical pronouncement "Let us not allow the Christmas Man to replace Jesus." Another uprising simultaneously flared in Sydney, Australia, after a Christian day-care center decided that "Santa was taking the Christ out of Christmas."

The charge that Santa was guilty of undermining Christmas' Christian order had a specific substance in the German-speaking world. It was here that the Christkind, whom Santa had seen off in America, held sway over gift-giving. In many parts, particularly in the Protestant north, the pointedly angelic and gender-free Christkind was not given to making appearances; the only evidence of its visit were the presents stacked beneath the Christmas tree and the chime of the bell that traditionally marked its passage. In the southern city of Nuremberg, however, the local toymakers had long made tinsel angel dolls in commemoration of Christkind. It became the tradition that a local girl was chosen for the coveted role and dressed in a white robe, blond curly wig, and tall gold crown; by the twentieth century, she had assumed civic functions, visiting the city's schools and hospitals and reading stories to the children there, who provided her with their Christmas wish lists. Christkind had, however, acquired unsavory Aryan associations in the process; Nuremberg's Nazis under the mayor revived the city's lapsed traditions when they displayed a Christkind girl, alongside swastika flags, at the opening of the Christmas market in 1933.

The irony was that Santa, though he might be regarded as an intrusive American, actually boasted the older lineage here. He was the same individual, though evidently unrecognized, that Luther had moved against in the sixteenth century. The issue was further complicated by the fact that the original St. Nicholas had survived Luther's maneuverings, though not without injury. This meant the uncomfortable coexistence of Nicholas and Santa, with both claiming gift-giving functions. The original one, doubtless to accommodate the hagiophobic Protestants, had lost his sainthood and was celebrated as plain Nicholas, grave and episcopal, on December 6, when he brought the children traditional oranges, chocolate, and nuts. As for the proper presents, the ones that interested the children, they were under the distribution of Christkind at Christmas. Nicholas' continued existence meant that Santa's encroachment on the central European Christmas was regarded by many as plain greed, a brazen attempt to secure for himself an influential gift-giving festival when his better half already presided over one three weeks earlier. It was plain why he was not always welcome in these parts. The Christmas Man now seemed a pointedly neutral tag rather than a merely clumsy one. It served to keep him at arm's length, branding him an outsider.

Christkind, besides, was on home ground. It drew support from defenders of traditional Christmas culture as well as from the church, and so found itself far better equipped to compete with Santa than it had in America. The truth was that European trouble had been brewing for decades, originally with the French, who have a long history of defending their culture, notably their language and food, against outside incursions. Père Noël, as the French knew Santa, finally experienced the ultimate persecution that he had side-stepped many centuries earlier when he was burned in effigy outside the cathedral at Dijon in 1951, by chance the twentieth anniversary year of the Coke deal. "This spectacular execution," wrote *France Soir,* "took place in the presence of several hundred Sunday-school children. It was a decision made with the agreement of the clergy who had condemned Père Noël as a usurper and heretic. He was accused of paganizing the Christmas festival and installing himself like a cuckoo in the nest, claiming more and more space for himself." The Dutch Reformed Church in the Transvaal banned Santa Claus from Christmas church appearances in 1957.

Nor was that the extent of Santa's problems. The new millennium was to prove disastrous when he found himself taking fire on another front entirely. Having coped with central European conservatives who saw him as a cultural invader, he now had to deal with cosmopolitan liberals intent on creating ethnically inclusive Christmas cultures in what might be regarded as his Anglo-Saxon heartlands. In 2001, the township of Kensington, Maryland, banned Santa, who would normally arrive on a fire truck and join the mayor in the ceremonial lighting of the community Christmas tree, because some families in the community did not celebrate Christmas and felt excluded by him. Similar diktats appeared in Britain in 2004, with a number of major shopping centers in cities such as Birmingham banning his grotto on the pretext of sensitivity to "people of other religions over the festive period." To cap it all, the Internet ether was thick with Santa's anagrammatical associations. "Friend," urged one Web site, "don't glorify Satan by giving the glory and attributes of Jesus Christ to Santa Claus! Santa is a counterfeit God, and you are honouring Satan when you teach your children to believe in Santa." It now struck me what had caused us and thousands of others to make the journey to Lapland that year: Santa's magic had begun to fail in the wider world.

Santa had wandered into a sometimes wild cross fire of denunciations, and the charges that lay behind them grew more insistent as the twenty-first century broke: of self-interest, of soulless consumerism, and of pandering to a commercial monoculture. To all these charges Santa had left himself grievously exposed, not least by the ill-judged association with Coca-Cola. The patron of children had become stooge of the retailers who saw children as the marketplace's winter fuel, useful to stoke profits through the dark months. It was time to remind himself and the world, if he was not too late, what he really stood for.

There was no question that Santa's overwhelming commercial interests—he had a delivery empire, after all, to establish from scratch—had cast a deep shadow over his charitable renown during the nineteenth and twentieth centuries. But they had not blotted it out. It was easy to forget that Christmas had long been an occasion for helping the needy. In England it had been the tradition to acknowledge services supplied during the year by placing tips in the counter boxes provided, and this was not always done entirely willingly. "I shall be undone here with Christmas boxes," wrote the irascible Jonathan Swift in 1710. "The rogues at the coffee house have raised their tax." Over the 1800s, however, Christmas charity was broadly revitalized, not least by galvanizing works of literature including *A Christmas Carol* and Louisa May Alcott's 1868 novel *Little*

Women, whose famous opening scene depicts a family donating their Christmas breakfast to destitute neighbors. Charity became extremely fashionable in New York and London; and to this cause Santa Claus had tied his colors long before he committed to Coca-Cola. For every Santa coining it in American department stores, there was another on the street soliciting donations for the Salvation Army, a tradition that dates from the end of the nineteenth century and that bell-wielding Santas continue there today. The Santa Claus Association was founded in New York in 1914 to collect and act upon the letters addressed to Santa by the city's destitute children. The practice has recently been revived by Operation Santa Claus, which distributes the letters among the public who commit to meet the requests they contain.

In England, Father Christmas has an equally hectic philanthropic schedule. The Santa Claus Home for Crippled Children was established in Highgate, London, in 1881. The Santa Claus Fund was founded in 1894, when a group of young men set about distributing white muslin stockings that contained warm clothes, sweets, a toy, an orange, and a party favor to the houses of poor London children late on Christmas Eve. By 1905, the fund had fourteen branches and hundreds of volunteer workers who delivered more than 6,500 stockings annually. More recently, Santa Claus has visited the kids in foster homes and hospitals and has appeared at charity carol services. It had for some years been the custom of the Round Table charity in a number of towns, Bath included, to co-opt him for fund-raising evenings before Christmas and parade him around the town on an open-topped double-decker tour bus. I met up with the other volunteers on a frosty evening in a carpark where the throbbing bus, a tinsel ark with a Christmas tree flashing its lights on the upper deck, awaited us. A man called Mike was handing out yellow bibs and collection buckets.

"For those of you who are new to this," he said, "we work the front doors of the houses. When they answer, explain that we're collecting for the hospice appeal; that's to say, funding care for the terminally ill. You'll find people will be expecting us by the din from the sound system. Once we're done with a particular area, we'll ferry you to the next one, which means you'll need to be getting back on the bus. That covers everything, except that we need a Santa tonight."

I had intended a modest amount from that evening in late December;

bearing witness, in Santa's defense, that he remained true to his charitable beginnings, would have been plenty. Mike's words, however, sent the strangest feeling through me; and with it came the realization that the evening was about to be transformed. I had shadowed a man through seventeen hundred years; I might now become him merely by raising my hand. Was Santa's great journey to end at me? There were excellent reasons why I of all people might have passed up the chance. Following Santa was one thing; but playing him after a lengthy biographical immersion was surely to risk an inextricable fusion, with psychological consequences. Then there were the children, and the confusion I risked visiting upon them if a friend were to tell them what she had seen their father doing. So: I would do it.

"A volunteer at last," said Mike. "Here's the costume." Mike had called him Santa, but the costume I stepped into was traditional Father Christmas, a long red gown trimmed in white and topped with a cowl, along with the belt, an elasticized white beard, and the charity bell.

"That's it," said Mike. "And once we're under way, ring the bell and wave at the children. By the way, there's no slipping out of Santa halfway through the evening. And when it's over, the one thing you don't do is get out of the outfit until you're safely back out of sight."

Then I lifted the musty cowl, pinged the itchy beard into place, and went up the stairs of the bus.

Father Christmas took up position next to the Christmas tree. The bus turned off the main road into a residential street, slowing to a crawl. "White Christmas" blared from the sound system. The yellow-bibbed volunteers streamed from the bus and made for the front doors with their buckets. An old lady was the first to appear, waving at Father Christmas as she dug in her purse. And as he raised his arm to wave back and swung the bell in his other hand, he felt a suitably aged stiffness steal upon him. Curtains twitched, then drew back. Father Christmas had an excellent vantage point. He could see hob pots steaming through fugged-up kitchen windows, and grandparents arranged on sofas in living rooms, their wan faces caught in the flicker of the television. At the sound of the carols, they rose unsteadily and found their purses while their sons and daughters appealed to their partners for small change from the foot of the stairs. Parents grabbed babies from high chairs or hollered to the children in their rooms. Doors opened to glimpsed interiors: halls and stairways, where school bags and shoes lay discarded. Families gathered in the rectangles of light, framing themselves to wave and lifting the limp wrists of the infants in their arms. At the upstairs windows, mothers drew back the curtains and pressed their babies close to the glass. Through one window, a man's slack bottom was hurriedly lowered into a pair of pants, and Father Christmas allowed himself a smirk in the knowledge that his beard concealed it.

It was not long before Father Christmas was waving constantly, to the houses on either side of the road, and to the families along the pavement who were trailing the bus up the street. He was so busy, what with all the waving and ringing and bobbing to the rhythm of the carols, that he barely noticed the propped plastic and paper representations of himself which had become a Christmas staple in many of the fairy-lit windows. He did find time, however, to register a less familiar sight: he was not always alone in those windows. Of late, he had been increasingly aware of an upstart white figure leaving the decorative sidelines, to the point of trespassing on his Christmas territory. He must keep a sharp eye on the snowman. Now, however, was not the time to worry about what was merely the latest in a long series of challenges, and one that could hardly compare with what he had been through. Now was Father Christmas' time, and it felt good. He clanged the bell with fresh enthusiasm. Everybody was waving at him. Parents and children were smiling, and swaying to the sound of "Jingle Bells." An elderly lady even blew him a kiss. All that devotion and persecution, and he had finally come to this: smiles and kisses in an English suburb. Only now did he realize—after all the churches and icons, the prayers, the shrines and bonfires, the cargoes and the toyshops—how he had done more than merely survive or even flourish: his gift was to bring joy. He had contributed. This recognition finally gave meaning to every inch of his journey, with all its triumphs and reverses. It even made up for the itchy beard. It gave him new heart. He would win back those he had recently lost. He would see off the likes of the snowman. Perhaps he had finally arrived at the place where he might settle, with a bright-eyed child dandled on his knee. The bus rounded a corner, revealing the town beneath him blanketed in a stipple of tiny lights; there were worse places to be.

Then "Jingle Bells" ground to a halt and Mike said, "You can come down now." I made my way downstairs and threw off my costume. Volunteer faces were ruddy from the cold. They handed in their coin-heavy buckets; over three evenings, they had collected £1,070 for the hospice. Father Christmas had redeemed himself, and it was time to get home. Tomorrow was Christmas Eve.

24

A ND THEN, SANTA WAS no longer there. It was very sudden. He had
made himself so familiar that he might at least have given notice, just
as the birds gathered on the October wires. But with the last of his appearances he just went, slipping away without any of the fanfare, the parades and the grand openings, that had marked his arrival in the towns and
cities weeks before. One day he was there and the next he was not; and that
next day was Christmas Eve. Staff in the stores, the town squares, and the
hospitals fended off dangling tinsel and stepped among gift-wrapped cardboard cartons as they pulled the doors on his abandoned grottoes. Many
of them would leave work early, but Santa was not done. In fact, he had
never been busier. Christmas Eve merely marked the end of his visible
phase. He would not be seen in his defining act, just as he had once intended it at the window.

Even so, Anna and Lizzie could sense it: the clouds of frozen breath and
bobbing night lights, the laden sleigh and the reindeer straining at their
harnesses, and the elfin shouts that all was ready; and in a dark wood the
door of a hut, smoke wreathed about the chimney, opening as it had opened
to them some weeks earlier. They could feel that he was coming; besides,
a Web site showed him somewhere over a place called Indonesia, arcing
across the sky toward them. Their anticipation reminded me how I had
felt each time Ash's labor had begun; a loved one whom I already seemed
to know crossing vast distances toward an arrival.

At Christmas, I sometimes felt like the second man in the family. Certainly, it seemed that the girls were waiting for someone else. They had
done all they could to hasten his arrival, checking his progress across the
globe's orbed surface. They had opened the double window on the Advent
calendar; the baby Jesus, they said, though they seemed to wonder what he
was doing there. They had written more letters in the way of reminders,
which we would send up the chimney before bedtime. They had circled the

Vintage Austrian postcard. (Courtesy of St. Nicholas Center, www.stnicholascenter.org)

Christmas tree for one more look at the present pile and, though they had been warned off, gave inquisitive pokes to the ones which carried their names. They had put out a mince pie and a glass of sherry by the chimney. And they had laid out their stockings. Bedtime, if they could only be patient, would finally come around.

He came as they slept, as he had come to their parents; with pencils and notepads, stickers and oranges. And sacks of golden coins.

The author's name and the complete title are given with the first citation of any source. In subsequent mentions, works are cited by the author's surname; where the author is responsible for multiple titles, short forms are given. Full citations may also be found in the bibliography.

Chapter 1

4 **in the case of Nicholas:** Bernard Newman, *Tito's Yugoslavia*, 232.

Chapter 3

15 **"And going down to the metropolis":** I. Sevcenko and N. P. Sevcenko (trans. and eds.), *The Life of St. Nicholas of Sion*, 29.

20 **Charles Texier:** Charles Texier, *Asie Mineure*, 691.

20 **Hans Rott:** Hans Rott, *Kleinasiastische Denkmaker*, 324–42.

Chapter 4

25 **its brutal termination:** The persecutions began in A.D. 303, with Diocletian's decree that Christian services were to be banned, places of worship destroyed, and scriptures burned. An edict of A.D. 304 ordered all Christians to sacrifice the pagan gods. After Diocletian's death, the persecutions in the East continued under Galerius until A.D. 311.

25 **Eusebius evoked willing Christians:** Eusebius, *The Ecclesiastical History*, vol. 2, Bk. 8, 263, 271, 275.

26 **Tertullian:** a Carthage theologian, Quintus Septimius Florens (c. A.D. 160–220), quoted in John McManners, *Illustrated History of Christianity*, 43.

28 **Only the restorers could answer that question:** By 2005, the restorers at Demre had identified fragments of what they took to be the missing fresco. It appeared to show a person lying on a bed, with another figure in a red tunic standing beside the bed.

28 **it was left to Symeon:** Symeon, known as Metaphrastes, was a principal compiler of saints' lives during the late tenth century.

28 **A prosperous nobleman:** Symeon's account of "Three Daughters" appears in Charles W. Jones, *St. Nicholas of Myra, Bari and Manhattan,* 53–57.

29 **Cyprian of Carthage:** Thascius Cyprianus. See Robin Lane Fox, *Pagans and Christians,* 14–15.

29 **Ignatius, the bishop of Antioch:** Brian Moynahan, *The Faith,* 111.

29 **Carthage once again exemplified Christian charity:** Jonathan Sumption, *Pilgrimage: An Image of Medieval Religion,* 251.

Chapter 5

31 **a ship carrying St. Paul:** Acts 27: 5–6.

32 **the natural point of final departure:** "The harbour of Myra seems to have been the great port for the direct cross-sea traffic to the coasts of Syria and Egypt. It was the seat of the sailors' god to whom they offered their prayers before starting on the direct long course, and paid their vows on their safe arrival." W. M. Ramsay, *St Paul the Traveller and Roman Citizen,* 298.

32 **"I knew enough of Greek navigation":** Alexander Kinglake, *Eothen,* 61.

33 **"hung up like a barometer":** ibid., 64.

34 **He made two sixth-century pilgrimages:** Sevcenko and Sevcenko, 31, 51.

35 **D. E. Colnaghi:** C. R. Newton, *Travels and Discoveries in the Levant,* appendix.

35 **Colnaghi witnessed pine logs:** ibid., appendix.

Chapter 6

37 **a French officer:** Texier, 690.

38 **Texier had disembarked at Andriake:** Texier, 691.

38 **the British writer Freya Stark:** Freya Stark, *The Lycian Shore,* 149.

39 **Symeon introduced Nicholas' childhood:** Jones, 49.

39 **Jacob of Varazze:** Jacobus de Voragine (c. 1230–1298), archbishop of Genoa and author of the *Golden Legend,* dated c. 1260.

42 **"In a short time":** Jones, 52.

Chapter 7

48 **"When he came to the very advanced age":** Jones, 65.

48 **"marble tomb":** William Granger Ryan (trans.), the *Golden Legend,* vol 1, 25.

49 **A Phoenician wreck found off Kaş:** Artifacts from the site are displayed in the Uluburun wreck hall, St. Peter's Castle, Bodrum.

49 **Christians first began visiting:** For early pilgrimages to the Holy Land, see Stephen Runciman, *A History of the Crusades,* vol 1, 38.

49 **Bishop Melito of Sardis:** Sumption, 89.

50 **"the river of his baptism":** quoted in ibid., 89–90.

51 **The Bordeaux pilgrim:** See A. Stewart (trans.), "The Bordeaux Pilgrim," *Itinerary from Bordeaux to Jerusalem.*

51 **the first archaeological investigations:** See Shigebumi Tsuji (ed.), *Survey of Early Byzantine Sites in Olu Deniz Area, First Preliminary Report.* I am also indebted to David Price Williams for giving me access to his unpublished notes on the Gemiler ruins.

54 **visits to Symbola:** Sevcenko and Sevcenko, 91.

54 **bishop of nearby Pinara:** ibid., 103.

Chapter 8

58 **Its two basilicas were dedicated:** The lower church at Levisi is variously dedicated but the Orthodox community on the Greek island of Kastellorizo, which has strong historical links with Levisi, knows it as belonging to St. Nicholas.

Chapter 9

63 **St. John the Russian:** Renée Hirschon, *Crossing the Aegean,* 186.

63 **their revered St. Gregory:** ibid.

66 **Justinian's historian Procopius:** Jones, 12–13.

67 **as many as twenty-five over the centuries:** See Raymond Janin, *La Géographie Ecclesiastique de l'Empire Byzantin.* Part 1, vol. 3: *Les Eglises et les Monastères,* 381ff.

67 **a Russian archbishop visiting:** Anthony, archbishop of Novgorod. See W. R. Lethaby and Harold Swainson, *Sancta Sophia Constantinople: A Study of a Byzantine Building,* quoted in Laurence Kelly (ed.), *Istanbul, A Traveller's Companion,* 81.

68 **St. Euphemia:** Euphemia of Chalcedon, martyred A.D. 305. Her relics lie in the St. George Chapel of the Ecumenical Patriarchate, Istanbul.

71 **a *podvoriye*:** Owen Matthews, "Dome from Dome: The Russian Churches of Karakoy," *Cornucopia,* vol. 5 (2003), 76–91.

73 **When Russian merchants and traders:** One version has it St. Nicholas was first introduced to the Russians by Myra shipwrights sent to work in the Russian shipyards.

73 **Novgorod on the River Volkhov:** Fitzroy Maclean, *Holy Russia,* 272.

73 **at Pskov . . . on the Kamenka at Suzdal:** ibid., 283–85.

74 **At Yaroslavl:** ibid., 311.

74 **a common source of general assistance:** The St. Cassien story is recounted in Helene Iswolsky, *Christ in Russia*, 152–53.

Chapter 10

80 **abounded with Christians:** Walter F. Adeney, *The Greek and Eastern Churches*, 19–20.

80 **three hundred bishops:** Arthur Penrhyn Stanley, *Lectures on the History of the Eastern Church*, 93.

81 **"On that momentous occasion":** George Poulos, *Orthodox Saints*, St. Nicholas entry.

81 **"The admirable Nicholas":** Jones, 63

82 **Le Père de Bralion:** Barbier de Montault, *Revue de l'Art Chrétien*, vol. 26 (1883), 279.

Chapter 11

87 **"the most charitable and the best known":** Jones, 57.

89 **the chancel arch of an island church:** Karja Church, Saavemaa Island.

89 **basilica of St. Francis of Assisi:** an early-fourteenth-century fresco in the St. Nicholas Chapel called *St. Nicholas Throwing the Gold Bars to Three Poor Girls* (1300–1301), by Palmerino di Guido. See B. Kleinschmidt, *Die Wandmalerei der Basilika San Francesco in Assisi* (Berlin, 1930), fig. 115.

89 **Lippo Vanni:** documented as painter and illuminator in Siena between 1344 and 1375.

89 **Agnolo Gaddi:** 1369–96. The 1380s fresco is in the Castellani Chapel, Church of Santa Croce, Florence.

89 **Paolo Veneziano:** influential early-fourteenth-century Venetian painter. In the Contini Bonacossi Collection, Uffizi, Florence.

89 **Ambrogio Lorenzetti:** Sienese artist active between 1319 and 1347, whose *Scenes of the Life of St. Nicholas* was painted circa 1332. At the Uffizi, Florence. Another rendering of "Three Daughters" by Lorenzetti is at the Louvre, Paris.

89 **Gentile da Fabriano:** Ca. 1370–1427. *St. Nicholas and Three Poor Maidens* was painted in 1425. At the Pinacoteca Vaticana, the Vatican.

89 **Masaccio:** Florentine painter, 1401–1428. The painting was included in the altarpiece of the chapel of St. Julian at the church of Santa Maria del Carmine, Pisa. At the Gemaldegalerie, Berlin State Museum.

89 **Lorenzo di Bicci:** Florentine artist, ca. 1350–ca. 1427. At the Metropolitan Museum of Art, New York.

89 **Fra Angelico:** 1387(?)–1455. The painting, originally part of the altarpiece at the chapel of San Niccolo in the church of San Domenico, Perugia, is at the San Marco Museum, Venice.

89 **Fra Filippo Lippi:** 1406–1469. The scene was painted at the Martelli chapel at San Lorenzo Church, Florence, date unknown.

89 **Lorenzo di Pietro:** Di Pietro, also known as Il Vecchietta, lived from 1410 to 1480. At the Diocesan Museum, Pienza.

89 **Francesco Pesellino:** Florentine painter, 1422–1457. At the Casa Buonarotti, Florence.

89 **Gerard David:** Dutch painter, ca. 1460–1523. *Three Legends of St. Nicholas* is at the National Gallery of Scotland, Edinburgh.

Chapter 12

93 **the ceiling paintings were extravagantly rococo:** They were the work of Charles Rosa of Bitonto between 1661 and 1673.

94 **a beautiful Norman basilica:** Charles Homer Haskins, *The Normans in European History* (241), calls the basilica "that great resort of Norman pilgrims."

96 **Bari's archbishop, Andrew:** The defection is described in Richard Fletcher, *The Barbarian Conversion from Paganism to Christianity*, 298, and in T.M.P. Duggan, "*Conversion of Archbishop in 1066 Inspires Theft of St. Nicholas' Bones?*"

97 **ancient taboos:** see W. M. Ramsay, *Cities and Bishoprics in Phrygia*, vol. 2, 497.

97 **Revelation:** Revelation 6: 9–10.

98 **Theodoret of Cyrus:** Ca. A.D. 393–466; quoted in Sumption, 28.

98 **manna, ambrosia:** Manna in this context derives from the honeylike substance exuded by the manna-ash tree (fraxinus orsus) and traditionally harvested in Greece. Ambrosia was the life-giving drink and anointing oil of the Greek gods.

98 **Barbier de Montault:** de Montault, 296–308. Katherine Hooker, *Through the Heel of Italy*, 93, describes the liquid as having "a nauseous taste suggesting brown sugar and water."

99 **holy earth:** F. W. Hasluck, *Christianity and Islam under the Sultans*, vol. 2, 671–72.

99 **the preparation of his corpse:** In John 19: 39–40, "a mixture of myrrh and aloes, about an hundred weight," is brought to embalm Christ. And wine mingled with myrrh is offered to Christ on the cross in Mark 15: 23.

100 **"The town of Makri":** *Pilgrimage of the Russian Abbot Daniel in the Holy Land 1106–1107*, 6–7.

101 **the greatest saint in the hierarchy:** Anna Comnena, *The Alexiad*, book 10, 255, 258.

101 **Caliph Hakim:** Sumption, 133.

Chapter 13

103 **a Bari clerk named Nicephorus:** Nicephorus' Bari translation account appears in Jones, 176–93.

104 **Charles Texier:** Texier, 691, refers to "three or four monks" in 1836.

106 **halting the oxen:** C. Grant Loomis, *White Magic,* 56.

106 **St. Millan:** Sumption, 34.

106 **A Muslim fleet had tried to steal his relics:** The event is recounted by Theophanes (d. A.D. 818); see N. Sevcenko, *The Life of St. Nicholas in Byzantine Art,* 20.

108 **Perdicka, or Partridges:** Robert S. Carter, "A Turkish Exploration by Boat," various refs.

110 **The pope had convened a council:** Jones, 217.

Chapter 14

114 **a prime assembly point:** For the Crusaders at Bari, see Runciman, vol. 1, 154.

115 **"many took the shorter route":** Jones, 220.

115 **"his excessive love for the blessed confessor Nicholas":** ibid., 211.

116 **William the Conqueror:** Adrian De Groot, *St. Nicholas: A Psychoanalytical Study of His History and Myth,* 33.

116 **"to the memory of Nicholas":** Comnena, book 4, 105.

117 **one liturgical statement:** Francis Dvornik, *Byzantine Missions Among the Slavs,* 241.

117 **insecure prison transfer:** Iswolsky, 150.

117 **in a frigate:** T.A.B. Spratt and E. Forbes, *Travels in Lycia,* 126.

117 **They were duly installed at St. Nicholas' Cathedral:** It is not known what subsequently became of these relics.

118 **he laid an image of St. Nicholas:** Harmon Tupper, *To the Great Ocean,* 85.

Chapter 15

123 **Martino da Canale:** John Julius Norwich, *Venice: A Travellers' Companion,* 117–18.

124 **"so sweet that had all the spice shops":** da Canale, quoted in Norwich, *Venice: A Travellers' Companion,* 118.

124 **"Mark is moving":** ibid., 118.

126 **St. Nicetus:** Or Nicetas. Sir Ashley Clarke, *Restoring a Venetian Church,* 1150.

126 **the acquisition from Montpellier of St. Roch:** Jan Morris, *Venice,* 162.

126 **Flaminio Corner:** quoted in Norwich, *Venice: A Travellers' Companion,* 118–19.

127 **"The History of the Translation of the Great St. Nicholas":** *Receuil des Historiens des Croisades,* vol. 5. For a detailed French précis of the text, see preface, xlv–liii, and for the Latin text, 253–92.

130 **They soon breached the walls:** The fall of Constantinople is recounted in Gibbon's *Decline and Fall of the Roman Empire*, quoted in Kelly (ed.), 75.

132 **Sion did have an uncle:** Sevcenko and Sevcenko, 21, 23, 25, etc.

Chapter 16

136 **A Norman knight, William Pantulf:** Thomas Forester (trans.), *Ordericus Vitalis*, book 7, ch. 8, 395–97.

136 **The duke of Puglia:** Runciman, vol. I, 166.

137 **"brought us to Patara":** *Account of the Pilgrimage of Saewulf to Jerusalem and the Holy Land in the Years 1102–3*, 4.

137 **a French clerk at the Bari shrine:** *Receuil des Historiens des Croisades*, preface, lii.

137 **Carcere, Rome:** J.A.S Collin de Plancy, *Dictionnaire Critique des Reliques et des Images*, 215; and de Montault, *Revue de l'Art Chrétien*, 294.

137 **a chapel on the Ostian Way:** Chapel of the Church of St. Paul. Collin de Plancy, 215.

137 **Ventimiglia in Liguria:** Collin de Plancy, 215.

138 **Halberstadt, eastern Germany:** de Montault, 294.

138 **Gembloux, Belgium:** It is the church of St. Marie Evergete at Gembloux; see de Montault, 294.

138 **Heisterbach, near Köln:** Collin de Plancy, 215.

138 **Corbie, northern France:** The grand prior placed a finger of St. Nicholas there in 1333; see de Montault, 295.

138 **Soissons in Picardy:** St. Jean des Vignes; a fragment of St. Nicholas' arm, burned there in the sixteenth century. See de Montault, 294.

138 **Benevento, near Naples:** De Montault describes Nicholas' bones and fragments at other churches in the area, 295.

138 **Aarhus, Norway:** de Montault, 295.

138 **treasury of the Austro-Hungarian empire:** now at the Orthodox Patriarchate, Istanbul.

138 **a reliquary containing several more pieces:** now at the Antalya Museum.

138 **associated occupations:** See Jones, 269–75, and De Groot, 164.

Chapter 17

145 **London skeptics removed statues:** Eamonn Duffy, *The Stripping of the Altars*, 381.

145 **"utterly forbidden to make":** ibid., 400–401.

145 **"and not to repose their trust":** ibid., 407.

146 "scour candlesticks": John Bale, quoted in Thomas J. Heffernan, *Sacred Biography: Saints and the Biographers in the Middle Ages,* 13.

146 "sent over the seas": Bale, quoted in ibid.

147 "good for a salad": Wendelmoet Claesdr, quoted in Alastair Duke, *Reformation and Revolt in the Low Countries,* 24.

147 When a Delft priest abandoned Catholicism: ibid., 123.

148 "whole streets of that sort of ladies of pleasure": Norwich, *Venice: A Travellers' Companion,* 363.

148 "the nobleman determined to sell": Jones, 54.

148 "Justinian's consort Theodora": Procopius, *The Secret History.* Richard Atwater, trans., 48.

149 "men of years, benevolence and social standing": J. H. Browne, *Great Metropolis: Mirror of New York,* 537.

Chapter 18

151 The house, now a museum: It is the Museum Amstelkring, Oudezijds Voorburgwal 40.

152 Henry Machyn: John Gough Nichols (ed.), *The Diary of Henry Machyn,* 121.

153 Hospinian: John Brand, *Observations on the Popular Antiquities of Great Britain,* vol. 1, 419.

153 Thomas Naogeorgus: ibid., 420.

156 Amsterdam's magistracy passed a statute: Simon Schama, *The Embarrassment of Riches,* 184.

156 an insurrection of eleven-year-olds: ibid.

156 The modern chimney: Paul Oliver (ed.), *Encyclopaedia of Vernacular Architecture of the World,* vol. 1, 431.

Chapter 19

159 the *Unity* of the Dutch West India Company: The *Eendracht* (*Unity*) sailed two months before the *New Netherland,* although the latter is more commonly cited as the first settler ship to New Amsterdam.

159 a port on Haiti's northwestern corner: Jones, 326.

160 Not Nicholas' bones: Some relics of Nicholas were enshrined at St. Nicholas Church, Flushing, Queens, on December 5, 1972. See Edward B. Friske, *New York Times,* December 6, 1972.

160 "the goodly image of St. Nicholas": Washington Irving, *Dietrich Knickerbocker's A History of New York,* vol. 1, 75.

163 Catelyn Trico: Trico's deposition, given late in her life, is recorded in J. Brodhead and E. B. O'Callaghan (eds.), *Documents Relative to the History of the State of New York,* vol. 3, 49–51.

164 "simple woman" and "empty flourbag": Duke, 41.

165 to indicate where New Amsterdam's fort: Irving, vol. 1, 107.

165 a much earlier St. Nicholas Church: ibid., 120.

166 "a spacious room": Henri and Barbara Van der Zee, *A Sweet and Alien Land,* 15.

166 tax-free alcohol: ibid., 358.

166 the new church: Ellis H. Roberts, *New York: The Planting and Growth of the Empire State,* 48.

166 "two images on the mantelpiece": Van der Zee, 298.

167 part-time work as a symbol of New York's Dutch origins: Jones, 333ff.

167 And manufactured toys: Mary Audrey Apple, "German Toys in Antebellum America," *Magazine Antiques,* December 2002.

168 "four hundred and fifty kinds of Christmas presents": Stephen Nissenbaum, *The Battle for Christmas,* 134–35.

168 "drawing forth magnificent presents": Irving, vol. 1, 145.

Chapter 20

172 "A stream of presents": Quoted in Clement A. Miles, *Christmas in Ritual and Tradition,* 168.

173 "a bad custom": ibid., 230.

173 congregations in parts of Germany: ibid., 108.

173 At Crimmitschau in Saxony: ibid., 112.

173 the Polos had spoken of: Marco Polo, *The Travels,* book 1, chapters 13 and 14. The Magi's relics were subsequently recorded in Milan in 1162, when the city was stormed and the relics removed to Köln. There they currently reside.

174 Tuscans rang earthenware bells: "A Tuscan Christmas," from a correspondent in Florence, *The Times* (London), December 24, 1935.

176 of greater moment than his actual nativity: Miles, 20–21.

176 "a glass of cherry-bounce": Jones, 342.

176 "endless variety of European toys": Penny Restad, *Christmas in America,* 67.

177 "transferred the observance": "H.," "Custom Observed on the Eve of St. Nicholas," *Gentleman's Magazine,* May 10, 1827, 408.

177 "noted St. Nicholas, vulgarly called Santeclaus": Jones, 342.

178 a woodcut of St. Nicholas: Nissenbaum, 70.

179 "Left his lodgings": Quoted in full in Edwin G. Burrows and Mike Wallace, *Gotham: A History of New York City to 1898,* 417–18.

180 "the good St. Nicholas": Irving, vol. 1, 145.

180 Irving would add a typically Dutch wagon: In the 1812 edition, vol. 1, 106: "the good St. Nicholas came riding over the tops of the trees, in that self-same wagon wherein he brings his yearly presents to children."

182 "anniversary of St. Nicholas": *Rivington's Gazeteer,* Dec. 23, 1773; quoted in Jones, 333.

183 "the priviledge to breake open": Miles, 308.

183 "certain grave injuries": Dora Robertson, *Sarum Close,* 84.

183 "mortally wounded by the Vicar": ibid., 87.

183 "superstitious and childish observances": Brand, vol. 1, 428.

183 Foolish ceremonials, masquerades: Nissenbaum, 49ff.

184 "small white mask": Restad, 46.

184 "is too firmly riveted": Burrows and Wallace, 463.

Chapter 21

187 "Santa Claus, or, St. Nicholas": Nissenbaum, 170.

188 "mysterious chimney friend 'Chriscringle'": Restad, 144.

188 an 1848 illustration: The illustration appeared in the first book edition of "A Visit from St. Nicholas" (Nissenbaum, 79).

188 "an ample cloak of scarlet and gold": From the *New York Herald.* Quoted in Restad, 145.

188 a tricorn hat and silver-buckled shoes: Jones, 352.

188 "often heard Santa Claus described": Restad, 145.

189 "It may be noted as a fact": Susan Warner, *Carl Krinken: His Christmas Stocking,* 1.

189–90 The words from St. Matthew's gospel: Matthew 25: 35–36.

190 "being so stately that one": Jonathan Israel, *The Dutch Republic,* 358.

190 a series of paintings in 1626: Gary Schwartz, *The Dutch World of Painting,* 70.

190 "to look for four poor virgins": Maureen Flynn, *Sacred Charity: Confraternities and Social Welfare in Spain, 1400–1700,* 59.

191 customized by a shop in Albany: Nissenbaum, 171.

192 "almost exactly standardized": *New York Times,* November 27, 1927.

192 **Stars and Stripes:** *Harper's Weekly,* cover illustration, January 3, 1863.

193–94 **a strategic partnership with Coca-Cola:** Mark Prendergast, *For God, Country and Coca-Cola,* 181–82.

194 **Haddon Sundblom:** Barbara Charles and J. R. Taylor, *Dream of Santa: Haddon Sundblom's Advertising Paintings for Christmas, 1931–1964.*

Chapter 22

196 **by appearing on the card in a horse race:** "Sporting Intelligence, Epsom Races," *The Times* (London), May 29, 1861.

196 **William Brockie:** Jacqueline Simpson and Steve Roud, *A Dictionary of English Folklore,* 314.

196 **the Royal Academy's summer exhibition:** "Royal Academy Exhibition," *The Times* (London), June 2, 1879.

196 **"only lately been told":** *Notes & Queries* (5s: 11 [1879], 66), quoted in Simpson and Roud, 314.

196 **a high-crowned hat and long beard:** Phyllis Siefker, *Santa Claus: Last of the Wild Men,* 101.

197 **"the sterling old Dutchman":** Nissenbaum, 171.

198 **"kind in the extreme":** John Franklin, *Narrative of a Second Expedition to the Shores of the Polar Sea,* xviii.

199 **"out to the North Pole":** "State of the Army Before Sebastopol," *The Times* (London), May 3, 1855.

199 **"just arrived from the North Pole":** "Devonshire Superstitions," *The Times* (London), November 2, 1837.

200 **"Santa Claus and His Works":** The poem is reproduced in full in E. Willis Jones, *The Santa Claus Book,* 72–78.

200 **"St. Claus, North Pole":** *Harper's Weekly,* January 4, 1879.

200 **depicted two children:** "Santa Claus' Route," *Harper's Weekly,* December 19, 1885.

201 **"It was the grievance that explorers":** "Commander Peary on His Expedition," *The Times* (London), May 4, 1910.

201 **"very much the same as any other part":** "The North Pole. Commander Peary on His Journey," *The Times* (London), September 15, 1909.

201 **"Santa Claus, Lapland, North Pole":** "Kindly Postal Clerks," *The Times* (London), December 29, 1927.

203 ***The Children's Friend:*** *The Children's Friend: A New Year's Poem to the Little Ones from Five to Twelve.* New York, 1821.

203 **"Old Santeclaus with much delight"**: quoted in Jones, 349.

203 **"upward of two thousand"**: John Franklin, *Narrative of a Journey to the Shores of the Polar Sea in the Years 1819–22*, 214ff.

204 **"In winter when he drove his sleigh"**: From Lura Beam, *A Maine Hamlet*. Quoted in Charles and Samuella Shain (eds.), *A Maine Reader*, 302.

204 **"Painted sleighs"**: Hodgson in 1821, quoted in Jane Louise Mesick, *The English Traveller in America*, 86–87.

204 **"an open carriage on two runners"**: John M. Duncan, *Travels Through Parts of the United States and Canada in 1818/9*. Glasgow, 1823.

Chapter 23

208 **An organized insurrection:** "Austria Leads Festive Purge of Santas," *Sunday Times* (London), December 15, 2002.

209 **"This spectacular execution"**: Quoted in Claude Levi-Strauss, "Father Christmas Executed." In Daniel Miller (ed.), *Unwrapping Christmas*, 38–39.

209 **Dutch Reformed Church:** John Pimlott, *The Englishman's Christmas: A Social History*, 150.

210 **"people of other religions"**: quoted in "Now Do You Believe in Santa Claus?," the *Sunday Times Magazine* (London), December 12, 2004.

210 **"I shall be undone here"**: quoted in Nissenbaum, 110.

211 **Salvation Army:** ibid., 253.

211 **The Santa Claus Fund:** "Christmas and the Poor" and Mary St. Helier, letter to the editor, *The Times* (London), December 25, 1897, and November 12, 1906.

Adeney, Walter F. *The Greek and Eastern Churches*. Edinburgh: T. & T. Clark, 1908.

Anichkof, Eugene. "St. Nicholas and Artemis." *Folklore 5* (1894), 108–120.

Anrich, Gustav. *Hagios Nikolaos*. Leipzig, 1913.

Baynes, N. H. "The Supernatural Defenders of Constantinople." In N. H. Baynes, *Byzantine Studies and Other Essays*. London: Athlone Press, 1955.

Bean, George. *Lycian Turkey*. London/New York, 1978.

Beaufort, Francis. *Karamania: or a Brief Description of the South Coast of Asia Minor*. London, 1817.

Bond, Francis. *Fonts and Font Covers*. Oxford, Eng.: Henry Frowde/Oxford University Press, 1908.

"Bordeaux Pilgrim." *The Itinerary of the Bordeaux Pilgrim*. A. Stewart, trans. London: Palestine Pilgrims' Text Society. Vol. 5, 1887.

Boullet, F. and C. *Ex-Votos Marins*. Editions Maritimes et d'Outre Mer, 1978.

Brand, John. *Observations on the Popular Antiquities of Great Britain*, revised by Sir Henry Ellis. London, 1877.

Brodhead, J. and E. B. O'Callaghan, eds. *Documents Relative to the Colonial History of the State of New York*. Albany: Weed, Parsons, 1853–1858.

Brown, Peter. *The Cult of the Saints*. Chicago: University of Chicago Press, 1981.

Browne, J. H. *Great Metropolis: Mirror of New York*. Hartford, Conn.: American Publishing Co., 1869.

Burrows, Edwin G., and Mike Wallace. *Gotham: A History of New York City to 1898*. New York/Oxford: Oxford University Press, 1999.

Cahier, Le Père Ch. *Caracteristiques des Saints dans l'Art Populaire*. Paris, 1867.

Caiger-Smith, A. *English Medieval Wall Paintings*. Oxford, Eng., 1963.

Carroll, Rory. "Bones of Contention." *The Guardian* (London), December 22, 2000.

Carter, Robert S. "A Turkish Exploration by Boat." *Archaeology*, May/June 1985.

Charles, Barbara, and J. R. Taylor, *Dream of Santa: Haddon Sundblom's Advertising for Christmas, 1931–64*. New York: Gramercy, 1992.

Cioffari, Gerardo. *The Basilica of Saint Nicholas*. Bari, no date.

Clarke, Sir Ashley. "Restoring a Venetian Church." *Country Life*, October 30, 1975, 1150–51.

Collin de Plancy, J.A.S. *Dictionnaire Critique des Reliques et des Images Miraculeuses*. Paris, 1821.

Colnaghi, D. E. "A Tour of Lycia by Mr. D. E. Colnaghi, 1854." Appendix to C. R. Newton, *Travels and Discoveries in the Levant*. London, 1865.

Comnena, Anna. *The Alexiad*. Elizabeth Dawes, trans. London: Kegan Paul, 1928.

Daniel. *Pilgrimage of the Russian Abbot Daniel in the Holy Land, 1106–1107.* Annotated by Colonel Sir C. W. Wilson. Vol. 4. London: Palestine Pilgrims' Text Society, 1897.

De Groot, Adrian. *St. Nicholas: A Psychoanalytic Study of His History and Myth.* The Hague/Paris, 1965.

De Selincourt, Beryl, and Mary Sturtle Henderson. *Venice.* London: Chatto & Windus, 1907.

Douglas, David. *The Norman Achievement 1050–1100.* London: Eyre and Spottiswoode, 1969.

Duffy, Eamon. *The Stripping of the Altars.* London: Yale University Press, 1992.

Duggan, T.M.P. "Conversion of Archbishop in 1066 Inspires Theft of St. Nicholas' Bones?" *Turkish Daily News,* Ankara, February 21, 2001.

Duke, Alastair. *Reformation and Revolt in the Low Countries.* Hambledon, 1990.

Duncan, John M. *Travels Through Parts of the United States and Canada in 1818/9.* Glasgow, 1823.

Dvornik, Francis. *Byzantine Missions Among the Slavs.* Boston, 1956.

Eusebius. *The Ecclesiastical History.* John Ernest Leonard Oulton, ed. London: Heinemann, 1932.

Flynn, Maureen. *Sacred Charity: Confraternities and Social Welfare in Spain, 1400–1700.* London: Macmillan, 1989.

Fellows, Charles. *An Account of Discoveries in Lycia.* London, 1841.

Figes, Orlando. *A People's Tragedy: The Russian Revolution, 1891–1924.* London: Jonathan Cape, 1996.

Fletcher, Richard. *The Barbarian Conversion from Paganism to Christianity.* Berkeley: University of California Press, 1997.

———. *The Cross and the Crescent.* London: Allen Lane, 2003.

Foss, Clive. "The Lycian Coast in the Byzantine Age." *Dumbarton Oaks Papers* 48 (1994), 1–52.

Franklin, John. *Narrative of a Journey to the Shores of the Polar Sea, in the Years 1819–22.* London, 1823.

———. *Narrative of a Second Expedition to the Shore of the Polar Sea, in the Years 1825–27.* London, 1828.

Girling, Richard. "Now Do You Believe in Santa Claus?" *Sunday Times Magazine* (London), Dec. 12, 2004.

Groom, Nigel. *Frankincense and Myrrh: A Study of the Arabian Incense Trade.* London, 1981.

"H." "Custom Observed on the Eve of St. Nicholas." *Gentleman's Magazine,* May 10, 1827, 407–408.

Hamilton, Mary. *Greek Saints and Their Festivals.* Edinburgh: Blackwood, 1910.

Hanson, Michael. *The Story of Christmas.* London, 1951.

Hare, Augustus J. C. *Sketches in Holland and Scandinavia.* London: Smith, Elder, 1885.

Harrison, M. "Churches and Chapels in Central Lycia." *Anatolian Studies* (Journal of British Archaeological Society at Ankara), 13 (1963), 117–51.

Haskins, Charles Homer. *The Normans in European History.* Boston: Houghton Mifflin, 1916.

———. *Studies in Medieval Culture.* Oxford, Eng.: Oxford University Press, 1929.

Hasluck, F. W. *Christianity and Islam under the Sultans.* 2 vols. Oxford, Eng.: Oxford University Press, 1929.

Haynes, Sybille. *Land of the Chimaera*. London: Chatto & Windus, 1974.

Highfield, Roger. *Why Reindeer Fly*. London: Weidenfeld & Nicolson, 2001.

Hirschon, Renee. *Heirs of the Greek Catastrophe*. Oxford: Clarendon Press, 1989.

————, ed. *Crossing the Aegean*. New York/Oxford: Berghahn, 2003.

Hooker, Katherine. *Through the Heel of Italy*. New York: Rae D. Henkle, 1927.

Housepian, M. D. *Smyrna: The Destruction of a City*. New York: Harcourt Brace, 1966.

Irving, Washington. *A History of New York from the Beginning of the World to the End of the Dutch Dynasty . . . by Dietrich Knickerbocker*. New York, 1809. 2nd ed., with alterations and in two volumes, New York, 1812.

Israel, Jonathan. *The Dutch Republic: Its Rise, Greatness and Fall, 1477–1806*. Oxford: Clarendon Press, 1995.

Iswolsky, Helene. *Christ in Russia*. Kingswood, Surrey, Eng., 1962.

Jacobus de Voragine: *The Golden Legend*. William Granger Ryan, trans. 2 vols. Princeton, N.J.: Princeton University Press, 1993.

Jameson, Mrs. *Sacred and Legendary Art*. London: Longman, 1848.

Janin, Raymond. *La Géographie Ecclesiastique de l'Empire Byzantin: Les Eglises et les Monastères*. Paris, 1953.

Jones, E. Willis. *The Santa Claus Book*. New York, 1976.

Jones, Charles W. *St. Nicholas of Myra, Bari and Manhattan*. Chicago: University of Chicago Press, 1978.

Kelly, Laurence, ed. *Istanbul: A Travellers' Companion*. London, 1987.

Kennedy, P. J., ed. *Butler's Lives of the Saints*. New York, 1963.

Ladas, Stephen P. *The Exchange of Minorities in Bulgaria, Greece and Turkey*. New York: Macmillan, 1932.

Lane Fox, Robin. *Pagans and Christians*. London: Viking, 1988.

Leigh Fermor, Patrick. *Mani*. London: John Murray, 1958.

Lemos, Andreas. *The Greeks and the Sea*. New York/London: Cassell, 1976.

Leong, Albert, ed. *The Millennium: Christianity and Russia 988–1988*. Crestwood, NY: St. Vladimir's Seminary Press, 1990.

Lindsay, Jack. *Byzantium into Europe*. London: Bodley Head, 1952.

Llewellyn Smith, Michael. *Ionian Vision: Greece in Asia Minor 1919–1922*. London: Allen Lane, 1973.

Loomis, Grant C. *White Magic*. Cambridge, Mass.: Medieval Acad. America, 1948.

Mango, Cyril. *Byzantium: Empire of the New Rome*. London: Weidenfeld & Nicolson, 1980.

Matthews, Owen. "Dome from Dome: The Russian Churches of Karaköy." *Cornucopia* no. 28 (2003), 76–91.

McManners, John, ed. *Illustrated History of Christianity*. Oxford, Eng.: Oxford University Press, 1990.

Meisen, Karl. *Nikolauskult und Nikolausbrauch im Abendlande*. Düsseldorf, 1931.

Mesick, Jane Louise. *The English Traveller in America*. New York, 1922.

Miles, Clement A. *Christmas in Ritual and Tradition*. London: T. Fisher Unwin, 1912.

Miller, Daniel, ed. *Unwrapping Christmas*. Oxford, Eng.: Clarendon Press, 1993.

Morris, Jan. *The Great Port*. London: Faber, 1970.

————. *Venice*. London: Faber, 1960.

Moynahan, Brian. *The Faith*. London: Aurum Press, 2002.

Muir, William Auld. *Christmas Traditions.* New York: Macmillan, 1931.

Naogeorgus, Thomas (Kirchmayer). *The Popish Kingdome, Englyshed by Barnabe Googe.* R. C. Hope, ed. London, 1880.

Newman, Bernard. *Tito's Yugoslavia.* London: Robert Hale, 1952.

Nichols, John Gough, ed. *The Diary of Henry Machyn.* London: Camden Society, 1848.

Nissenbaum, Stephen. *The Battle for Christmas.* New York: Alfred Knopf, 1996.

Norwich, John Julius. *A History of Venice.* London: Allen Lane, 1982.

———. *The Normans in Sicily.* London: Penguin, 1992.

———, ed. *Venice: A Travellers' Companion.* London: Constable, 1990.

Notes & Queries. London, 1843 (12 S I. FEB 26, 1916, 173–74).

Oliver, Paul, ed., *Encyclopaedia of Vernacular Architecture of the World.* 3 vols. Cambridge, Eng.: Cambridge University Press, 1997.

Orderic. *Vitalis Historiae Ecclesiasticae Libri Tredecim.* Thomas Forester, trans. London, 1854.

Ozgur, M. Edip. *The Church of St. Nicholas in Myra.* Antalya, Turkey, 1998.

Paludet, L. G. *Ricognizione Delle Reliquie Di S. Nicolo.* Vicenza, Italy, 1994.

Phelps Stokes, I. N. *The Iconography of Manhattan Island.* New York: Robert H. Dodd, 1915–28.

Pimlott, John A. R. *The Englishman's Christmas: A Social History.* Sussex, Eng.: Harvester Press, 1978.

Polo, Marco. *The Travels.* Manuel Komroff, ed. New York: Boni & Liveright, 1926.

Poulos, George. *Orthodox Saints.* 2 vols. Brookline, Mass.: Hellenic College Press, 1976.

Prendergast, Mark. *For God, Country and Coca-Cola.* New York: Scribner, 1993.

Procopius. *The Secret History.* Richard Atwater, trans. Ann Arbor: University of Michigan Press, 1961.

Psalty, François. "Saint Nicolas, Successeur de Neptune et Père Noel." *Belletini* (journal of TTOK [Turkish Touring and Automobile Club], Istanbul), January 1952, 27–28.

Ramsay, W. M. *Cities and Bishoprics of Phrygia.* Oxford, 1897.

———. *St. Paul the Traveller and Roman Citizen.* London: Hodder & Stoughton, 1898.

Reau, L. *Iconographie de l'Art Chrétien.* 6 vols. Paris, 1955–59.

"Monachi Anonymi." "An Anonymous Lido Monk's History of the Translation of Great Nicholas, His Uncle Nicholas and Theodore, Martyr, from the City of Myra to the Monastery of St. Nicholas on the Lido." In *Recueil des Historiens des Croisades,* vol. 5. French preface, pp. xlv–liii. Latin account, 253–92. Paris: Académie des Inscriptions et Belles-Lettres, 1844–1906.

Restad, Penny. *Christmas in America.* Oxford: Oxford University Press, 1995.

Revue de l'Art Chrétien. Lille, 1857.

Rex, Richard. *Henry VIII and the English Reformation.* London: Macmillan, 1993.

Robert, Louis. *Documents de l'Asie Mineure.* Paris, 1897.

Roberts, Ellis H. *New York: The Planting and Growth of the Empire State.* 2 vols. Boston and New York, 1887.

Robertson, Dora. *Sarum Close.* London: Jonathan Cape, 1938.

Rott, Hans. *Kleinasiatische Denkmaler.* Leipzig, 1908.

Runciman, Steven. *A History of the Crusades.* 3 vols. Cambridge: Cambridge University Press, 1951–54.

Saewulf. *Account of the Pilgrimage of Saewulf to Jerusalem and the Holy Land, in the*

Years 1102–3. Bishop of Clifton, trans. Vol. 4. London: Palestine Pilgrims' Text Society, 1897.

Schama, Simon. *The Embarrassment of Riches.* London: Collins, 1987.

Schwartz, Gary, ed. *The Dutch World of Painting.* Exhibition catalogue. Vancouver, Canada: Vancouver Art Gallery, 1986.

Sevcenko, Nancy P. *The Life of St. Nicholas in Byzantine Art.* Turin, Italy: Bottega d'Erasmo, 1983.

Sevcenko, I., and N. P. Sevcenko, trans. and eds. *The Life of St. Nicholas of Sion.* Brookline, Mass.: The Hellenic College Press, 1984.

Shain, Charles and Samuella, eds. *The Maine Reader.* Boston: Houghton Mifflin, 1991.

Shorto, Russell. *The Island at the Center of the World.* New York/London: Doubleday, 2004.

Siefker, Phyllis. *Santa Claus, Last of the Wild Men.* Jefferson, N.C: 1997.

Simpson, Jacqueline, and Steve Roud. *A Dictionary of English Folklore.* Oxford: Oxford University Press, 2000.

Spratt, T.A.B., and E. Forbes. *Travels in Lycia, Milyas and the Cibyratis in Company with the Late Rev. E. T. Daniell.* London, 1847.

Spring, Roy. *Salisbury Cathedral.* London, 1987.

Spufford, Francis. *I May Be Some Time.* London: Faber, 1996.

Stanley, Arthur Penrhyn. *Lectures on the History of the Eastern Church.* London: John Murray, 1862.

Stark, Freya. *Alexander's Path.* London: John Murray, 1958.

———. *The Lycian Shore.* London: John Murray, 1956.

Sumption, Jonathan. *Pilgrimage: An Image of Medieval Religion.* London: Faber, 1975.

Texier, Charles. *Asie Mineure.* Paris, 1862.

———, and R. Pullan. *Byzantine Architecture.* London, 1864.

Thurston, Herbert S. J., and Donald Attwater. *Butler's Lives of the Saints.* London, 1956.

Tristram, E. W. *English Medieval Wall Painting.* Oxford, Eng.: Oxford University Press, 1944.

Tsuji, Sh., ed. *The Survey of Early Byzantine Sites in Olu Deniz Area: 1st Preliminary Report.* Osaka, Japan: Osaka University, 1995.

Tupper, Harmon. *To the Great Ocean.* London: Secker & Warburg, 1965.

Van Rensselaer, Mrs. Schuyler. *History of the City of New York in the Seventeenth Century.* New York: Macmillan, 1909.

Van der Zee, Henri and Barbara. *A Sweet and Alien Land.* London: Macmillan, 1978.

Vlassios, Antonas, and Despina Sideri. *Reminiscences of Myra and Antifilo,* extracted and translated by Nicholas Pappas from archives of the Centre for Asia Minor Studies, Athens. Unpublished.

Waits, William B. *The Modern Christmas in America.* New York, 1994.

"Warner, Susan" (Elizabeth Wetherell). *Carl Krinken: His Christmas Stocking.* New York, 1854.

Yewdale, Ralph Bailey. *Bohemond I, Prince of Antioch.* Princeton, N.J., 1924.

Yiannakis, John. *Megisti in the Antipodes.* Carlisle, Western Australia, 1996.

Young, Karl. *The Drama of the Medieval Church.* 2 vols. Oxford, Eng.: Oxford University Press, 1932.